To: Duke

From: Mary

Valentine's Day - 1963

GUNS of the OLD WEST

GUNS of the

OLD WEST

BY

Charles Edward Chapel

Coward-McCann, Inc.   New York

Contents

An Episode in the Opening Up of the Cattle Country. Painting by Frederick Remington.

Foreword

THE story of American firearms is one with the saga of America's west-ward-pushing frontier.

The story might begin in the echo of Daniel Boone's long-barreled flint-lock, rocketing among the frosty hills near the present eastern Kentucky border in 1767. It was Boone's first trip beyond the Appalachians, and the rifle he carried was yet to be misnamed "Kentucky." No matter what a man called it—"Meat-getter," "Ol' Betsy," "Hair-saver," were some of its affectionate nicknames—it could be trusted to get him out of a tight corner against redskins with their iron-barbed arrows, against redcoats with their Brown Bess smoothbore muskets.

Boone died in 1826, but already the voice of the Kentucky had been heard in the fastness of the Rockies and in the remote rugged country to the west and south. It helped to guard the burdens of pack animals weighted down with the furry wealth of beaver plews and bull boats, riding low in the turbid flood of the Big Muddy, St. Louis-bound. That gun knew Bent's Fort on the Arkansas; it traveled southward with the high-wheeled freight wagons to Mexican Sante Fe. Later, perhaps altered from flintlock to the new and more efficient percussion firing system, it was to accompany the covered caravans overland, after word that gold had been found at Sutter's Mill swept the East like a flame. The useful life span of that great rifle was to last from about 1730 approximately over a century and a half; it was always the arm of the restless, rugged men who had to answer the challenge of the unmapped country that lay over the western horizon.

While the Kentucky "long rifle" and its companion piece, the Kentucky pistol, were at work on the wilderness frontier, back on the Atlantic seaboard, a young man whose name was to become emblazoned in the history of the American West was engaged in manufacturing a quite revolutionary kind of weapon.

Samuel Colt had already secured foreign and U. S. patents on his revolver before he set up his factory in Paterson, N. J., in 1836, taking advantage of the Passaic River's water power. There he made not only his celebrated hand gun, but also revolving rifles and shotguns. History seemed to have favored the inventor, for one of his guns played an important part in the Texans' war for independence against Mexico, and is famous among collectors today as the Texas Paterson .34 caliber five-shot revolver. However, after a promising beginning, the company failed in 1841. The Mexican War saw him back in business with government orders, first arranging with Eli Whitney, inventor of the cotton gin, to fill his contracts at Whitney's arms plant at Whitneyville, Connecticut, later in his own factory at Hartford.

It was here that Colt enters more definitely and at least semi-officially into the picture of the Old West with the adoption by Wells Fargo Express Company of one of his revolvers (usually considered as the 1849 model) for use by their stagecoach messengers. However, the company did not issue one make or model of gun to their guards, but supplied their men with the revolvers of various manufacturers, of different models and calibers. Also, that the Colt generally was a favorite in the cattle country of the high plains country was no accident.

The revolver, from the first, was the natural weapon of Texans; the Colt —as well as other makes, such as the Remington and the later Smith & Wesson—had served them well in two wars; they knew it and liked it. Texas was primarily a cattle-raising country. The end of the Civil War found its grazing lands overstocked with longhorns, and its cattle a drug on the few local markets. The lush grass of the high plains country answered the feed problem. At the same time the railroad was pushing westward into Kansas, and the East was hungry for beef.

The green prairies to the north offered, at the very least, survival to the

Texas cowmen, and with a good chance for high profits. It was not long before the thunder of millions of longhorn hoofs was heard along the trails leading northward to Oklahoma, Wyoming, and Montana. And with them came Texas cowboys riding Texas ponies and armed with the Colt six-shooters that were as necessary to their way of life as their saddles. Indeed, the Colt six-shooter, from the old Dragoon models to the celebrated "Peacemaker" and "Frontier" guns seemed to belong primarily to the cattle country.

Other arms—both shoulder pieces and hand guns—played major roles in the winning of the West. Among the famous rifles were the Winchester, the Spencer and the Henry, both as military (U. S. Martial) arms and as private weapons. There was the Remington—pistol, revolver and shoulder weapon. And there was also the deadly little product of Henry Deringer, Jr., whose short-barreled, heavy-calibered pistol in various types and in its many imitations had the great advantage of being easily concealed and murderous at short range. Here was a weapon for gamblers, bankers, bartenders and also for the honkytonk girls who might feel the need of personal protection. It was a town gun, a house gun, and it, too, made history in the frontier West. And there were others. . . .

The purpose of this book is to discuss, describe and picture these weapons as they were used in that colorful but indefinite place-in-time we call the Old West.

Where does the West begin? It might plausibly be argued that one of our first Western frontiers lay within blunderbuss range inland from Plymouth Rock. To begin there, however, would embrace far too much in territory and time for our purpose. Instead, we'll have to make an arbitrary limit and focus our attention on the era of American westward expansion, generally from the middle of the eighteenth century to about the close of the nineteenth. To make it a little simpler, we can take the nineteenth century alone, after this new nation had been established as a free and independent union of states—say roughly from 1800 to 1900. In every historical sense that hundred-year span was one of remarkable richness: It was to see the acquisition, by purchase and grant, of all the vast stretch of country from the Mississippi to the Pacific Coast. It was to see the exploration of that almost unmapped wilderness, its development from a raw and lawless frontier of natural wealth to a relatively well-ordered and secure land.

The new West that lay beyond the Mississippi held everything to sharpen the appetite of a young, independent and vigorous people. What did you want? Tired of sweating out a meager living from the rocky New England hillside farm? Hitch up the team and get the wagon loaded; we're heading West to take up government land; a farm so big a man can't see where it

[3]

ends. Sick of the endless hum of the mills of Lawrence and Lowell, with their dollar-a-day wage? Head for Kansas, for Independence or Westport, where the Santa Fe trade route starts. A smart, handy lad might get a job with the wagons. In a few years—who knows?—he might be on his way to a fortune as a trader, possibly with fifty or more high-wheeled freighters rolling into Santa Fe, piled with Yankee goods—pots and pans, hardware, bolts of calico, tools, knives and guns—and rolling back again with leather sacks of Mexican gold and silver bars. . . .

Gold? Why, they say you can pick it up in glittering chunks in camps like Rough and Ready, Hangtown, Last Chance or Shirt Tail Canyon. You can scoop it up in your tin washpan from the creeks tumbling down from the Sierras. But it's rough country, and sooner or later a man will need a gun if he aims to keep on living. . . .

Gold? The West was filled with it. Or talk of it, anyhow. It was in the dust-churned tracks of beef herds driven to the cattle cars at railhead, bound for Kansas City and Chicago. It was in the raucous little board-and-canvas towns which would mushroom into thriving commercial centers day after tomorrow, and which offered wide-open entertainment for tonight. It was evident in the roaring mining camps that stretched from Nevada down through Arizona and New Mexico. For a man tough enough to hold his own against blizzard and drouth, against raids of hostile Indians and equally savage whites, this country would prove a rainbow's end.

It was not surprising that the nineteenth century was moving day for an adventurous nation heading West. They came by horseback, prairie schooner, by steam train and stagecoach, by sail around the Horn or across the steaming Isthmus of Panama. One way or another, throughout all that time, they were bound for their golden frontier, a turbulent, a fighting one. They knew it, and they kept their guns close to hand.

Just what kinds of guns they carried to this raw, new country and used there, we shall soon see.

GUNS of the OLD WEST

I

How Guns Began

FIREARMS, like people, have ancestors, and the frontier guns were no exception. Just as did most of the men and women who carried them, these weapons had their early roots in Europe. We can trace their lineage back to the sieges of the walled cities of the thirteenth and fourteeth centuries, to a primitive weapon called the hand cannon.

Don't be misled by the name, for the first versions of this arm bore little resemblance to the old pistols and shoulder weapons you see in museums or the shops of antique gun-dealers today. The word "hand" merely indicates that this was a semi- or fully portable cannon, at first maneuvered and fired by two men, and the early models were very crude indeed.

These were merely tubes made of welded iron bars strengthened by hoops and covered with leather. The explosive they used was called "serpentine powder," a mealy mixture of saltpeter, sulphur and charcoal, and it took a large quantity in each charge to give sufficient velocity to the missiles—at first stones, then lead, brass and iron balls—to penetrate enemy coats of mail. Although it was not long before the barrels began to be cast of iron or bronze, they continued to be not only loaded, but also ignited from the muzzle by torch or red-hot iron.

The name of the inventive genius who first bored a small hole at the top of the barrel near the breech is, alas, lost to history. By putting a little black powder into this touchhole and spilling a bit around it, then applying the torch, this unsung hero literally blazed the way for breech firing. Perhaps he had experienced some personal casualty in firing from the muzzle, for that operation could be both awkward and dangerous. Only after the torch had been applied to the muzzle did the gunner have time to get the piece set to aim and to absorb the recoil, and it's conceivable that

[5]

premature explosions often occurred. All of which might well have inflicted more casualties on the gunners themselves than on their human targets, making that type of weapon the enemy's best friend.

The process of forming gunpowder into grains, discovered in the fifteenth century, worked a change. By this method of "corning," as it was called, one could vary the size of the grains, and therefore the strength of the powder. To charge adequately a hand cannon, it was not necessary to fill half the barrel with powder, when a smaller amount of the larger grains would do the job. The natural consequence of this was the introduction of one-man hand cannon—the forerunner, or remote ancestor, of the hand gun and shoulder arm used on the constantly shifting American frontier. Yet—characteristically of all firearms—this improvement does not imply that the former type of muzzle-firing weapon was obsolete. Hand cannon, both muzzle- and breech-firing types, were used right alongside the crossbow, for the development of new types of firearms was slow and often like the way to heaven, one step forward and two steps back. We will discuss this phenomenon a little later—for phenomenon it is when compared to the history of almost all other mechanical devices.

Use of the fifteenth-century hand cannon is shown by figures 1 and 2, for infantry, and in figure 3 as it was used by mounted men, usually knights or men of high estate who could afford such expensive armament.

When used by horse soldiers the hand cannon was called a petronel, and it was secured to the horseman by a thong or chain about his neck, attached to the butt of the weapon. His armored breastplate was just as necessary in absorbing the heavy recoil as it was in fending off enemy missiles. So, filled with sound and fury, his charger pounding ahead at full gallop, with one gauntleted first clenching a flaming torch and the other steadying his petronel in its forked metal rod, this knight must have struck terror to the hearts of a less combat-wise enemy. And that's probably all that he did strike, for his armament—despite all its noise and fire and smoke —was far more frightening in appearance than deadly in performance.

Just how effective these ancient weapons were is something we may never accurately know. We do know that historians of that period were wont to rely on hearsay, gossip and their own personal biases. Objective, on-the-spot reporting was unknown, and usually literacy was limited to monasteries and princes of the church and the realm. Moreover, history and the stories of battles were often not written until decades had passed after the engagements. However, for what it is worth, an Italian writer in 1430 described the use of hand cannon in the siege of Lucca in this manner:

"The Luccanians invented a new weapon. In their hands they held a block of wood, about one and one-half yards long, fastened to which was an iron tube filled with sulfur and saltpeter which threw iron bullets by

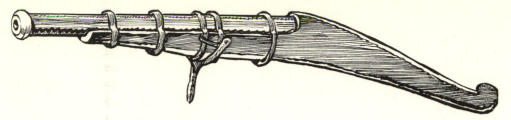

1. A Small Hand Cannon Called a Hand Culverin.

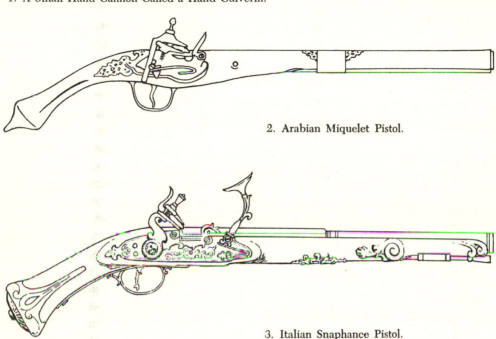

2. Arabian Miquelet Pistol.

3. Italian Snaphance Pistol.

the force of fire. The blow, when it struck, brought certain death, and neither armor nor shield were a sufficient protection; then not seldom did a single bullet penetrate a file of two or three men."

Before going further, we might warn the reader who may be new to gun lore that it is impossible to assign various types of guns to neat little boxes, labeled by dates and specific kinds of arms. No strict chronological division is possible, because no gun authority would care to say, for example, just when the flintlock period ended and the percussion era began. Even though, in the latter case, we are more or less agreed upon dates of patent, first model, the time of general public acceptance and the date of government use for martial arms, from first date to last there's a time-stretching spread of over three decades. Even when authorities agree—as they rarely do—who is to say if the percussion period began with the granting of patent, the completion of the first model, or the time when the system came into general public use? And even today not only percussion pieces, but flintlocks and almost every other form of historic firearm are in use in some part of the world. When does an era in gun design end? Apparently not quite yet.

So it is throughout the history of guns: the various periods of development and progress are like a number of overlapping circles, each with its own center and each cutting over the circumference of the others.

What happened to old guns? Sometimes they were converted from an old firing system to a newer type. Sometimes they were melted down for their metal, or sold for junk, or gathered dust and rust in the attic. But a surprising number of them are somewhere in regular use.

Madison Avenue, New York, is Advertisingland and it is governed by the Priests of Pursuasion. One of their great basic laws is that obsolescence is the life of trade. This may apply to household equipment, automobiles, toys, clothes, and to other things we use, but within the scope of our book, that law very rarely was valid, and then only as applied to Martial Arms (that is, arms actually contracted for by the government and put into active military use). The guns that come within our purview originally attracted no seeker for prestige; their hidden motivation stayed cozily hidden and they carried no keeping-up-with-the-neighbors snob appeal. The only prestige, motivation and snobbery when a man obtained a gun was a great desire to remain among the living, and a gun was a tool that would help him mightily to do just that. Considerately cared for and used with skill, a gun would argue loud and persuasively for you against man and nature when both were hell-bent on your immediate personal destruction.

New arms, manufactured on the Atlantic seaboard and shipped overland by wagon or by sail to the Coast, were costly, and the pioneer usually had little cash. He was accustomed to "making do"; he was characteristically thrifty, largely because he had to be, but anyway he liked things that had served him well and would still do so. Old buckskins grew soft and comfortable with use; a good horse or mule was one that was seasoned and disciplined to the dangers and hardships of the wilderness trails; a knife might be honed to stiletto thinness and be the better for it, and a well-cared-for rifle might have had the lands so worn with shooting that the barrel had to be rebored for a larger ball, but the gun was still an old friend, and could still be trusted to do a job. Why change it for a more modern weapon, unless there was a good and definite reason?

With the exception of some famous makes of firearms, whose development and descriptions are treated in separate chapters, we will follow the usual method of following the progress of these forebears of Western guns —according to their ignition, or firing, system. Since strict chronological divisions are nonexistent in gun history, the changing method of setting fire to the powder charges in weapons has come to be accepted as the logical line which—no matter how vaguely in point of time—sets off one period of firearm development from another. The reason for taking this mechanism as a kind of yardstick is simple: On the ignition system depend the various loading, aiming and rifling methods—in other words, how the gun is fired determines how it is used, and how effective the arm is for its purpose.

We can see that very clearly below, in a development of a system and a weapon which was the natural outgrowth (or development or evolution, if you wish) of the hand cannon. This is called . . .

The Matchlock

Although the matchlock was probably invented in Europe about 1450, it was possibly developed in Asia before that date. In its first stage it was a vast improvement on the hand cannon, for, instead of the awkward hot irons and torches used to ignite the priming powder, this new gun was equipped with a burning wick, attached to what we would call the hammer, but what in the illustration is an s-shaped piece of metal that became known as the serpentine. The wick was called a match, thus giving the piece its name. This device was a considerable step forward, for it allowed the shooter to aim and fire at the same time.

In the meantime (again see the illustration) gunmakers moved the touch-hole from the top of the barrel to the side, where they placed a tiny pan, called the flash pan, and which held the priming powder for setting off the main charge. Various changes were to follow, chief among them being the introduction of a match soaked in a saltpeter solution, dried and then issued in four- and five-foot lengths. This, however, proved both awkward and unsatisfactory and resulted in the snapping type of serpentine, which was by this time called a cock, held back by a spring until released by pulling the trigger. The cock then fell with a quick blow, igniting the priming powder in the pan. The long, awkward match of the nonsnapping type was replaced by a short piece of match held in the cock by a tube, instead of by the former clamp.

Many shoulder arms and some pistols using the older nonsnapping type of matchlock were introduced to America by the original settlers, and continued in use until the latter part of the seventeenth century. The chief advantages, accounting for their long span of usefulness, were that they were simple to make and easy to repair. They were also very inexpensive—a fact not without attraction, especially for the Indians, who used this arm well into the eighteenth century, probably during the French and Indian War in what was then our Western frontier.

The serpentine, or nonspanning, type of matchlock (see illustration) worked like this: First the end of the match is lighted (A), being held by

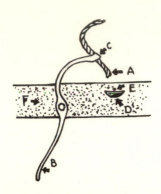

the clamp (C) at the upper end of the serpentine in which the match is carried. The lower end of the pivoted, s-shaped piece of metal—later to be known as the trigger—(B) is then pulled to the rear, which lowers the burning end of the match into the pan (D) that holds the fine priming powder. This is ignited and starts a fire going through the touchhole (E) into the rear of the barrel. The main charge of powder is thus ignited, causing the explosion that propels the bullet from the barrel.

Almost three-quarters of a century was to pass before the next development in ignition locks appeared, and as usual this new invention was designed to overcome the defects of the older type. Although the outstanding advantage of the matchlock lay in its simplicity and cheapness, its exposed wick almost precluded game-hunting or human hostilities during damp or rainy weather. Other practical disadvantages were that the matchlock took a long time to prepare for firing, and the burning wick was too often an unwelcome advertisement of the shooter to wild game or human enemy.

For these defects, a remedy of sorts appeared with the application of what was even then an ancient ignition principle—flint and steel. Thus was born what might be termed the great-great-great-grandfather of the later and justly famous flintlock. It was called . . .

The Wheel Lock

Although this marked a definite milestone on the strangely twisting road of gun development, even less than other innovations did it replace its predecessors in popularity. During its lifetime its effect on the general use of matchlocks and even longbows and crossbows was negligible.

Probably invented in Germany about 1515, this mechanism, for its period, seems of almost Rube Goldberg complexity after the primitive and simple systems preceding it. The device consisted of a notched steel wheel motivated by a straight spring and cam. The spring was wound with a keylike tool called a spanner, and when the trigger was squeezed, the cock, its jaws holding a piece of flint, descended against the whirling wheel and a shower of sparks ignited the priming powder in the pan. The rest of the process—the fire in the pan running through the touchhole in the rear of the barrel, and so forth—was the same as we have seen in other ignition types. The hardness of the flint, however, wore down the notches in the wheel rim, so iron pyrites, the brassy yellow mineral called "fool's gold," was successfully substituted.

While this was almost weatherproof, and had the further advantages of one's being able to conceal it on the person, and greater accuracy than the matchlock when fired from horseback, it suffered two major intrinsic liabilities. For one thing, the mechanism was both complicated and delicate, and as temperamental as a privileged courtesan. When something went wrong with the wheel lock—oftenest, you may be sure, at a crucial moment in hunting or in combat—nothing less than the services of a skilled locksmith were required. Another built-in disadvantage was the high cost of its construction; the average yeoman or knight of modest means simply could not afford this fancy firearm. Even sovereigns, barons and rich merchants who habitually equipped large units of fighting men from their own private purses, balked at the price of issuing this arm, and as a military gun it was in relatively scant supply. This was just not the stuff to feed the troops; and the crossbow, hand cannon or matchlock that was good enough for grandfather was plenty good enough for the ordinary levied soldier or huntsman. It is probable, however, that our yeoman would not have traded his clumsy but dependable old weapon for the costliest wheel lock that ever lost a nobleman an eight-point buck—or his own life on the battlefield.

This weapon, a rich man's personal arm and often richly ornamented with inlaid ivory, silver and gold, was never in use on the American frontier. It does, however, deserve mention because of its important place in the story of guns, and because it brings us closer to a firing system which, on musket, rifle and pistol, was to play a long and active role in the history of the pioneer West.

The development of guns, as we have seen, was a slow and almost a reluctant process. Improvements and refinements appeared very gradually and over a relatively long period of time. This is specially noticeable when we consider the comparatively breath-taking pace in the changes of other mechanical devices for use in homes, offices and in commerce generally, from the post-Civil War years onward.

The very nature of early firearms—always precision instruments and skillfully hand-wrought to last for generations—precluded any sudden, sweeping dramatic changes which overnight would make yesterday's guns fit only for the junkyard. An exception may be entered here in the case of martial arms; but even then, no matter how vitally urgent the need, alterations took time to design and produce. To offset improvements in enemy weapons—if and when it could be done—meanwhile taxed to the utmost both military and civilian ingenuity and courage until the new guns were available for the field.

Rare indeed was the invention that could revolutionize the entire field of firearms. Later on, however, we shall explore some of the startling inventions, along with their applications, which seeemed to accomplish exactly that. Miracles could do no less.

It is not too surprising, then, that it took thirty-five years after the introduction of the wheel lock for the next ignition system to make its appearance. This lock had a peculiar-sounding name to our ears; it was of Dutch or German origin and is said to have originally meant either "chicken thieves" or "pecking fowls." Although it was spelled in various ways, we may settle for . . .

The Snaphance

About 1550, there originated in any one—or more—of five countries: Spain, Holland, Germany, Scotland or Sweden, a new and sorely needed simplification of the flint-and-steel principle. This used a hammer, and—as in the wheel lock—its jaws, called the cock, held a piece of flint. The hammer, again, was connected to a spring, and a pressure on the trigger caused it to fall forward with a snap onto a piece of steel called the hen, sending a shower of sparks into the pan containing priming powder and connected through the touchhole to the main charge of powder in the barrel.

Today, gun experts identify the snaphance by a sliding cover for the priming pan and a separate piece of steel for the flint to strike, as opposed to an arm that had the pan cover and steel plate in a single piece. The steel plate against which the flint strikes is called a "frizzen," or a "battery." Either is correct, and both words refer to the same part. To avoid possible confusion with other meanings of the latter word, we'll use frizzen in this connection when speaking of the steel plate.

Not only does the snaphance have an established place in gun genealogy, but it was also used in both shoulder arms and hand guns by American hunters during frontier times. Until fairly recently some gun collectors classified this system as a flintlock, and it is very likely that the buckskin-clad frontiersmen—usually noted for a cavalier attitude toward the niceties of nomenclature—referred to their snaphance-equipped guns by that same name.

At about the same time that the snaphance made its appearance, a slightly different form of flint-and-steel lock was made in Spain, and it forms another of the transition pieces between the wheel lock and the true flintlock. This is called . . .

The Miquelet

The name comes from a corps of armed men known as Miqueletes who acted as escorts for distinguished persons and shipments of valuable cargoes in Spain. They were named for one of their leaders, Miquel de Prats, an armed retainer of Cesare Borgia, who might have personally equipped the guards with guns of this type.

In the miquelet the heavy mainspring and hammer assembly are outside, as distinguished from the snaphance, with its mechanism protected inside a lock plate where it cannot be easily injured. In this respect, the miquelet is inferior to the snaphance, but it still has one advantage in that the frizzen and pan cover are in one piece, so that the pan is uncovered automatically when the flint hits the frizzen.

Another advantageous feature was incorporated by pure chance. It was the introduction of a safety catch, made necessary by a defect in the design of the lock that permitted the cock to slip when in the half-cock position. Here the safety catch consists of a bolt at right angles to the lock plate, and a nose on the front of the cock that, in the half-cock position, rests on the bolt. The first part of the pull on the trigger releases the bolt, leaving the cock now free to strike the frizzen. Another distinguishing feature of this lock is the hammer. It is invariably a straight piece of metal as opposed to the s-shaped hammer used on other locks, a descendant of the old serpentine of the hand cannon.

Both pistol and shoulder miquelets were used for centuries in the Mediterranean countries, and it was probably introduced into the American West via New Spain and California. The weapon was doubtless used by Mexicans in their revolution against Spain in the first decades of the nineteenth century. About the same time American mountain men and trappers obtained these guns from Mexicans, since Mexico held most of the land from what is now eastern Texas westward to the Pacific Coast, a rich country for beaver and other peltry. Later, these guns probably figured in the Santa Fe trade.

Because they were neither expensive nor complicated, and readily adapted to a great range of firearm types and calibers, they continued in use in various remote parts of the world long after flintlocks became obsolete in the more settled regions.

It is the true flintlock firing system that was used for the first models of the famous Kentucky rifle and pistol. In the next chapter we shall take a brief look at the pre-Kentucky flintlocks, and then concentrate on the story of the Kentuckies, called the first true American firearm.

II

The Kentucky Rifle and Pistol Head West

But Jackson, he was wide awake
And wasn't scared of trifles;
For well he knew the aim we'd take
With our Kentucky rifles . . .

STOMPING, whooping and hollering, the crowd of tough-fisted keelboat men jamming the New Orleans music hall that sticky May night of 1822, shook the walls as they shouted the chorus of the new song, "The Hunters of Kentucky." For the song had a special meaning to most of these men, who, seven years before, had trekked from the wilderness of the Kentucky and Tennessee countries to join General Andrew Jackson in the cypress swamp at New Orleans. With them, of course, went their personal weapon—the beautifully and meticulously made long-barreled flintlock, with its graceful lines and burnished tiger-flame maple stock that snuggled into a man's shoulder as sweet as a girl at a log-cabin hoedown.

But the voice of the Kentucky rifle that eighth of January, 1815, wasn't raised in any dance tune. Its deadly accuracy sent Packenham's 5,000 red-coated regulars reeling back once, and then again from the molasses-barrel and spongy log entrenchments before the Crescent City. It accounted for almost as many British casualties as the entire American defending force of some 3,000, while Jackson's loss was eight killed and thirteen wounded in the greatest American land victory of that war.

Although the victory had no effect on the war's outcome—the battle was fought two weeks after the Peace of Ghent was signed, and more than a month before news of it reached America—the part played by that great

[15]

native shoulder arm was to be important in the history of the growing nation. It acted as a powerful restorative to national pride, since our land operations in the war had been largely dismal failures; and, in creating a new American hero, thirteen years later it helped to blaze the trail from Monticello in Tennessee to the new White House in Washington, where Old Hickory would begin his two terms as President.

This was not the first time that the Kentucky had won its battle honors. Nor would it be the last.

There was that sultry day in July, 1755, when 400 backwoodsmen, carrying their own Kentuckies and under Lieutenant-Colonel George Washington, picked their way westward through the Pennsylvania wilderness as part of General Braddock's expedition against the French Fort Duquesne on the Monongahela. Surprised and surrounded by a force of French and Indians, Braddock's regulars, closing ranks and firing volleys from their smoothbore Brown Bess muskets, were mowed down by the enemy, while Washington's men, firing from behind trees and carefully aiming every shot, picked off the Indians and managed to cover the retreat of the remnants of the ill-fated expedition.

Later in the same war, again the accurate fire of the Kentucky in the hands of Pennsylvania Provincial troops, clearing the way for General Wolfe's British regulars against the French advance guard, counted heavily in the capture of that ancient French stronghold. With it, Canada was won for the British Crown.

A quarter century went by. Now the fire of the Kentucky was coming uncomfortably close to the powdered wigs of the British Parliament in distant London, as those gentlemen listen to a report of their War Office:

"The settlers from the backwoods of America used their hunting rifles with so much effect that the only effective rejoinder was to pit rifle against rifle; for this purpose Jägers were recruited on the Continent."

The Jägers, coming largely from Hesse, were riflemen and most of them had been foresters and gamekeepers before being levied. But their arms could not compare in accuracy with the Kentucky, nor their spirit as mercenaries compare with that of men who were fighting for their farms and families.

Such American victories as that at King's Mountain, in 1780, when the frontiersmen's skill accounted for British losses of 400 to 88 of the Americans', also gave rise to heated debates in Parliament. There were many suggestions for adopting the rifle as a military arm, but it was not until 1794, eleven years after Cornwallis' surrender at Yorktown, that a single British battalion was exclusively equipped with rifles. That battalion, it is safe to say, was not in evidence at the Battle of New Orleans.

At this point, two facts may strike the general reader as calling for some sort of explanation. One is that since the rifling of gun barrels had been known for over two centuries (it was invented in Germany sometime between 1515 and 1550, and the Kentucky rifle was not developed until about 1728) why hadn't it come into more widespread use? And, second: Since the effectiveness of the Kentucky had long been recognized and tested in military actions, why wasn't it issued by the government as an official martial weapon?

To hazard an explanation of the first question, we must remember, as always, that firearm development was an extremely slow process, especially before tools of engineering and mechanics were perfected into efficient instruments. Frequently it was a process of trial and error that lasted over decades or more. The primitive German gunsmiths were on the trail of a revolutionary idea, but it would be a great many years before a rifled barrel would be a part of an effective arm. Although the rifling was known to have added impact to the projectile, the pitch of lands and grooves seldom gave the ball an accurate spin—sometimes the rifling was straight instead of spiraling inside the barrel—and the weapons were clumsy, short-barreled and, in fact, like most other shoulder pieces of the time. They were meant to be fired at short range, like a shotgun, and were. Perhaps the only advantage was that the rifling permitted the ball to strike harder—sometimes—than the ball of the more popular musket. As we have seen, it was not until the Kentucky had been proving itself for about seventy years that rifling came into its own, and the rifle became a widely recognized shoulder arm, distinct and separate in many ways from the musket or the shotgun.

Governments are notoriously slow in giving their official sanction for the use of technical improvements, and the young United States was no exception. As a former British colony, its soldiers and officers had long been used to the British government-issue arm—the Brown Bess smoothbore musket. This venerable piece was named for Elizabeth I of England, who ordered one of her regiments equipped with matchlock shoulder guns with browned barrels and fittings. The piece, with various ignition changes, survived until the British adoption of the percussion system in 1836.

During the Revolution, firearms of any kind and condition were in short supply and badly needed by the Continentals. Aside from scattered private gunsmiths in their small shops, we had no government armories nor was there time to establish any. France, the first European power to recognize the new nation, was a potential ally and supplied the Continental Congress with several shipments of the French Model 1763 Flintlock Musket, caliber .69, commonly called the Charleville Model, after the city where it was made. It was upon this design that the first regulation United States shoulder arm was made after the War—U. S. Model 1795 Flintlock Musket, caliber .69, at the Springfield Armory. Comparatively few Kentuckies were bought during the Revolution for regulation issue to troops.

To begin with, between 200 and 500 individual gunsmiths were engaged in making the Kentucky, and almost never were any two alike, except in quality of workmanship. Decoration, calibers, over-all lengths and lengths of barrel not only differed with each maker but—since they were usually made to individual order, for a certain type of man and to serve a specific purpose—each gunsmith might work in certain variations of his own, or of the hunter buying the gun. It was not easy to hit upon an exact standard model to use as a pilot. Also, it was a private, personal weapon made expressly to meet the needs of the highly specialized man who used it with superb skill—the frontiersman. And the backwoodsman, because of his environment, already had one or more of those rifles. The city man and townsman, the farmer in a relatively settled community, were not too handy with firearms in any event, and would do just as well with the Charleville smoothbore. Or so the thinking of the time probably went. And, as always, both time and money were commodities all too rare. It was cheaper to bring rifles in from abroad—and a great deal quicker than making them.

During the flintlock period, the Kentucky was the queen of rifles in America, and we shall investigate the various types of these remarkable guns further on. Before we discuss the details of the Kentucky rifle and pistol, however, it is high time to explore the type of firing system they used—the flintlock.

Like many other types of firearm ignition, the flintlock was not invented at any particular time or place or by a specific gunsmith. Topsy-like, it just grew, the result of a gradual development that began to appear as a distinct type about 1630 and reached its final form about 1675. In its last stage the frizzen was made in one piece with the cover of the priming pan. As the trigger was pulled the hammer, striking the frizzen, made sparks and at the same time the hammer knocked the cover of the priming pan out of the way so that the sparks could ignite the priming powder.

It might be mentioned in passing that a few breech-loading flintlocks were made, but were unsuccessful in operation. With the use of loose powder, they had a strong tendency to blow open at the breech, an action not conducive to the peace of mind or the health of the shooter. Several flintlock revolvers were also made, but these, too, were born ahead of their time; both the breech-loading arm and the revolver had to wait for the introduction of the percussion ignition—the "cap and ball" type in the first half of the nineteenth century—before coming into general use.

In the early 1700's the town of Lancaster, Pennsylvania, could still be called a frontier settlement; that is, settlers nearby were by no means immune to savage Indian attacks. It was also in good hunting country, and hunting at that time was a necessity rather than a sport. The locality had been largely settled by Germans and Swiss, people adept by tradition at precision work, so it was not strange that they would follow hereditary occupations, which included gunmaking. Both time and place, about 1725–1730 and from Virginia to the Jerseys, happily brought together the man who needed a special kind of gun and the craftsman who could make it.

The available shoulder arms were of little use to the frontiersman. The smoothbore musket was no good for accurate work at a distance, and the Central European rifle, as we have already indicated, was short-barreled, large-bored, badly sighted and usually inaccurate because it was necessary to ram down the ammunition with such force that the lead balls were jammed out of shape and the muzzle frequently warped. Moreover, the balance was so far to the rear that it was almost impossible to hold the rifle steady on the target, and the recoil—once experienced—was vicious enough to make the staunchest marksman instinctively flinch. Altogether, the pioneer could have done as well with a boomerang.

What the settlers wanted was simply this: a rifle both easy to carry and to fire, accurate at the usual ranges against all kinds of game and marauding Indians. Above all, it should be loaded easily and swiftly with a few simple tools, and of uncomplicated mechanism so that it could be repaired in the wilderness without having to go back to a gunsmith's shop. Also of vast importance, the rifle should be economical in the use of powder and lead. Ammunition not only cost money, but it burdened down a man's shoulders. When you head out across the mountains for the Western Territories, you can get a long distance from a base of supplies, and if you have to pack as much fodder for a gun as you would for a wife and young'uns—well that's no kind of gun to carry. So the frontier rifle must do its job, and keep lean and handy while doing it.

In response to these demands, the Lancaster gunmakers reduced the caliber of the European rifle from about .70 to about .45; increased the average barrel length from about 31 to about 42 inches; made the trigger guard smaller and stronger; used curly maple for the stock; gave the rifle plain open sights both front and rear, fixed to the barrel by a grooved slide which permitted adjustment horizontally; and ornamented the rifle with an eight-pointed brass star sunk into the cheek piece on the left side, this last feature being a strictly American idea which survived to the end of the Kentucky flintlock period. The barrel was made full octagon. On the right side of the stock was placed a box, five inches long by one and one-half inches wide, covered with a hinged brass lid, in which the hunter could keep patches of tallow-greased buckskin. These patches were about the size of a dollar; wrapped around a bullet made about 3/100 of an inch smaller than the bore, the greased patch enabled the shooter to load without the pounding required for the old German guns, thus cutting the loading time to about one fourth the number of seconds formerly consumed.

This description fits the average Kentucky in the early part of its history, but about 1790 the gunsmiths began to give the butt a distinct crescent shape, use imported locks, make the barrels longer, and employ a great deal of carving and silver or brass mounting; flat key pins for fastening the barrels to the stocks replaced the round ones of the early period. This fancier, but not necessarily better, rifle was popular until about 1830 when calibers were reduced to about .33, barrels made shorter and less attention was paid to the quality of workmanship.

From about 1830, the Kentucky declined in general use until, by 1850, it had almost disappeared as an important hunting arm. The reasons were that sizable wild game had been greatly reduced in numbers, the frontiers had moved on westward, and the more convenient breech-loading percussion arms, including magazine rifles, were in general use against game, predatory animals, hostile Indians and lawless whites. The chief targets left for the old muzzle-loading flintlocks were squirrels and turkeys.

The Kentucky rifle, however, by no means suffered a total eclipse. In many remote localities the frontiersmen took a dim view of the percussion cap-and-ball weapons. Why spend good money and send far away for caps, when flint or iron pyrites could be picked up off the ground for nothing? After a useful life of over a century, the Kentucky, like the man who fired it, was mighty tough to kill; and as personal weapons the old flintlocks as well as percussion models were used by both the North and South during the Civil War.

Kentucky (Pennsylvania) Flintlock Rifle.   FULLER

There seems to be no record of just what the Kentucky rifle was called before it accompanied the early hunters and trappers to the wilderness west of the Alleghenies. Since it originated with the Lancaster, Pennsylvania, gunsmiths, it might have been popularly known as a Lancaster, or a Pennsylvania rifle, or by the name of the individual gunsmith who made it, or just called a hunting rifle. But from about 1766, when hunters and trappers started carrying the rifle into the broad spread of land now including southern Ohio and Indiana, Kentucky and northern Tennessee—that was generally called the Kentucky country—the rifle had its name, and it was a name that stuck with it for almost two centuries, despite efforts to change it to "the Pennsylvania rifle," certainly a more logical choice. However, a name that was used since before the Revolutionary War is not easily changed. Kentucky it was, and Kentucky it remains.

The author of this text once spent a week examining a representative collection of forty-three Kentucky rifles, all authentic flintlock pieces in their original condition and probably made before 1800. The average caliber (that is, the diameter of the inside of the muzzle, measured between the lands) was .439, the average barrel length was 44.31 inches, average total length was 58.14 inches, and the average weight was 9.546 pounds.

A rifle of caliber .439 would fire bullets whose weight was such that about 57 balls could be made from one pound of lead, depending upon how tightly the ball fitted the rifling and whether or not a greased patch was used. These figures we have given are only averages. In reality, of the forty-three rifles, sixteen used 60 balls to the pound, four used 80 to the pound, four used 52 balls to the pound, and six fired 120 balls to the pound. The number of balls to the pound of lead for the remainder of this group varied greatly. Furthermore, each man who made Kentucky rifles had his own ideas and never made two rifles exactly alike, hence any figures we give are only indicative.

An examination of more than two hundred early Kentucky rifles, all of which appeared to be in their original flintlock condition, and including some made by Henry Deringer, Sr., showed that the average bore diameter of this group is 0.45-inch, the average weight is 9 pounds, and the average barrel length is 40 inches, although there was evidence that many of the rifles were originally longer.

This large group of representative Kentucky flintlock rifles was also examined for rifling. Thirty-three per cent were rifled with 7 grooves, 25 per cent were rifled with 8 grooves, 5 per cent were rifled with 6 grooves, 2 per cent were cut octagon, 2.5 per cent were straight cut, and 30 per cent of the whole lot were smoothbore. This requires a little explanation.

When the rifling (system of lands and grooves) wore down, the owner could have a gunsmith rifle the barrel to a larger caliber, or he could have it made into a smoothbore and thus fire it either as a musket or a shotgun.

Several kinds of native American wood were used for the stocks, but the average stock was made of curly maple, and the butt is what we call the shotgun type. The furniture, which means the butt plate, trigger guard, patch box, and other metal fittings, are almost always of brass, although other metals are sometimes found.

Those made after 1800 usually have a thinner buttstock, the butt plate is more crescent-shaped, carving is rarely found, and there are usually more inlays. The reason for these changes is that the Kentucky rifle in the Eastern states was becoming more of a sporting arm than an absolute necessity for shooting game for food and for protecting oneself and family against the British, the French, or the Indians. However, this was merely a lull before a storm, because Kentucky rifles were used in the War of 1812 against the British, and continuously, both in flintlock or percussion form, against enemies of the United States, domestic and foreign, up to the middle 1860's.

As for decoration, a European influence on the very earliest Kentucky rifles is found in the incised carving and the raised carving sometimes executed in panels, often for the whole length of the stock on the better grade specimens. Those made after 1790 generally lack the beautiful carving, but have metal inlays, usually silver on the more expensive pieces, but more often brass on those for the frontiersmen.

Since Lancaster, Pennsylvania, where the Kentucky rifle developed as a unique type, was also the center of the witchcraft known as "hex," the inlays on Kentucky rifles, during both the flintlock and the percussion periods, often included a crooked heart with the bottom or point turned to one side as a charm against an enemy. The barrel is sometimes found with X-marks, usually on the underside, to protect the owner from evil spirits, witches, and demons, and especially against a "hexer," which could be either a male or female practicing witchcraft.

One of the oldest decorations is an eight-pointed star. Another early embellishment was a crescent moon, with or without a star. The Chinese yin-yang emblem of male and female characteristics is found on many early specimens. Animals, birds, fish, leaves, acorns, and other emblems of botany and zoology are common. Fraternal symbols, such as the square and compass of Ancient Free and Accepted Masonry, are present on many.

The Kentucky Pistol

While the general reader might believe it the most natural thing in the world for the gunsmiths who turned out the Kentucky rifle also to make a pistol that shared some of the same characteristics, the discovery and classification of that arm as a distinct type of weapon is relatively recent.

It was while the author was working on the first edition of his book, *The Gun Collector's Handbook of Values*, that—more or less by the pure blind luck that sometimes blesses an arms collector and hobbyist—he learned of the work of Calvin Hetrick, of New Enterprise, Pennsylvania. Hetrick was probably the first to recognize the Kentucky pistol as a separate type of small arm, the first to acquire a collection of representative pieces, and the first to tell any author about his discovery. Therefore, when the first edition of the above-mentioned *Handbook of Values* came off the press, it brought to public attention for the first time this important type of hand gun.

Others were quick to confirm the accuracy of this classification: Joe Kindig, Jr., of York, Pennsylvania, an authority on the Kentucky rifle, and Richard Steuart, of Baltimore, Maryland, an expert on Confederate arms. Later, Herman P. Dean, an expert in this field and owner of the Standard Printing and Publishing Company, Huntington, West Virginia, acquired a large collection of Kentucky pistols, and also agreed that this was an area of firearms study that required special treatment.

Probably most of the Kentucky pistols were made in eastern Pennsylvania, although a few were made in the neighboring states of New York, New Jersey, and Ohio, and a smaller number in Maryland and Virginia. Later, when the Kentucky rifle was being slowly changed in design to meet the needs of the Far Western explorers and trappers, the long hunters and the mountain men, the Kentucky pistol also underwent changes to meet the suggestions of those purchasers. By this time, a good many of the gunsmiths followed their market westward with the shifting of the frontier, and the pistol, along with the modified Kentucky, sometimes called the Plains rifle, followed.

One of the more striking features of this pistol is that it is usually unmarked. This is particularly true of those made during the Revolution—as it is true of muskets and rifles—for the gunsmiths of that troubled time had no desire to invite British reprisals, as they would if it were known that they were furnishing arms to the colonists. Another theory for the lack of marking is that very few of these hand guns were made and there was simply not the incentive for the gunsmith to put his name on them, as there was for him to sign his rifles. While most of the makers of Kentucky rifles turned out hundreds in a lifetime, the average rifle-maker, it is estimated, turned out less than ten, and probably not more than six, pistols. No arm could take the place of the Kentucky rifle, but obviously the pistol was in less demand, despite its fine workmanship. They are carefully balanced; the stocks are slender and graceful, and the furniture—the metal fittings such as the trigger guard, ramrod thimble, muzzle cap, etc.—are of the same material and design as on the rifles.

These pistols are full-stocked. A half-stocked pistol is regarded as a freak or hybrid specimen and not as a true Kentucky type. Except for the details already mentioned, the design varies greatly with the maker. Kentucky pistols and rifles are as individual as the pioneer Americans who made them.

The Kentucky pistol is treated separately from other American flintlock and percussion pistols because the design and construction were entirely different from those of the American martial, secondary martial and non-martial flintlock and percussion pistols. Aside from the brief remarks we have made about the unique characteristics of the Kentucky pistol, an examination of the illustrations and a comparison with pictures of other single-shot flintlock and percussion pistols will convince anyone in a few minutes that we are here discussing something entirely American, completely untouched by European influences of the period during which they were made.

Typical Specimens

In a large collection of genuine flintlock Kentucky pistols, in their original condition, most of them are either caliber .44 or caliber .48, smoothbore. The barrel length varies from 7.5 inches to 10 inches, and the average barrel length is slightly less than 9 inches. The average total length is 14.25 inches. The barrel, the lock, or the lock plate, or all three of these parts, may or may not be marked, and sometimes all three have different markings. The reason for this is that the barrel was sometimes made by one man, the lock by another, and the lock plate by a third. Furthermore, although these were definitely American-made arms, English-marked locks were often used when the gunsmith was in a hurry or was not adept at making locks.

Kentucky flintlock pistols converted to percussion varied greatly in caliber, but were almost always smoothbores. During the percussion period, the old fear of British reprisals had ceased and more and more gunmakers began to put some identifying mark on the pistols.

When the gunsmiths began to make Kentucky pistols as outright percussion arms, and not as conversions, the caliber varied even more and so did the total length and weight. For example, although some were of large martial caliber and size, a few were small pocket pistols, probably made for gamblers, steamboat captains, and frontier dance-hall girls. This was before Henry Deringer, Jr., became famous as the maker of the small, single-shot percussion pistol, and before the pepperbox emerged as the forerunner and antecedent of the true revolver.

A representative group of Kentucky pistols is shown in Plate 1, which includes five made as flintlocks, one converted from flintlock to percussion, and one which was made as a percussion pocket pistol, described as follows:

Kentucky Flintlock Pistol, Revolutionary period, caliber .36, rifled, with eight deep grooves; 9.5-inch octagon barrel; 14.875 inches over all. Kentucky-rifle-type front and rear sights. Engraved lock, 4.125 inches. Iron pan with fence. High-quality full burl maple stock fastened to barrel with dart-shaped silver pins. Silver butt cap, finely engraved silver inlays on each side of grip, silver barrel pin escutcheons and name plate. Brass trigger guard, engraved brass lock-pin escutcheons, ramrod thimbles, and muzzle cap. Silver-tipped hickory ramrod. Weight 2 lbs. This is the only early rifled Kentucky flintlock pistol in the Hetrick collection. It is extremely rare. It is unsigned, but it is known that this particular piece was the personal arm of Captain William Cowan, of Chester County, Pa., who carried it at the Battle of Yorktown in the Revolutionary War. Plate 1, figure 1.

Kentucky Flintlock Pistol, Colonial period, about 1740; caliber .48 smoothbore; 7.5-inch, brass, half octagon, half round barrel; 13.375 inches over all. No sights. Engraved lock, 4.875 inches; iron pan with fence; no bridle over tumbler or frizzen pin; pan and plate separately forged and pinned together. Full stock, curly maple, round-pin-fastened; engraved brass butt cap and trigger guard, brass ramrod thimbles. No muzzle cap. Note very early type of grip. Ramrod and trigger not original. Unsigned. Probably one of the first pistols of the Kentucky type made in America. Extremely rare. Weight 1 lb. 12 oz. Plate 1, figure 2.

Kentucky Flintlock Pistol, probably pre-Revolutionary period; caliber .44, smoothbore; 9.125-inch, part octagon, part round barrel; 13.625 inches over all. No sights. Four-and-one-fourth-inch lock, severely plain with single vertical slash across tail. Marked on inside of plate "HVF." No frizzen spring. Iron pan and plate separately forged and fastened together with screws. Round-pin-fastened to stock. Full stock with bird's-head grip; brass butt cap extending toward tang; brass trigger guard, side plate, ramrod thimbles, muzzle cap. Simple, neat engraving on butt cap, guard, and side plate. Ramrod not original. Early, wide trigger with curl to rear. The stock is exceptionally slender for a pistol of this size, and of walnut. Unsigned except as noted. Weight 1 lb. 11 oz. Plate 1, figure 3.

Kentucky Flintlock Pistol, Revolutionary period, caliber .44, smoothbore; 8.75-inch, brass, part octagon, part round barrel; 14.25 inches over all. No sights. Plain lock, 4.25 inches, with curved slash across tail of plate; roller on frizzen; pan separately forged; iron pan with high fence. Full stock, maple, dark finish, with silver butt cap extending toward tang; silver trigger guard; silver name plate with monogram; silver ramrod thimbles, muzzle cap, side plate. Butt cap, guard, side plate, barrel, and tang simply but tastefully engraved. Fine relief carving on stock at rear of tang; incised carving on fore stock. Excellent workmanship. Ramrod not original. Not signed on barrel or lock, but inside of plate is marked with a large, curiously curved "H." Early-type trigger guard. Plate 1, figure 4.

Kentucky Flintlock Pistol, period of 1812 or later; caliber .48, smoothbore; 9-inch octagon barrel; 14.5 inches over all. Barrel is round-pin-fas-

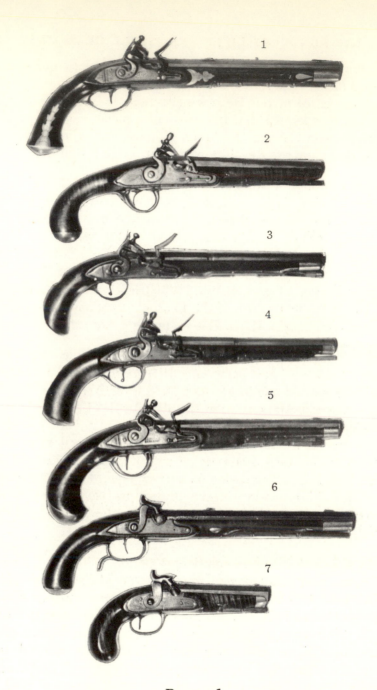

Plate 1

1. Kentucky Flintlock Pistol, Revolutionary period.
2. Kentucky Flintlock Pistol, Colonial period.
3. Kentucky Flintlock Pistol, pre-Revolutionary period.
4. Kentucky Flintlock Pistol, Revolutionary period.
5. Kentucky Flintlock Pistol, 1812 or later.
6. Kentucky Pistol, converted.
7. Kentucky Percussion Pocket Pistol.

tened. Kentucky-type front sight; no rear sight. Plain lock, 4.25 inches, with vertical slash across tail of plate. Iron pan with fence. Lock marked "J. J. Henry Boulton." Full stock, maple, red violin finish with heavy brass furniture: butt cap extends upward toward tang at rear; trigger guard, ramrod, thimbles, side plate, muzzle cap. Not marked on barrel. Hickory ramrod, Kentucky rifle type. Weight 2 lbs. 1 oz. Plate 1, figure 5.

Kentucky Pistol, converted from flintlock to percussion, period about 1800; caliber .34, smoothbore; 9.75-inch octagon barrel; 15.375 inches over all. Plain, handmade lock, originally flint, with vertical slash across tail of plate, marked, in script, "A.J." Attractive dark-finished curly maple full stock with brass butt cap, trigger guard with spur, ramrod thimbles, long muzzle cap. Barrel is flat-pin-fastened. Silver name plate. Kentucky front and rear sights. Very slender and graceful in design. Barrel not signed. Kentucky-type hickory ramrod. Weight 2 lbs. Plate 1, figure 6.

Kentucky Percussion Pocket Pistol, probably pre-Civil War period, about caliber .32, 4.875-inch octagon barrel, rifled with 7 grooves; 8.75 inches over all. Front and rear sights. Lock, 3.25 inches long, marked "T. Howell Philadelphia." Barrel marked "J. Fleeger, Allegheny." (This was the John Fleeger who was proprietor of the Allegheny Iron Works, Pittsburgh.) Tang extends well toward butt, which has no cap. Fine, natural stripe, full curly maple stock. Brass trigger guard and ramrod thimbles. Silver muzzle cap. Flat-pin-fastened. Weight 1 lb. 3 oz. According to tradition, a few of this type were made for captains of steamboats plying between Pittsburgh and New Orleans, to keep order among the passengers and crew. Plate 1, figure 7.

Early American Colonial Dog-lock Kentucky Pistol

Plate 2 contains only one picture, that of an American colonial Kentucky flintlock pistol of the dog-lock type, made about 1670, from the collection

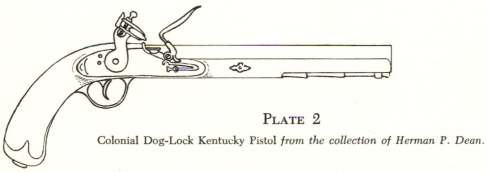

PLATE 2

Colonial Dog-Lock Kentucky Pistol *from the collection of Herman P. Dean.*

[27]

of Herman P. Dean. This type is a great rarity among Kentucky flintlock pistols and is illustrated here to emphasize the fact that the Kentucky pistol did not suddenly appear as a distinct type and then disappear without going through many changes.

Plate 3 and Plate 4 both consist of Kentucky flintlock pistols from the collection of Herman P. Dean and clearly show the common characteristics of this type of pistol and at the same time the individual differences, not only as to caliber, barrel length, total length, and weight, but also the details of design and construction.

Percussion Kentucky Pistols

Plate 5 and Plate 6 illustrate percussion Kentucky pistols from the Herman P. Dean collection. Notice the two, side by side, at the bottom of Plate 6, which are saw-handle dueling pistols made in Albany, New York. However, several of the other Kentucky pistols illustrated in this text, both flintlock and percussion, could be regarded as dueling pistols.

Kentucky Shoulder Arms

Plate 7 shows various Kentucky rifles.

Probably the greatest collection of shoulder arms ever assembled in the United States was that of Claude E. Fuller of Chattanooga, Tennessee, whose writings on guns are listed in the bibliography in the appendix of this book. Some years ago, this arms expert went through his entire collection and selected those specimens which he thought should illustrate any discussion of shoulder arms—U. S. martial, U. S. secondary martial and other muskets and rifles that played a part in the winning of the West.

Mr. Fuller and the present author did not agree completely on several points; viz.: in the designation of the year models for firearms; in the organization of his illustrations which did not follow the same chronological order as that used by the present author in his book, *The Gun Collector's Handbook of Values,* and in his description of the accompanying illustration of a Kentucky rifle as a "typical" Kentucky.

There is simply no such thing as a "typical" Kentucky rifle, any more than there is such a specimen as a "typical" man or a "typical" woman, merely because they belong to the human family. No two Kentucky rifles were alike, even if made by the same gunsmith, in the same shop and with the same tools. Each one was a custom-made, hand-built product, and those men who crafted the Kentucky rifle were, in a sense, artists, and each weapon turned out varied in some details from the preceding one.

Mechanically, however, Mr. Fuller was correct, to an extent. We have already examined the pre-1800 Kentucky rifle in its original flintlock con-

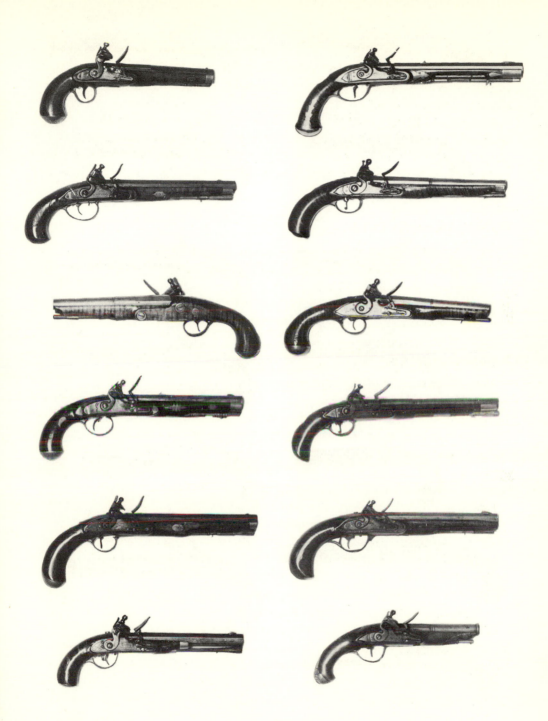

PLATE 3
Kentucky Flintlock Pistols *from the collection of Herman P. Dean.*

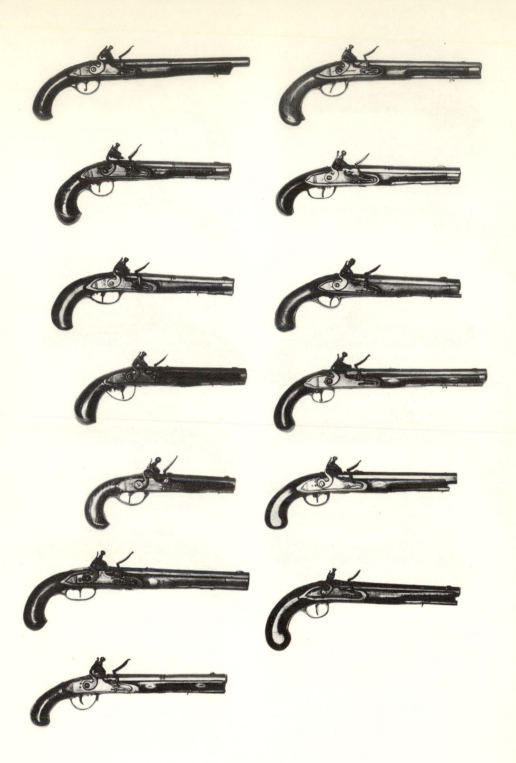

PLATE 4

Kentucky Flintlock Pistols *from the collection of Herman P. Dean.*

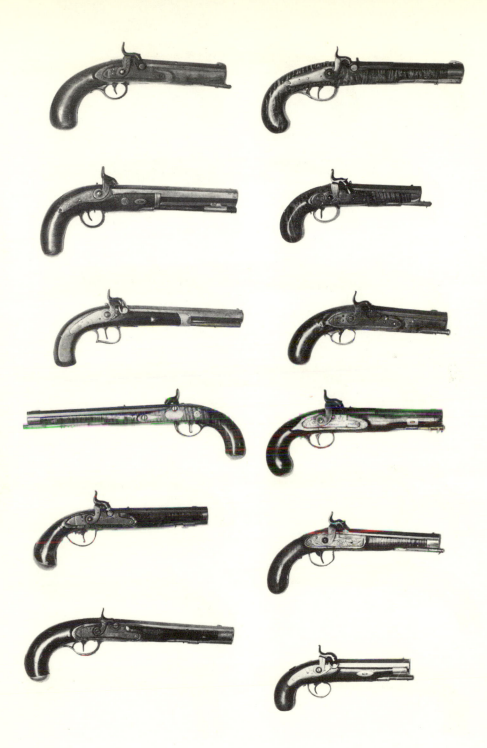

PLATE 5

Kentucky Percussion Pistols *from the collection of Herman P. Dean.*

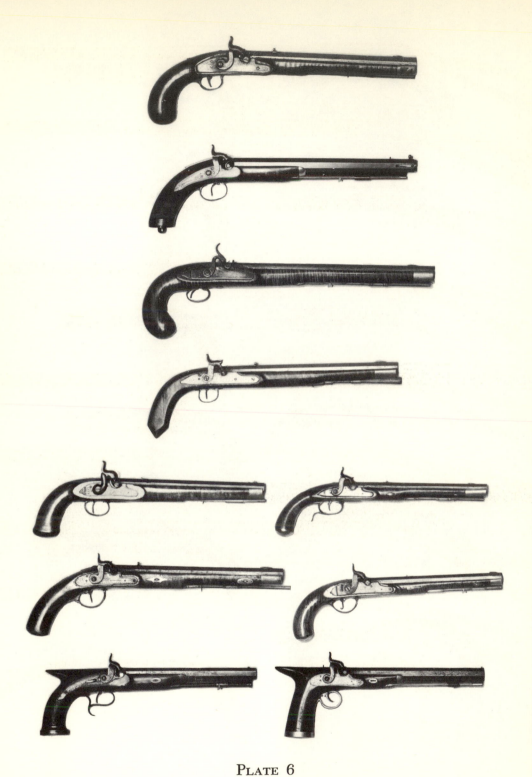

Plate 6

Kentucky Percussion Pistols *from the collection of Herman P. Dean.*

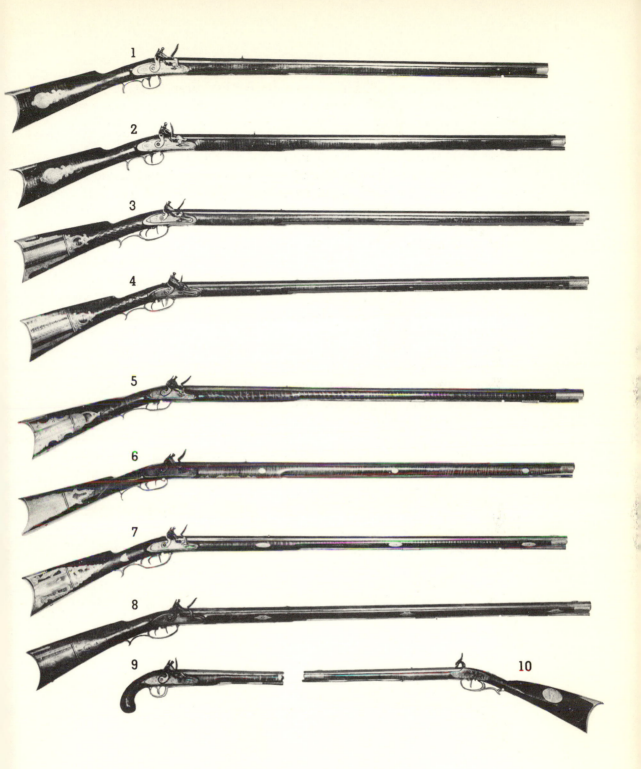

PLATE 7. Kentucky (Pennsylvania) Arms.

1. H. Leman, Lancaster, Pa., Kentucky Rifle.
2. H. Leman, Lancaster, Pa., Kentucky Rifle.
3. M. Fordney, Lancaster, Pa., Kentucky Rifle.
4. M. Fordney, Lancaster, Pa., Kentucky Rifle.
5. J. H. Johnson Kentucky Rifle.
6. Eichholtz & Bros., Lancaster, Pa., Kentucky Rifle.
7. A. Gumph, Lancaster, Pa., Kentucky Rifle.
8. H. Gibbs, Lancaster, Pa., Kentucky Rifle.
9. C. Isch, Lancaster, Pa., Kentucky Pistol.
10. John Settle, Pa., Boy's Kentucky Rifle.

dition to get the average bore, weight, barrel and over-all length, and this one would seem generally to fit into the average. However, those averages pertained to the early Kentucky, and during the later years barrels were shortened and other modifications made.

Moreover, about 1940 great quantities of counterfeit "genuine Kentucky rifles in their original flintlock condition" began to flood the market. True, some of these at one time might have been as represented, and had been changed by their owners to percussion pieces. Many others had probably been made with the percussion lock as original equipment. The counterfeiters were highly skilled, and they very carefully changed these to flintlocks, because the original flintlocks are relatively rare and demand a higher price than the later specimens. This work of faking was done by experts—something like the business of counterfeiting old paintings and antique furniture that even fool acknowledged authorities in those fields.

Often the combined knowledge of a metallurgist, machinist, master woodworker and specialized historian would be required to distinguish the genuine Kentucky flintlock from the fake. And to make everything look good, the same fakers made "genuine Kentucky flintlock rifles converted to percussion," and sold them at a slightly lower price. So you can begin to see the difficulties in judging accurately a Kentucky—let alone a "typical" example of that type of weapon.

The illustrations Mr. Fuller supplied for this book, especially those in Chapter IV, constitute a material contribution to our better understanding of the arms history of our nation.

III

Flintlock Pistols on the Frontier

ONE of the challenging aspects of the historical study of guns, as we have pointed out, is that there is no possible way of fitting them into neat little chronological boxes. To a limited extent, the same holds true when we speak of martial arms, although we do have a definition accepted by experts that covers almost all military firearms, and those of the United States for almost any given period. However, throughout our history, martial arms have also been used as personal weapons; because the soldier coming home used to take his musket or rifle with him. The discharged service man may not do that today, but government arms of all types are available for purchase at the so-called "surplus" stores, as well as at many gun-dealers'.

Therefore, this chapter is devoted to flintlocks which fit primarily the definition of martial arms. In this case, that is, United States flintlock pistols are those made in the government armories at Harpers Ferry, Virginia, and at Springfield, Massachusetts, or those made by private individuals or commercial manufacturers under contract to the United States for use by federal forces, or for distribution by the United States to the various states under federal jurisdiction.

These hand guns, then, were used by the armed forces of the government, and especially by troops operating or stationed along our changing frontier. With certain rare exceptions, infantry privates were not issued pistols; they were permitted to own and use their own weapons, but this did not make those military arms. The hand gun was generally the weapon of officers, along with their swords; of the cavalry along with their sabers or carbines; and frequently of artillerymen.

The pistol was always found in the belt or holster of the frontiersmen, for close work when a rifle would be awkward and useless. Also, because they

[35]

were handy and not too difficult to conceal, the hand gun—even the flint-lock in its smaller versions—was the favorite of outlaws and the gentry who transact their business in lonely places and along shadowed trails in the dark of the moon. In the truest sense, the pistol is a private and personal weapon; it is loaded with a full charge of mystery, intrigue and romance.

Not quite so romantic, and a proved fact perhaps difficult to believe today, is the knowledge that the United States, since the beginning of the Republic, was officially supplying Indians with its own martial weapons. These, of course—at least at the time—were not given to known hostile Indians, but Indians who wanted U. S. guns badly enough could usually get them un-officially, by capture in battle or by trading with those who had them. During one period of our post-Civil War history, politics and graft played a major role in seeing that even hostiles were supplied with the latest model of shooting irons. That was not a happy surprise for the troops having to face the murderous fire of new repeating carbines with old-issue single-shot rifles.

Like other good guns, the flintlocks were built to last a long time. They were in common use in the West by settlers, by Indians, by various men and groups on the dodge from the law. It is entirely possible that they are still in use somewhere on the continent of North America, perhaps among some primitive Indians of the Northwest.

The following United States Flintlock pistols are illustrated on Plate 1:

U. S. Pistol, Model 1805 (1806), Harpers Ferry, caliber .54, smoothbore; 10.625-inch, round barrel, key-fastened with projecting rib. Lock plate 4.875 inches long and 1 inch wide, marked with spread eagle, "US," and "Harpers Ferry," with date, which may be 1806, 1807, or 1808. Walnut half-stock 11.75 inches long. Total length 16 inches. Trigger guard 5.75 inches long with round rear end. Weight 2 lbs. 9 oz. Flat double-neck hammer. Steel ramrod on most specimens, but original may have been hickory. Small brass front sight, but original may have been made without sight. Brass-mounted. The manufacture was authorized Nov. 13, 1805, hence the correct model date is 1805. Most specimens were made in 1807. Plate 1, figure 1.

U. S. Pistol, Model 1807–1808, made by contractors, sometimes called an officer's pistol and also called a militia pistol, but used by regular enlisted men of the federal forces, and possibly carried by officers as well as enlisted militiamen; resembles U. S. Pistol, Model 1805 (1806), Harpers Ferry, except that it was usually pin-fastened and often full-stocked, somewhat resembling a Kentucky pistol. It was made under contracts in 1807 and 1808 with several gunmakers, probably including the following: William Calderwood; Jacob Cooke; A. & J. Ansted; O. & E. Evans; Abraham Henry; Joseph Henry; Henry Pickel; De Huff, Gonter & Dickert; Adam Leitner; John Shuler; Winner, Nippes & Steinman; John Miles; Martin Frye; Wm. & Hugh Shan-

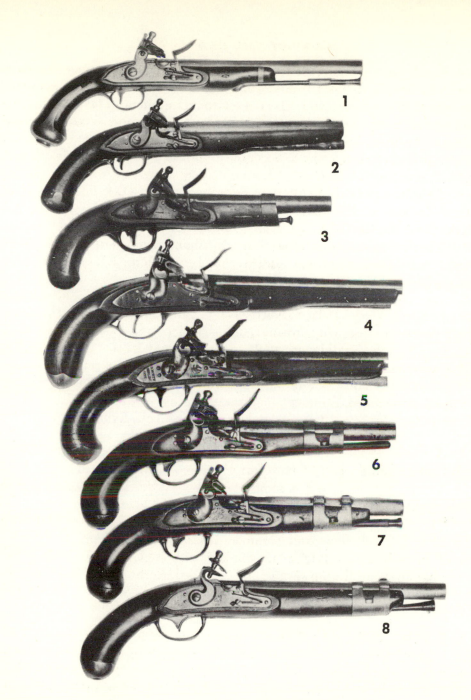

PLATE 1. U. S. Martial Flintlock Pistols.

1. U. S. Pistol, Model 1805 (1806), Harpers Ferry.
2. U. S. Pistol, Model 1807-1808, Contract Type, made by I. Guest.
3. U. S. Pistol, Model 1807-1808, Contract Type, made by O. & E. Evans.
4. U. S. Pistol, Model 1808, S. North, Navy.
5. U. S. Pistol, Model 1811 (1810), S. North, Army.
6. U. S. Pistol, Model 1813, S. North, Army.
7. U. S. Pistol, Model 1816, S. North, Army.
8. U. S. Pistol, Model 1817 (1818), Springfield.

non, and I. Guest. Values vary greatly according to the contractor and his workmanship. It is possible that contractors other than those mentioned here made this type of pistol. There is a strong argument in favor of classing this as a U. S. martial flintlock pistol; hence it is described here in general terms, but similar specimens of this general type are described under the names of their makers as U. S. Secondary Martial Flintlock Pistols. Plate 1, figure 2, made by I. Guest.

In addition to pistols of the type described above, O. & E. Evans made one under one of the 1807–1808 contracts which resembles the French Model Year IX (1800–1801) Cavalry Pistol; caliber .689, 7.87-inch barrel, total length 14.564 inches. Brass butt cap, band, side plate, and separate trigger bow. Lock plate may or may not be marked "Evans" and has a rounded face at the rear end. Plate 1, figure 3.

U. S. Pistol, Model 1808, S. North, Navy, caliber .64; 10.125-inch round, smoothbore, pin-fastened, browned, unmarked barrel. Walnut stock to ¼-inch from muzzle. Total length 16.25 inches. Weight 2 lbs. 14 oz. No sights. Brass-mounted. Double-necked hammer. Horizontal brass pin with fence. Brass mountings. Hickory ramrod. Iron belt hook on left. Lock plate marked "U. States" between hammer and frizzen spring, with an eagle, and "S. North Berlin Con." in 3 lines behind hammer. Plate 1, figure 4.

U. S. Pistol, Model 1811 (1810), S. North, Army, caliber .69; 8.625-inch round, smoothbore, pin-fastened barrel marked with "V," and eagle head with letters "CT" within the same oval. Walnut stock extends to ¼-inch from muzzle. Total length 15 inches. Weight 2 lbs. 11 oz. Lock plate 5.188 inches long and 1.05 inches wide. Brass trigger guard 6.25 inches long with pointed ends. Double-necked hammer. Brass pan with fence. Umbrella-shaped brass butt cap. Lock plate marked with eagle and "U. States" between hammer and frizzen spring, and "S. North Berlin Con." in 3 lines behind hammer. Usually listed as either Model 1810 or S. North, Berlin, 1st Contract. Plate 1, figure 5.

U. S. Pistol, Model 1813, S. North, Army, caliber .69; 9-inch, smoothbore, round barrel with semioctagonal breech, banded to stock with double straps, the forward one of which is not fluted, marked "P" and "US." Walnut stock, about 12.69 inches long, ends at forward edge of barrel band. Total length 15.3 inches. Weight 3 lbs. 6 oz. Trigger guard 5.56 inches long with round ends. Brass pan without fence. Double-necked hammer. Lock plate marked "S. North," followed by an eagle and "US MIDln Con." but sometimes marked only "S. North US." Plate 1, figure 6.

U. S. Pistol, Model 1816, S. North, Army, caliber .54; 9-inch, round, smoothbore barrel marked with "P," "US" and initials of either proof tester or barrel maker. Stock 13.25 inches long. Total length 15.3 inches. Lock plate 5.25 inches long, 1.125 inches wide, flat, beveled in front, rounded at rear, and marked "S. North," with an eagle, "US," and "MIDLn Con." between the pan and the hammer. Weight 3 lbs. 3 oz. Trigger guard 5.56 inches long with round ends. Iron-mounted. Double-strap barrel band. Iron butt strap. Brass front sight. Brass pan without fence. Hickory ramrod. Double-necked hammer. Plate 1, figure 7.

U. S. Pistol, Model 1817 (1818), Springfield, caliber .69; 11.06-inch, round, smoothbore barrel held by a double-strap iron band with a brass sight on front strap, and marked over the breech plug "1818," and also marked on some specimens with an eagle head between "P" and "V." Lock plate marked "Springfield 1818" in 3 lines behind hammer, and "US" under an eagle between the frizzen spring and the hammer. To be a Model 1817 (1818), Springfield, it should have an ordinary frizzen, a lock plate with a blunt rear end, and a double-necked hammer in addition to the markings described. If it has a frizzen resembling that of the French Charleville musket, with a turned-up toe; and a lock plate resembling that of the Charleville, with a sharp teat-shaped rear end, it may be classified as a U. S. Pistol, Model 1807, Springfield. There is doubt whether the Model 1817 (1818) was issued to the Army for service use. Plate 1, figure 8.

The following United States Flintlock pistols are illustrated on Plate 2:

U. S. Pistol, Model 1819, S. North, Army, caliber .54; 10-inch, round, smoothbore, browned barrel with brass sight on muzzle, held by a single spring-fastened band, and marked "P," "US," and the initial of the proof tester. Full stock, walnut, 13.75 inches long. Total length 15.5 inches. Weight 2 lbs. 10 oz. Lock plate 4.625 inches long and 1 inch wide, marked "S. North," eagle, "US," and "Midltn Conn." with date, which may be 1820, 1821, 1822, or 1823. Trigger guard 5.25 inches long with round ends. Iron-mounted. Brass pan without fence. Double-necked hammer. Sliding safety bolt on outside of lock near hammer. Peculiar catch behind cock on lock plate. Rear sight. Plate 2, figure 1.

Same, but bears additional marks, such as "S.N.Y." for State of New York.

Same, but Navy Model, with 8.5-inch round barrel, made without safety lock, and with belt hook on left. Iron-mounted. Swivel ramrod. No safety bolt. Double-necked hammer. Brass pan without fence. Lock plate marked "US" and "S. North" with date, usually 1827 or 1828. Plate 2, figure 2.

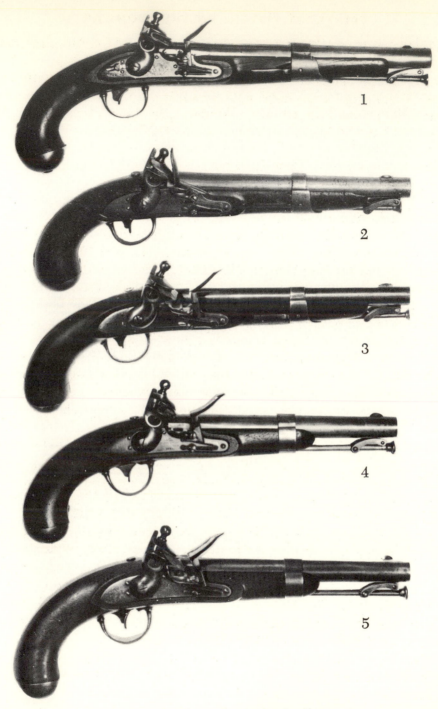

PLATE 2. U. S. Martial Flintlock Pistols.

1. U. S. Pistol, Model 1819, S. North, Army.
2. U. S. Pistol, Model 1819, S. North, Navy.
3. U. S. Pistol, Model 1826, S. North, Navy.
4. U. S. Pistol, Model 1836, R. Johnson, Army.
5. U. S. Pistol, Model 1836, A. Waters, Army.

U. S. Pistol, Model 1826, S. North, Army, caliber .54; 8.625-inch round, smoothbore, browned barrel held by single spring-fastened band, with brass sight on muzzle, and marked "P," "US," and initials. Total length 13.25 inches. Weight 2 lbs. 4 oz. Full stock, walnut. Iron-mounted. Swivel ramrod. No safety bolt. Double-necked hammer. Brass pan without fence. Lock plate marked "US" and "S. North" with date, usually 1827 or 1828.

Same, but Navy Model, with belt hook on left held by a separate screw and a pin. Plate 2, figure 3.

U. S. Pistol, Model 1836, R. Johnson, Army, caliber .54; 8.5-inch, round, smoothbore, bright barrel held on stock by single branch-band, and marked "US," "P," and initials. Three-quarter, walnut stock 11.125 inches long. Total length 14.25 inches. Weight 2 lbs. 10 oz. Flat, beveled lock plate 4.65 inches long and 1 inch wide, marked "US," "R. Johnson Middn Conn." and date. Rear sight. Brass front sight on barrel. Trigger guard 5 inches long with round ends. Polished iron mountings. Swivel ramrod. Double-necked hammer. Brass pan with fence. Plate 2, figure 4.

Same, but A. Waters, Army, marked on lock plate with eagle head and "A. Waters, Milbury, Ms." with date. Plate 2, figure 5.

United States Secondary Martial Flintlock Pistols: Definition and Classifications

United States Secondary martial flintlock pistols are single-barrel pistols of large caliber and size, which collectors and dealers are unable to honestly classify as United States martial flintlock pistols under the classification given above. The same is true of those which fall into one of the following categories:

1. Made by manufacturers having contracts with the United States; those who made pistols for state troops; and those who made and sold them to irregular and unofficial forces, such as Indian scouts, guides for the United States Army, etc.

2. Made by private manufacturers who had contracts with the state governments—not the United States—or contracts with semi-official state, county, or municipal organizations, military or naval.

3. Made by private manufacturers for sale to anyone who would buy the arms, such as federal officers, military, naval and civil; state officers, military, naval or civil; sheriffs, constables, marshals, or anyone else.

4. Made by private manufacturers as experimental, speculative, trial, or sample weapons in the hope of obtaining sales to the United States, the various states, or other organizations or individuals.

The following are typical examples:

[41]

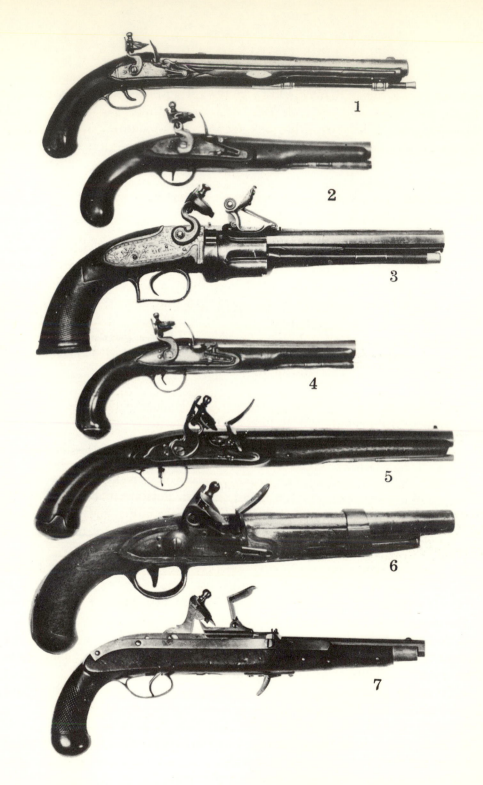

PLATE 3. U. S. Secondary Martial Flintlock Pistols.

1. Bird & Co. Pistol.
2. Booth Pistol.
3. Collier Flintlock Revolver.
4. Coutty Pistol.
5. Deringer U. S. Pistol, Model 1807-1808.
6. O. & E. Evans U. S. Pistol, Contract of 1807-1808, French Martial Type.
7. Hall Breech-loading Bronze-Barrel Pistol.

Bird & Co. Pistol, caliber .58; 12-inch, half-octagon, smoothbore, pin-fastened barrel. Total length 17 inches. Weight 2 lbs. 5 oz. Iron pan with fence, iron trigger guard, and other iron mountings. Gooseneck hammer. Lock plate marked "C. Bird & Co. Philada. Warranted." Full stock, walnut. Hickory ramrod. Plate 3, figure 1.

Booth Pistol, caliber .58; 8-inch, round, tapering, smoothbore, pin-fastened brass barrel marked "Philadelphia." Total length 13.5 inches. Weight 2 lbs. 5 oz. Brass-mounted. Iron pan with fence. Brass trigger guard. Full stock, walnut. Hickory ramrod. Lock plate marked "Booth." Plate 3, figure 2.

Collier Flintlock Revolver, caliber .34, 5-shot; 9-inch octagon barrel. Total length 17.5 inches. One specimen has a 4-inch barrel and a total length of 11.5 inches. Another specimen has a 6.125-inch barrel and a total length of 14 inches. Patented in 1818 by Elisha Haydon Collier, of Boston, Mass., an American citizen living in London. Plain metal finish. Brass-bead front sight. Raised-notch rear sight. Cylinder rotated by hand, although some had a spring arrangement for rotation. Collier returned to the United States. His patents were granted in England, France, and the United States; and although the known specimens in collections were apparently made in England, this rare and interesting weapon is listed here to provide for the occurrence of American-made specimens. Of course this is not a pistol, but it is listed here for convenience. Plate 3, figure 3.

Coutty Pistol, caliber .58; 7.75-inch, tapering, brass, pin-fastened, smooth-bore barrel marked "Philadelphia," with proof marks. Total length 13.5 inches. Weight 1 lb. 12 oz. Full stock, walnut. Iron pan with fence. Gooseneck hammer. Brass trigger guard. Hickory ramrod. Lock plate marked "Coutty." Plate 3, figure 4.

Deringer U. S. Pistol, Model 1807–1808, caliber .52; 10-inch, round, pin-fastened barrel. Total length 16.5 inches. Weight 2 lbs. 10 oz. Full stock, walnut. Brass trigger guard, butt cap and thimbles. Iron pan with fence. Flat double-necked hammer. Bevel-edged flat lock plate. Hickory ramrod. Lock marked "H. Deringer Phila." Barrel marked "M." Also see U. S. Pistol, Model 1807–1808. Plate 3, figure 5.

O. & E. Evans U. S. Pistol, Contract of 1807–1808, French Martial Type, caliber .69; 8.875-inch, round, smoothbore barrel fastened to stock with brass band, marked "PM" with date and "P." Total length 15 inches. Weight 2 lbs. 13 oz. Double-necked hammer. Oval brass trigger guard. Brass pan without fence. Steel ramrod. Iron back strap. Flat lock plate marked "Evans." This is supposed to have been patterned after the French Model Year IX (1800–1801) Cavalry Pistol, caliber .69, 7.9-inch barrel; total length 14.567 inches, with a round-faced, reinforced hammer; brass pan without fence; brass band, butt cap, side plate, and separate trigger bow; lock plate with rounded face at rear end. However, the usual specimen found in collections follows the description given. These contract-made pistols are classified sometimes as U. S. martial and sometimes as U. S. secondary martial. Plate 3, figure 6.

Hall Breech-Loading Bronze Barrel Pistol, caliber .50; single-shot; 5.562-inch, bronze, octagon, smoothbore, pin-fastened barrel. Weight 2 lbs. 13 oz. Full-length walnut stock. Checked butt. Brass, oval, pin-fastened trigger guard. Pan is part of bronze breech-block. Steel hammer, frizzen, and side plates. Bronze latch frame. No marks except what appears to be a serial number on right of breech-block, but this piece was undoubtedly made by John H. Hall, since it is similar in design to the U. S. Rifle, Model 1819, John H. Hall Breechloader. Plate 3, figure 7.

At this point it might be wise to interject a word of warning to those who might own an old gun with the letters "U.S." stamped somewhere on it. By themselves, the letters have little meaning, since anyone could—or can today—impress those letters on a weapon. The letters are no proof that the weapon is a United States martial arm; on the other hand, the absence of the letters does not prove that it is *not* one. Certainly, one would be most unlikely to find that stamp on such nonmartial flintlocks as . . .

Dueling Pistols Used in the West

Of course, there was "no sich animile" as a special kind of dueling pistol designed specially for frontier or Western use. In fact, a good many of the rough, tough frontiersmen weren't at all finicky about what kind of weapons they used to work off slights, grudges or insults, real or fancied, against someone else. Flintlocks, derringers, Colts, knives, fists or rocks, rifles or shotguns, when raw liquor and hot blood ran together—especially with the added catalyst of a pretty and flirtatious young woman—damage to the human body was sure to result and often it was fatal.

Dueling pistols from 1750 to 1800 were standardized as single-barrel flintlocks with a smooth bore 0.50-inch in diameter (that is, caliber .50). The barrel could not exceed 10.5 inches in length or be less than 9 inches long. The sights had to be fixed; that is, not adjustable. The grip, safety, and trigger system could be of any design or construction. Normally, dueling pistols were stocked to the muzzle, although from about 1740 on, they began to have half-stocks. The barrel was almost always octagonal in shape. For target practice, sights were used, but the arbitrary code of dueling made it unethical for the contestants to take deliberate aim. They were supposed to aim and fire on signal, or on command, as agreed upon by their seconds. Trigger pull could not exceed three pounds.

The so-called "hair triggers" were invented and developed so that it would be possible to fire a pistol by a very slight pressure on the trigger, so light that it would not disturb the aim. A small, powerful spring was first compressed, or to use the language of that period, it was "set" by pressing the trigger forward. Years later, set triggers were made so that they could be compressed or "set" by pressing a small button.

Poor or middle-class men could not afford to own a pair of dueling pistols. They were the property of the rich men, hence they were usually carefully made, with checkering of stocks, engraved metal parts, inlay work, and other forms of decoration, although a few were entirely lacking in decoration but without doubt showed the skill and care of the gunmaker.

Since dueling pistols were made for men of wealth, and had to be in pairs to conform with the dueling code, they were usually cased, and the case, or box, was of a quality suitable to the pistols. However, because of laws against dueling, in many instances neither the pistols nor the cases bore the marks or labels of the makers.

Dueling pistols were not martial pistols, either primarily or secondarily, hence they were used in warfare only incidentally. Some officers of the armed forces, who carried dueling pistols with them, fired them in preference to the regular martial pistols.

Plates 4 and 5 show additional illustrations of U. S. secondary martial flintlock pistols. Like Plate 3, they provide a vast array of makes, types, models, and variations used when the West was anything west of the Ohio River. These were definitely the side arms of the hunters, traders and trappers, including the long hunters and the mountain men.

Henry (J. Boulton) Pistol, caliber .60; 8.875-inch, round, smoothbore, pin-fastened barrel. Total length 14.25 inches. Full stock, walnut. Brass-mounted. Flat gooseneck hammer. Iron pan with fence. Brass butt cap and trigger guard. Hickory ramrod. Lock plate marked "J. Henry Boulton." Plate 4, figure 1.

Henry (J. J. Boulton) U. S. Pistol, Model 1826, caliber .54; 8.5-inch, round, smoothbore barrel held by single band. Total length 13.5 inches. Full-length walnut stock. Swivel, steel ramrod. Brass pan without fence. Double-neck hammer. Lock plate marked "J. J. Henry Boulton." Plate 4, figure 2.

[45]

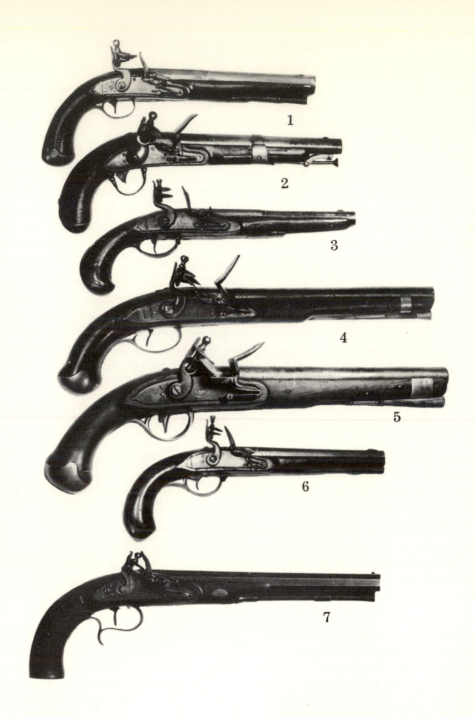

PLATE 4. U. S. Secondary Martial Flintlock Pistols.

1. Henry (J. Boulton) Pistol.
2. Henry (J. J. Boulton) U. S. Pistol, Model 1826.
3. Kuntz Pistol.
4. McCormick U. S. Pistol.
5. Miles Pistol, U. S. Model 1807-1808.
6. Moll Pistol.
7. North Dueling Pistol.

Kuntz Pistol, caliber .44; 9-inch, round, smoothbore, pin-fastened barrel marked "Kuntz Philad." Total length 12.75 inches. Full-length walnut stock. Bird's-head butt. Flat gooseneck hammer. Iron pan with fence. Brass trigger guard. Lock plate marked "J. K. Philad." Plate 4, figure 3.

McCormick U. S. Pistol, caliber .64; 10.25-inch, round barrel marked "U.S." with eagle head over "P" in an oval. Brass trigger guard, butt cap, and side plate. One brass thimble. Full-length walnut stock with brass band partly around barrel. Brass-tipped hickory ramrod. Flat lock plate marked "Ketland & Co." in front of hammer and "United States" in two curved lines behind hammer. Iron pan with fence. Flat gooseneck hammer. Stock marked "U.S." on left and "McCormick," the name of the U. S. contractor. The lock, of course, was made by Ketland in England. Plate 4, figure 4.

Miles Pistol, U. S. Model 1807–1808, caliber .58; 9.75-inch, round, smoothbore, pin-fastened barrel marked "Miles Philada P." Total length 15.5 inches. Full-length walnut stock. Brass-mounted. Flat double-neck hammer. Iron pan with fence. Hickory ramrod. Flat lock plate marked "Miles Phila" within an oval. Plate 4, figure 5.

Moll Pistol, caliber .38; 8.375-inch, brass, octagon, rifled, pin-fastened barrel marked "P. & D. Moll Hellerstown." Total length 14 inches. Full-length tiger-striped maple stock. Gooseneck hammer. Iron pan with fence, forged as part of lock plate. Brass trigger guard. Brass knife-blade front sight. Open rear sight, of iron. Hickory ramrod. Flat imported lock plate marked "London Warranted." Supposedly used by cavalry in War of 1812. Plate 4, figure 6.

North Dueling Pistol, caliber .50; smoothbore, 10.25-inch, octagon, browned barrel with a countersunk gold seal having "S. North Middletown Conn." in raised letters, and the word "Connecticut" engraved in Old English letters on the barrel itself. Single set trigger. Two iron thimbles. Engraved double-neck hammer. Safety lock. Gold-lined vent. Engraved tang. Horn-tipped walnut half-stock. Checkered grip. Square butt. Rib under barrel for horn-tipped hickory ramrod. Silver wedge escutcheons. Parts other than barrel are casehardened. Specimen described was one of a matched pair, each of which was numbered 11. This was not a martial weapon and is included here only for convenience in listing. Plate 4, figure 7.

Richmond-Virginia Pistol, caliber .54; 10-inch, round, smoothbore, key-fastened barrel with extending rib. Total length 16.625 inches. Weight 2 lbs. 13 oz. Walnut half-stock. Swivel ramrod. Brass-mounted. Double-neck

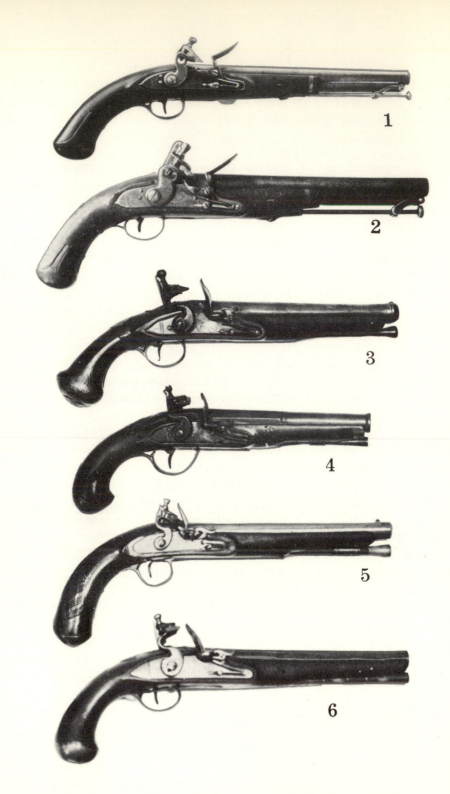

PLATE 5. U. S. Secondary Martial Flintlock Pistols.

1. Richmond-Virginia Pistol, marked "Richmond, Virginia."
2. Richmond-Virginia Pistol, marked "Richmond."
3. Walsh Pistol.
4. Halbach & Sons Pistol.
5. Lawrence Pistol.
6. Smith & Hyslop Pistol.

hammer. Iron pan with fence. Brass butt cap, trigger guard, ramrod thimble, and barrel reinforcing band. Lock plate usually marked "Richmond" with the date (somewhere between 1812 and 1816), and "Virginia." Resembles U. S. Pistol, Model 1805 (1806), Harpers Ferry except for the swivel ramrod design. Made for the Militia by the State of Virginia. Plate 5, figure 1.

Same, but marked "Richmond" and the date, without the "Virginia." Plate 5, figure 2.

Walsh Pistol, caliber .54; 8-inch, brass, tapering, cannon-shaped, smoothbore, pin-fastened barrel marked "J. Walsh Philad" inside an engraved panel. Total length 14 inches. Weight 1 lb. 15 oz. Full-length walnut stock. Gooseneck hammer. Brass pan and fence cast as part of lock plate. Brass mountings, lock plate, trigger guard, and name plate. Hickory ramrod. Lock plate marked "J. Walsh" inside an engraved panel. Plate 5, figure 3.

Halbach & Sons Pistol, caliber .50; 6.75-inch, rifled, bronze barrel, part octagonal and part round, with cannon muzzle, pin-fastened. Total length 12 inches. Bronze-mounted with butt cap ornamented with the American eagle, shield, and 13 stars. Flat gooseneck hammer. Iron pan with fence. Specimen illustrated is not marked, but some specimens are stamped on the lock plate "Halbach & Sons." This pistol was made in Baltimore, Md., about 1780. Plate 5, figure 4.

Lawrence Pistol, caliber .62; 9-inch, round, iron, smoothbore, pin-fastened barrel. Total length 15 inches. Flat gooseneck hammer. Brass-mounted. Marked "Lawrence" on the lock plate and "Philada" on the barrel. Lawrence was listed in the Philadelphia city directory as a gunsmith from 1821 to 1829. Plate 5, figure 5.

Smith & Hyslop Pistol, caliber .58; 8.75-inch, round, iron, smoothbore, pin-fastened barrel. Total length 14 inches. Late type gooseneck hammer. Brass-mounted. Lock plate marked "Smith & Hyslop New York Warranted." Full stock with checkered butt. The manufacturer was active in New York City in the 1820's. Plate 5, figure 6.

IV

Musket, Rifle and Carbine:
American Martial Shoulder Arms

THIS chapter will cover nearly three centuries in the history of American shoulder arms. The guns discussed and illustrated date from a matchlock which might have been carried by Captain John Smith when he first set foot on the New World in 1607, in the little river island that was to struggle for survival as Virginia's first colony. Or they could have been in the hands of another soldier, thirteen years later and leagues to the north; a bearded and steel-corseleted captain named Miles Standish. We close with a description of the U. S. Magazine Rifle, Caliber .30, Model 1896, Krag-Jorgensen—to give its official title. The U. S. Model, 1902, was used by the last of the Plains soldiers, and this improved type was issued and found wanting in the Spanish-American War, and also in the Philippine campaign. Later, it made way for the Mauser-like Springfield, 1903, as it is popularly called.

The Krag, however, was a perfectly good weapon for the state home guard units of World War I, and was used at times for training federal troops. A good many still lively gaffers recall, without nostalgia, the sore shoulders acquired on the rifle range with this gun in their youthful days of 1916–1917. What they called the Krag then was neither official nor polite, but it seemed to help at the time.

Guns have always been—and still are—built to last. So it's only natural that most of these weapons, even when they became obsolete for military use and lost favor with civilians who were able to beg, borrow or steal improved models, found their way to the wilderness frontiers as the varying and uneven tide swept slowly westward.

Most of these guns come under the classification of martial weapons, a special category described in a preceding chapter on martial flintlock pistols. Requirements for this classification are the same with martial shoulder arms, and that of course includes the musketoon and the carbine. The musketoon is a musket with a shortened barrel, designed for convenience in handling from horseback, just as the carbine is a rifle with a shortened barrel. As martial weapons they are cavalry guns. There is, incidentally, no official length of barrel for these saddle guns. It varies. When a government arsenal or a contractor designates a piece as a carbine or a musketoon, then that's what it is. It's that simple.

While the true Kentucky rifle, as it was made up to about 1830 and also in its Plains-rifle version as made by Hawken, was a favorite of the pioneer, it would be a mistake to assume that the famous weapon was used to the exclusion of any other shoulder gun. This is especially true as new ignition systems developed and came into general use. During the initial frontier stage, when only hunters, traders and trappers braved the wild country, the newer weapons were difficult to come by; freighter caravans, pack animals, and flatboats were all slow, definitely not on schedule—except perhaps, wishfully, a seasonal one—and they didn't go far from their destinations, which were the settlements rather than the rude and remote wickiups of the real frontiersman.

The hunter and trapper, rough-looking, smelly, dressed in greasy, smoke-stained buckskins, might get as far as one of the fur-trading posts with his catch of plews—or even as far as St. Louis—but as a rule, gold was no friend of a man who had spent one or three years in the mountain country, risking his life hunting beaver, mink and otter; then risking it once more against hostile Indians, though he might live with or have married into some band. It was not easy for a man to keep his wits and his money when he hit town with a strong hunger for a sky-high card game, the warmth of mellow whisky, the fierce, hot action of a gouging, chawing ba'ar-hugging tussle with a buckskin rival, or the friendly promise of girls—your choice of any shape, size and color! Well, boys, that's where the money goes; the promised new outfit, the newfangled percussion gun, all the froufrou for the squaw. Maybe a man was lucky to head back to the high country with his hair, his horse and his old flintlock. . . .

So it was often that well into the percussion era the flintlock continued to supply meat and peltry, both for clothing and for commerce. Too, it was well tested in fighting off enemies intent on scalps and loot, and it was always the rifle whose voice spoke loudest to the frontiersmen. Yet for the traders, the smoothbore had its uses. When they rode into an Indian village with their packs to deal for furs, smoothbore muskets were brought out—what matter if the bores were rusty or warped, the powder adulterated and the balls lopsided. Eventually, flame and smoke would spurt from the muzzles and the noise would rival the thunder itself. And if that wouldn't produce the prime furs, then tin mugs filled from jugs of water, alcohol, red pepper and burned sugar—with a few rattler heads stirred in it—would do the trick. For this was the traders' trap line, and as long as the gentle-men of New York, New Orleans, of London and Paris, demanded good beaver hats, and their fine ladies needed otter and mink for jackets or sleeve linings, this kind of trapping paid off handsomely.

It didn't take long for the Indian to learn the advantages of a rifle—again, even an old one—and later, that he could shoot faster still with a breech-loading piece. Nor was he at all backward in discovering the advantages of a magazine rifle. The government supplied good rifles to the friendly tribes, sometimes as a treaty compensation when a tribe was to be relocated to another area. Of course, if unsuspected gold or silver was found on these new lands, in some way or other the treaty terms would be forgotten in the rush. In those cases, the white settlers and gold-hungry prospectors would get an unpalatable taste of their own lead, served hot from their own brand of rifles. Or perhaps better ones.

The Indians could also get rifles by sporadic, swift raids on isolated stockaded outposts, on wagon trains, and even on small, remote settle-ments. For the Indian, generally speaking, was a born fighting man, a warrior. From the horse Indians of the high Plains—Apache, Comanche, and Kiowa in the Southwest, to the Sioux, Blackfeet, and Arapaho in the North, to say nothing of many other tribes—he was a real soldier, and won the profane respect of our most experienced generals. Afoot or on the back of a pony, an Indian with a rifle was no one to fool with, as the charred remains of many a burned wagon train and lonely ranch house testified.

So here in words and pictures are many of the shoulder arms that soldiers, civilians and Indians used when they wrote the dramatic—and sometimes desperate and tragic—history of our Western frontier.

Colonial Flintlock Musket, probably assembled in the American colonies prior to 1700; caliber .80; 30-inch barrel; total length 53.5 inches; weight 8.5 lbs. Black walnut stock made without butt plate. Brass mountings. Lock 7 inches long, 1.25 inches wide, with gooseneck hammer· Bone-tipped ram-rod. Lock has faint markings similar to English flintlock muskets of period before 1700, but remainder of musket apparently made in America. Plate 1, figure 1.

Matchlock Musket, type probably brought to America for the first mili-tary units of the new colonies, and is of the type used about the early or middle seventeenth century. Caliber .812, 41.5-inch, pin-fastened barrel; total length 55.5 inches; weight 9.25 lbs. Plate 1, figure 2.

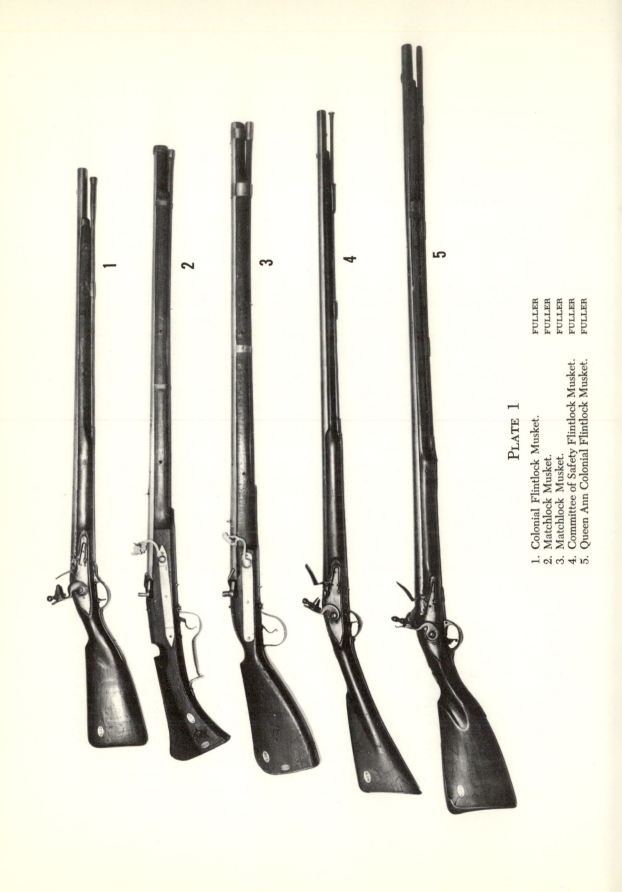

PLATE 1

1. Colonial Flintlock Musket.   FULLER
2. Matchlock Musket.   FULLER
3. Matchlock Musket.   FULLER
4. Committee of Safety Flintlock Musket. FULLER
5. Queen Ann Colonial Flintlock Musket.   FULLER

Matchlock Musket, caliber .812; 42.5-inch barrel; total length 57.5 inches; weight 10.25 lbs. When the regulations for firing muskets were changed so that they were fired from the shoulder instead of from the chest, larger butt stocks were provided, of which this specimen is an excellent illustration. This musket probably was used in America in the latter part of the seventeenth century. Plate 1, figure 3.

Committee of Safety Musket, caliber .72; 43-inch, pin-fastened barrel; total length 59 inches; weight 9 lbs. Brass mountings. Marked on lock plate "S. Barrett" and engraved on butt plate tang "Daniel Everet." Probably made by S. (Deacon) Barrett, who had a large water-power shop in Massachusetts in 1774. This may be described as a typical American colonial musket, but it is more accurately described as a typical musket of the type purchased by the Committees of Safety in the various American colonies to supply the people with arms for the coming Revolution.

There is no one definite, individual type, make, or model that can be placed in this classification to the exclusion of all other flintlock shoulder arms. Each Committee of Safety appointed one or more agents to obtain arms already made, and gunsmiths were chosen to make new arms, some of which followed the British Brown Bess of that period while others copied the French martial shoulder arms of the same era. Many of these arms were not marked. Some were assembled from parts made by different men; thus, a lock plate might have one name, and the barrel another name; parts from foreign-made arms were freely used. Fuller considered this particular specimen to be a representative piece. Plate 1, figure 4.

Queen Ann Colonial Musket, caliber .812; 49-inch barrel; total length 65.5 inches; weight 11 lb. English walnut stock or possibly Honduras mahogany, being light-colored but very hard. All mountings, including four ramrod pipes, guard and butt plate are heavy brass castings. Lock 7 inches long, 1.25 inches wide, with gooseneck hammer. Lock marked with a British crown, "AR," and arrow, similar to other British martial marks of the period. This type of musket was accepted by Fuller as characteristic of those arms brought to America in the period 1670 to 1700 and used by the American Colonial troops serving with the British in the French and Indian Wars. Plate 1, figure 5.

British Brown Bess Musket, or simply Brown Bess, was used by both British and Americans during the Revolutionary War. The arm was a smoothbore, muzzle-loading flintlock musket, varying in caliber from .684 to .758, the average being .753. A distinguishing feature is that the barrel is fixed to the stock by lugs under the barrel, and held by sliding pins through the stock, instead of being held by bands. There are many variations. The proof marks are those used by the British of that period. Not illustrated.

U. S. Musket, Model 1795, caliber .69; flintlock; smoothbore; 44.75-inch barrel; 56.5-inch stock. Total length 59.5 inches. Lock plate 6.625 inches long and 1.28 inches wide. Trigger guard 13 inches long with pointed ends. Three bands. Stamped "Springfield" in a curve at the rear of the lock plate. Marked "U.S." in script over an eagle on the lock plate in front of the cock. The year of manufacture was marked in shallow script on the tang of the butt plate. Head of the eagle faced to the rear. Iron pan with fence at the rear. Beginning in 1802, the word "Springfield" ran straight on the lock plate, but in 1804 the word was placed in front of the cock, and the "U.S." was placed over the eagle. The rear end of the lock plate was then marked with the year of manufacture. This model was copied from the French flintlock musket, Model 1763, known to collectors as the "Charleville Pattern." Butt plates were dated from 1799. Plate 2, figure 1.

U. S. Musket, Special Model 1795, similar to the regular Model 1795, except for minor variations. Plate 2, figure 2.

U. S. Musket, Model 1809 (sometimes called Model 1808), caliber .69; flintlock; smoothbore; barrel 44.5 inches long; stock 56 inches long. Lock plate 6.31 inches long and 1.31 inches wide. Trigger guard 10.75 inches long with round ends. Three bands. It is not possible to assign definitely the year 1808 to a model, but collectors for years have assumed that there is such a model. In 1808, parts from the Model 1795 were still being used to make muskets, but in 1809 the Springfield Armory began to make muskets which remained the same until the U. S. Musket, Model 1812, began to be assembled late in 1815; hence we should not speak of a Model 1808, but instead should list it as a Model 1809, already described. Some specimens marked on lock plate in front of cock with "U.S." in script over eagle, with "Springfield" in curved line under eagle. Rear of lock plate marked with year. This model closely follows the Model 1795 except for a change in the lock, the turning lug on the barrel, and the barrel tang lug, hence only a collector who specializes in these early martial shoulder arms can classify them accurately. Plate 2, figure 3.

U. S. Musket, Model 1812, caliber .69; flintlock; smoothbore; 42-inch barrel; 54-inch stock. Total length 57 inches. Lock plate 6.375 inches long and 1.31 inches wide. Trigger guard 11 inches long with round ends. Three bands. The grip does not extend into the stock as it did on previous models. The left side of the stock has a cheek recess if made at Springfield, which

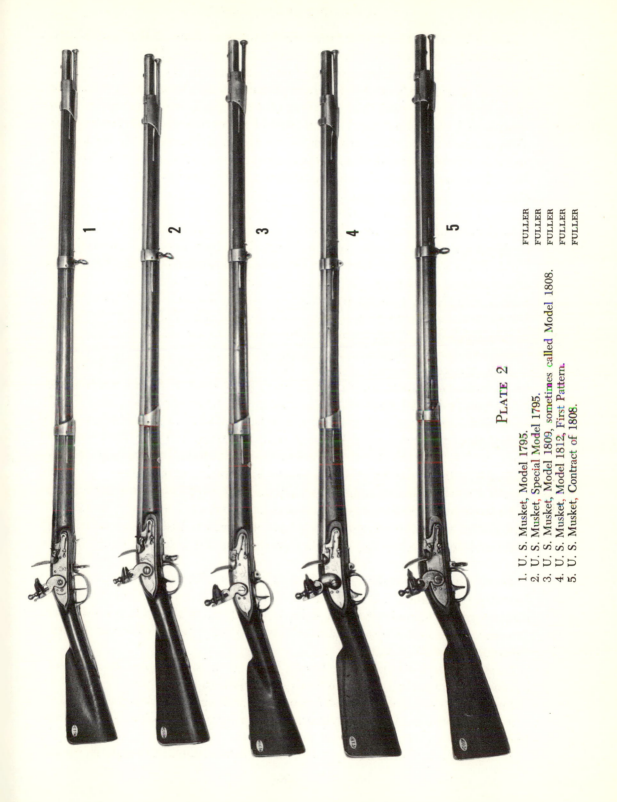

PLATE 2

1. U. S. Musket, Model 1795.
2. U. S. Musket, Special Model 1795.
3. U. S. Musket, Model 1809, sometimes called Model 1808.
4. U. S. Musket, Model 1812, First Pattern.
5. U. S. Musket, Contract of 1808.

FULLER
FULLER
FULLER
FULLER
FULLER

characterizes this model as distinguished from that made at Harpers Ferry. Some collectors divide this model into three patterns. There were three arrangements of band springs: The first had them to the rear; the second type had spring studs; and the third type had the band springs to the front. Since this was the period of the War of 1812, parts from various models were mixed in the field, to the confusion of historians and collectors. Lock plate marked with "U.S." in script over eagle and "Springfield" in curved line under eagle in front of cock. Year marked to rear of lock plate behind cock. The one illustrated in Plate 2, figure 4 is known as "First Pattern," with band springs to the rear.

Collectors and historians also recognize specimens made under contract by Henry Deringer, father of the Henry Deringer, Jr., who created the "Philadelphia Deringer Derringer," described elsewhere in this text, and also similar specimens made by Robert Johnson, in 1814. In addition, collectors recognize a somewhat similar contract musket made by Eli Whitney, although there are enough differences between the Whitney musket and the others to classify it under its own heading.

U. S. Musket, Contract of 1808, caliber .69; smoothbore, 42-inch barrel; 54.25-inch stock. Total length very slightly more than 57 inches. Lock plate 6.5 inches long and from 1.188 to 1.25 inches wide. Trigger guard 11.25 inches long with pointed ends. Three bands. Copied from muskets furnished as samples by the Springfield Armory and the Harpers Ferry Armory, and possibly the French Model 1763, Charleville Pattern. There was a vast amount of deviation from the average dimensions given above because muskets were made by many contractors, both skilled and semiskilled in the manufacture of firearms. There was a problem of obtaining materials, and there were not enough competent inspectors. Fuller described the specimen illustrated as the "Henkle Contract Musket." Plate 2, figure 5.

U. S. Flintlock Musket, Model 1812, caliber .69; smoothbore; 42-inch barrel; 54-inch stock. Total length 57 inches. The left side of the stock has a cheek recess if made at Springfield, which distinguishes this model from practically the same musket made at Harpers Ferry. Some collectors divide this model into three patterns:
First pattern: Bottom band retained by band spring 3 inches long to rear of band with usual lug on spring fitting into a hole in band.
Second pattern: Bottom band retained by stud spring forward of band.
Third pattern: Bottom band retained by spring 2.5 inches long, forward of band.
In addition to those made at the two United States National Arsenals

(often referred to as U. S. Armories), this model was made under contract by Henry Deringer, Sr., Robert Johnson, Eli Whitney, and others. Plate 3, figure 1.

U. S. Experimental Model Flintlock Musket, 1812, is what Claud E. Fuller described as "one of the interesting experimental pieces made by the government at Harpers Ferry." It is the third pattern of the U. S. Flintlock Musket, Model 1812, but it has a magazine primer which serves as a battery for the flint. When the projecting lever is turned one-half revolution, it permits enough powder for one priming to be fed into the pan. A screw cap made it possible for the shooter to fill the magazine with enough powder for several priming charges. Since there was a danger of the magazine exploding, it is probable that few were made. Although this arm did not reach the West, it was one step in the long road toward the development of the arms which won the frontier. Plate 3, figure 2.

U. S. Flintlock Musket, so-called Model 1831. This arm was so listed originally by Fuller, but recent research has shown that there was no model of that year made by the United States. Actually, it is U. S. Musket, Model 1821 (sometimes called Model 1822), caliber .69; smoothbore; barrel 42 inches long, with bayonet lug on top, and with the addition of a fence to the pan. Plate 3, figure 3.

U. S. Flintlock Musket, Model 1821. This is similar to the above, but is generally classified by collectors as either Model 1821 or Model 1822. Actually, there's no distinct model in either of those years. In addition to those made by the two national armories, thousands were made by private contractors, one of whom was Henry Deringer, Sr. Plate 3, figure 4.

U. S. Flintlock Musket, Model 1835 (Usually called Model 1840). This musket was manufactured at the Springfield Armory from 1840 to 1844, and by private contractors until 1848, as well as by the Harpers Ferry Armory, although the years of manufacture there are uncertain. Most of these muskets were converted from flintlock to percussion fire and were used by both the United States and the Confederacy in the Civil War. It was also used in vast quantities in the West, before, during, and after the Civil War, both by civilians and Indians. Plate 3, figure 5.

U. S. Flintlock Rifle, Contract Model 1814. Because he considered this rifle one of the most important transitional models in the story of American arms, Fuller includes this in his book, *The Whitney Firearms.* The rifle has a part-round, part-octagonal barrel, 33.312 inches long; marked at top flat

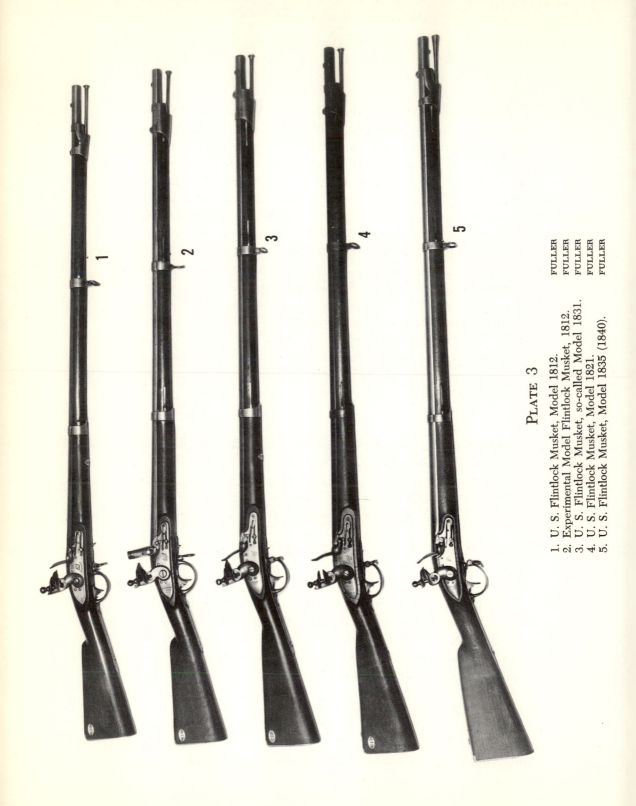

PLATE 3

1. U. S. Flintlock Musket, Model 1812.   FULLER
2. Experimental Model Flintlock Musket, 1812.   FULLER
3. U. S. Flintlock Musket, so-called Model 1831.   FULLER
4. U. S. Flintlock Musket, Model 1821.   FULLER
5. U. S. Flintlock Musket, Model 1835 (1840).   FULLER

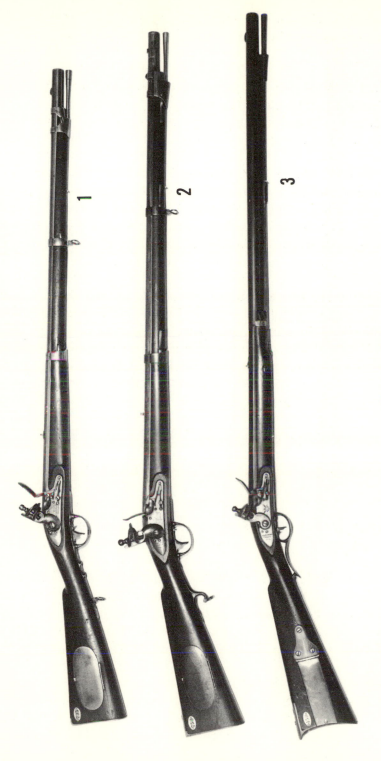

PLATE 4

1. U. S. Flintlock Rifle, Contract Model 1814.　FULLER
2. U. S. Flintlock Rifle, Model 1817.　FULLER
3. U. S. Flintlock Rifle, Model 1803, Harpers Ferry.　FULLER

at breech and on left flat at breech with names or initials of contractors. An oval iron patch box in the stock was carried over to the Model 1817 Common Rifle. Plate 4, figure 1.

U. S. Flintlock Rifle, Model 1817, also called The Common Rifle. Caliber .54; 36-inch barrel; 48-inch stock. This rifle, the second regulation U. S. rifle to be officially adopted and issued to the armed forces, was manufactured by the national armories and private contractors. Plate 4, figure 2.

U. S. Fintlock Rifle, Model 1803, Harpers Ferry. This rifle is also called Model 1800, and Model 1804; caliber .54; barrel averaging 33 inches long, and total length between 48 and 49 inches. It resembles the U. S. Rifle, Model 1814. This was the first regulation rifle adopted and issued by the United States, and shows the influence of the Kentucky rifle more than any of our other U. S. martial or secondary martial arms. Plate 4, figure 3.

Virginia Manufactory Flintlock Rifle, caliber .54, 39-inch octagon barrel. Total length 54.5 inches. Weight 9 lbs. 14 oz. Full-length walnut stock to end of barrel with brass tip. Brass butt plate, patch-box cover, and trigger guard. Patch-box-cover spring catch at bottom of stock. Wooden ramrod held by 3 brass ramrod ferrules. Lock plate marked "Virginia" between cock and pan, and "Richmond," which is arranged differently from that on Virginia Manufactory Flintlock Musket. Plate 4, figure 4.

Same, but converted to percussion.

Same, but caliber about .44, 44-inch octagon barrel. Total length 58 inches. Marked with Virginia State marks.

Note: Ornamental patch box, bearing some legend or motto, may be found on Civil War models.

U. S. Musketoon, Model 1839 (1840). Sometimes called Model 1840, this caliber .69 flintlock, smoothbore, 26-inch barrel arm has a bayonet stud 2 inches from the muzzle. The Springfield Armory production is considered to be the standard issue to the armed forces, while those made at Harpers Ferry are regarded as being model or pattern pieces. Plate 5, figure 1.

U. S. Musketoon, Artillery Model 1842. Fuller lists this as the U. S. Model 1842 Artillery Percussion Musketoon. This weapon derives from the U. S. Musket Model 1842, which was caliber .54; percussion (cap and ball); smoothbore; 32-inch barrel; 55-inch stock. This weapon had to be cut down

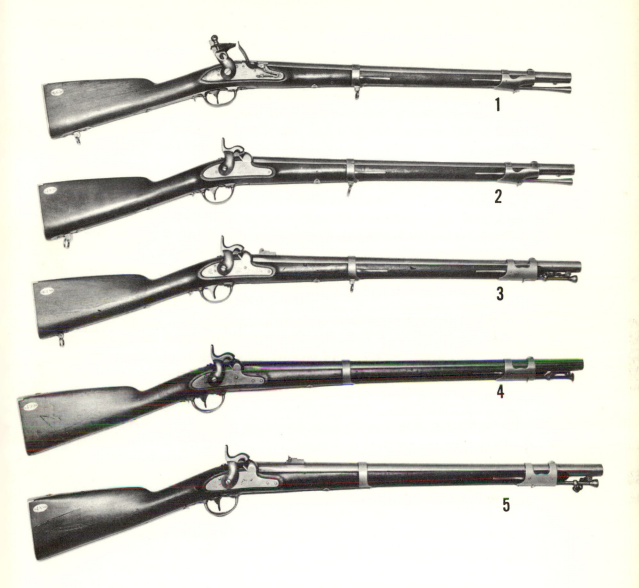

Plate 5

1. U. S. Musketoon, Model 1839 (1840).   FULLER
2. U. S. Artillery Percussion Musketoon, 1842.   FULLER
3. U. S. Model 1842, Cavalry, Musketoon, Chain Swivel.   FULLER
4. U. S. Model 1842, Cavalry, Musketoon, Regulation Swivel.   FULLER
5. U. S. Model 1842, Cavalry, Rifled, with chain swivel and
   butt stock loaded.   FULLER

in length for mounted use. Incidentally, those with genuine Confederate markings are worth more to collectors than those bearing only the marks of the Springfield and Harpers Ferry Armories. Plate 5, figure 2.

U. S. Model 1842 for Cavalry, Chain Swivel. This is Fuller's description and he means that it was a percussion shoulder arm with the barrel cut short at the armory for mounted use. Caliber .54; smoothbore. Plate 5, figure 3.

U. S. Model 1842 Musket, caliber .54; percussion, smoothbore, and **U. S. Rifled Musket, Model 1842,** were the same, but the latter arm was bored and rifled to caliber .58, with a long-range rear sight for the Model 1855 elongated, or Minié-type ammunition. Strictly speaking, we are dealing here not with separate types or models but with modifications or variations. Both the smoothbore musket, caliber .54, and the rifled musket, caliber .58, were shortened at the national armories for mounted use.

U. S. Model 1842, Cavalry, Regular Swivel, to most people looks like figure 3, but this has the regulation swivel instead of the chain swivel. This detail is very important to advanced collectors, dealers, and some historians. If you look closely at the forward end of the weapon, just under the barrel, you should be able to see the difference. Plate 5, figure 4.

U. S. Model 1842, For Cavalry, Modified. This is a modification of the chain swivel gun illustrated by figure 3, except that it has been rifled and the butt stock loaded. Plate 5, figure 5.

Muskets Converted from Flintlock to Percussion

In 1842, the War Department decided to inspect and classify all muskets made before 1832, and also those made later. Those in serviceable condition made after 1831 were to be retained without examination. Those in serviceable condition made from 1821 to 1831 were to be issued when needed and otherwise retained for alteration from flintlock to percussion. Those made from 1812 to 1820 were not to be considered satisfactory for issue to troops or for alteration, but were to be held in reserve for emergency. Those made before 1812 and all damaged or unserviceable arms not worth repairing were to be set aside for sale. In practice, this last class of arms was found to contain many weapons made from 1828 to 1831.

Briefly, the methods of altering flintlock shoulder arms to percussion were as follows: (1) using the old hammer with a side lug; (2) using a new hammer with a side lug; (3) providing a bolster lug with a clean-out screw; (4)

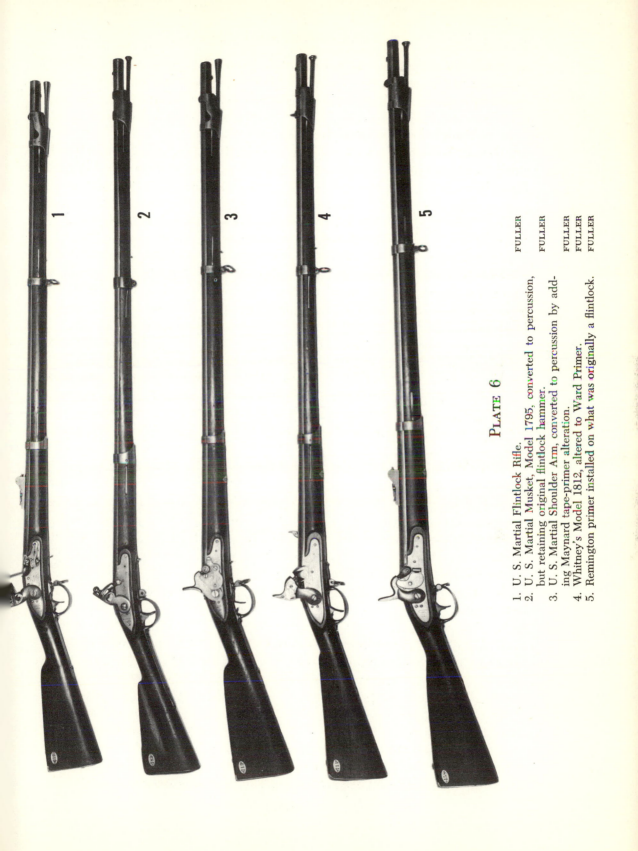

PLATE 6

1. U. S. Martial Flintlock Rifle.   FULLER
2. U. S. Martial Musket, Model 1795, converted to percussion,
   but retaining original flintlock hammer.   FULLER
3. U. S. Martial Shoulder Arm, converted to percussion by adding Maynard tape-primer alteration.   FULLER
4. Whitney's Model 1812, altered to Ward Primer.   FULLER
5. Remington primer installed on what was originally a flintlock.   FULLER

providing a bolster lug as part of a new barrel breech; and (5) screwing a cone into the top of the barrel. In all these cases, we are dealing with muzzle-loading, single-shot shoulder arms. Such converted weapons were used on both sides in the Civil War, by the Indians against the white people, and by the settlers against the Indians.

Some of these flintlock shoulder arms altered to percussion were originally rifled muskets and retained at their full length; some were rifled muskets cut down to become carbines; some were made originally in short length for mounted use; some were smoothbores and obviously remained smoothbores, regardless of their barrel length, although a small-caliber smoothbore in some cases could be rifled to provide a rifle of a larger caliber.

Plate 6 consists of five shoulder arms which Fuller thought should be grouped together to illustrate some of the problems encountered during the transition from one type of ignition to another. From top to bottom, they are:

1. U. S. martial flintlock which Fuller designated as Model 1842, although the U. S. Rifle, 1841 (also called 1842), was a percussion rifle. Actually, this was a rifle which, through some oversight, was not converted to percussion, and again clearly demonstrates an overlap between the flintlock and percussion periods.

2. U. S. Musket, Model 1795, converted to percussion, but retaining its original flintlock hammer.

3. Designated by Fuller as Model 1840 with the Maynard tape-primer alteration to percussion.

4. Classified by Fuller as Whitney's Model 1812, altered to Ward primer. The alteration consisted of welding to the barrel a large cone seat that supplied a high fence around the nipple, the removal of flintlock parts, and the installation of a hammer which contained a coil of primers (caps). The patent was issued July 1, 1856.

5. An example of the Remington primer installed on what was originally a flintlock.

U. S. Rifled Muskets and Carbines of 1855: The U. S. shoulder arms listed in *The Gun Collector's Handbook of Values* as 1855 Models are as follows:

(1) U. S. Rifled Carbine, Model 1855 (Also called Model 1854).
(2)   Same   (Maynard), made by U. S. Armories.
(3)   Same   (Maynard), made by contractors·
(4)   Same   (Maynard), with Confederate marks.
(5) U. S. Rifle, Model 1855 (Maynard), made as a rifle and not treated as a rifled musket, with variations from the above.
(6) U. S. Rifle, Model 1855 (Maynard), with Confederate marks.

[66]

(7) U. S. Pistol-Carbine, Model 1855, also classified as a U. S. Percussion Pistol.

(8) U. S. Pistol-Carbine, Model 1855, with detachable stock.

The Claude E. Fuller 1855 Specimens: Plate 7, figure 1, shows the Model 1855 as first issued. Figure 2 shows the Model 1855 with the improvements of 1859, including the patch box and sight.

U. S. Rifled Musket, Model 1861: Figure 3 shows one version of this model. *The Gun Collector's Handbook of Values* recognizes ten variations or modifications of this one shoulder arm, as follows:

(1) U. S. Rifled Musket, Model 1861; caliber .58; percussion. This was the principal infantry weapon of the Civil War, adopted because of dissatisfaction with the Maynard tape-lock model of 1855. There is no magazine for the Maynard primer, and the stock is not cut to admit the lock plate which would have the magazine. The mainspring is longer. Otherwise, it conforms to the Model of 1855.

(2) U. S. Rifled Musket, Model 1861, Cadet, total length 53 inches, but look out for fakes cut down to this length to raise value.

(3) Same as either of the above two, but with Confederate marks.

(4) U. S. Rifled Musket, Model 1861, Colt, same as previous specimens but marked on lock plate, "U.S. Colt's Pt. F.A. Mfg. Co. Hartford, Ct."

(5) U. S. Rifled Musket, Model 1861, with Confederate marks.

(6) U. S. Rifled Musket, Model 1861, Amoskeag, same as above described models but marked on lock plate, "Amoskeag Mfg. Co., Manchester, N.H.," with the date and an eagle between the U and the S in "U.S."

(7) U. S. Rifled Musket, Model 1861, Amoskeag, with Confederate marks.

(8) U. S. Rifled Musket, Model 1861, Lamson, Goodnow & Yale, same as above models except marked "L.G. & Y., Windsor, Vt." with "U.S." under the eagle and the date behind the hammer.

(9) U. S. Rifled Musket, Model 1861, Lamson, Goodnow & Yale, with Confederate marks.

(10) U. S. Rifled Musket, Model 1861, Civil War Contractors, made by several manufacturers, many of whom became famous later in making arms of their own design, such as Savage, Remington, etc.

U. S. Rifled Musket, Model 1863: Shown on Plate 7, figure 4. However, there are at least six versions or modifications of this model, as follows:

(1) U. S. Rifled Musket, Model 1863, First Type, caliber .58; percussion; 40-inch barrel; 52.5-inch stock. Total length, 56 inches. Marked "Springfield" with an eagle and the date behind the hammer.

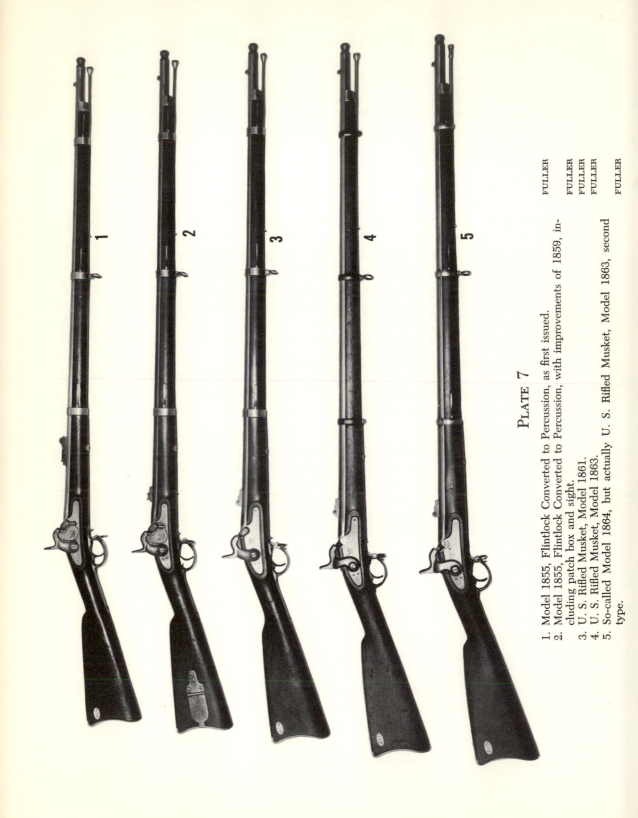

PLATE 7

1. Model 1855, Flintlock Converted to Percussion, as first issued. FULLER
2. Model 1855, Flintlock Converted to Percussion, with improvements of 1859, including patch box and sight. FULLER
3. U. S. Rifled Musket, Model 1861. FULLER
4. U. S. Rifled Musket, Model 1863. FULLER
5. So-called Model 1864, but actually U. S. Rifled Musket, Model 1863, second type. FULLER

(2) U. S. Rifled Musket, Model 1863, First Type, Made by Private Contractors, and so marked.

(3) U. S. Rifled Musket, Model 1863, Second Type, sometimes called the Model 1864. The rear-sight mortise in the barrel was eliminated and the method of attaching the rear sight to the barrel was changed. Although the First Type had no band springs, this model had band springs and solid bands.

(4) U. S. Rifle, Model 1863, Remington Arms Co. Contract, caliber .54, instead of the caliber .58 found on those described above. Percussion; rifled; 33-inch barrel; 44-inch stock. Three bands. Barrel and lock are like those of the Model 1841 Rifle. Bands and ramrod are copied from the Model 1863 Rifled Musket, Second Type. Butt plate, trigger guard, stock, and stock tip are copied from the Model 1855 Rifle. Marked "Remington's, Ilion, N.Y. 1863," with an eagle.

(5) U. S. Rifle, Model 1863, Navy, caliber .69; 34.25-inch, round, rifled barrel. Muzzle-loading. Lock marked "U.S." under eagle and "Whitney-Ville 1863." Finger spur rear of guard. Large ramrod tip. Known to collectors as the "Navy Plymouth Model," and also called the "Whitney-Ville Model." Not usually recognized as a distinct model.

(6) U. S. Double Musket, Lindsay, Model 1863, caliber .58; percussion; 41.375-inch barrel; 53-inch stock. Total length 56 inches. Marked "Lindsay's Patent Oct. 9, 1860." A single trigger operates two hammers centrally hung side by side, each of which ignites a percussion cap on one of the two nipples. Two charges are loaded into the barrel, one on top of the other. The fire from the cone of the right hammer ignites the forward charge, and the rear charge of powder is fired from the left hammer. This was an experimental model, hence it is not a U. S. martial shoulder arm in the strict sense of the term, but it marks another step in the long road toward rapid-fire, breech-loading arms, and it does bear the designation of "Model 1863."

U. S. Rifled Musket, So-called Model 1864: Illustrated by figure 5 is the so-called Model 1864, but actually it is the Second Type, U. S. Rifled Musket, Model 1863.

Cadet Models of both flintlock and percussion arms were supposed to be suitable for young men who were not yet physically strong enough to drill and execute the manual of arms with the shoulder gun of regulation weight, nor were they expected to carry such weapons into action. For many years cadets at the U. S. Military Academy, West Point, and midshipmen at the U. S. Naval Academy at Annapolis, have carried and fired the regulation shoulder arm issued to all our armed forces, thereby disproving this outmoded theory. However, during the flintlock and percussion periods, cadets

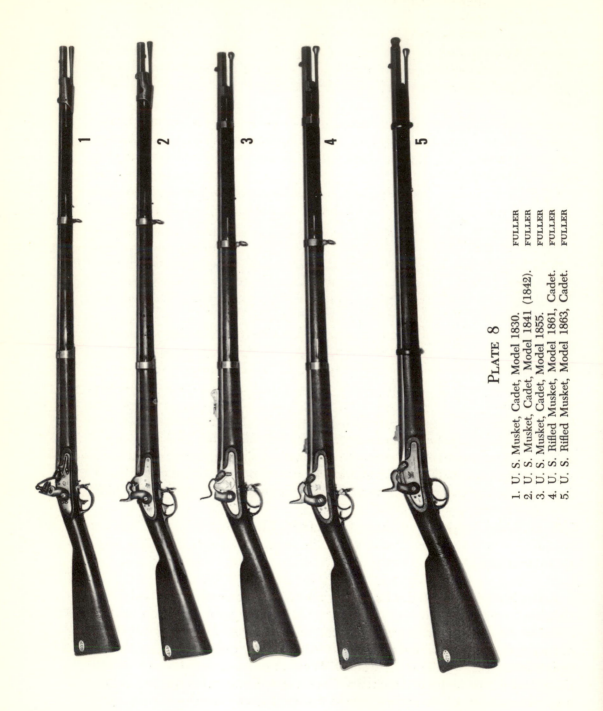

PLATE 8

1. U. S. Musket, Cadet, Model 1830.   FULLER
2. U. S. Musket, Cadet, Model 1841 (1842).   FULLER
3. U. S. Musket, Cadet, Model 1855.   FULLER
4. U. S. Rifled Musket, Model 1861, Cadet.   FULLER
5. U. S. Rifled Musket, Model 1863, Cadet.   FULLER

and midshipmen were accepted at the academies at a comparatively tender age. Even so, they were not too tender to manage and fire an arm weighing between 8 and 9 pounds and with a total length often equal or exceeding that of the young man.

Plate 8 of the Fuller collection consists of five Cadet models. Figure 1 is the Model 1830, described in *The Gun Collector's Handbook of Values* as U. S. Musket, Cadet, Model 1830, caliber .54; flintlock; smoothbore; 40.5-inch barrel; 43-inch stock; total length 55.75 inches. The more important parts were not made at Springfield but came from previous models made either at Harpers Ferry or by contractors. How and why this was termed a Cadet Model is a mystery.

Figure 2 is the U. S. Musket, Cadet, Model 1841 (1842); caliber .54; percussion; smoothbore; 40-inch barrel; made by Springfield Armory in 1844 and 1845.

Figure 3 is the U. S. Cadet Musket, Model 1855, which is the same as the U. S. Rifled Musket, Model 1855, but not equipped with the Maynard tape primer, and with the barrel 38 inches long; a total length of 53 inches, and weighing 8.5 pounds. This gives a slightly different length, of course, to the stock, barrel and rammer from that of the Rifled Musket cited above. From 1856 to 1860 the Springfield Armory produced 2,813 of these models. They are exceedingly scarce now, and appear so seldom on the market that they are not recognized for evaluation in *The Gun Collector's Handbook of Values*, although Fuller does list this model in his *Firearms of the Confederacy*.

Figure 4 is a U. S. Rifled Musket, Model 1861, Cadet, previously mentioned as one of the variations of the Model 1861. Here, the principal characteristics are a 38-inch barrel and a total length of 53 inches.

Figure 5 is the U. S. Rifled Musket, Model 1863, Cadet, which we have not listed before in this text and have not recognized in *The Gun Collector's Handbook of Values* because of its scarcity, the small number of reported sales and the probability that not many were made or issued.

The Lindsay Double Musket, and the Conversions. Shown in figure 1, Plate 9, is the U. S. Double Musket (Lindsay), Model 1863, which we have described before. Although this was strictly an experimental model, it stimulated the activities of inventors, manufacturers, and promoters.

Figure 2 is the Miller Conversion of the Springfield Musket, based upon a patent issued to William H. and George W. Miller, West Meriden, Connecticut, May 23, 1865. U. S. Patent No. 47,902.

Figure 3 is the B. S. Roberts conversion of the Springfield Musket, based upon a patent granted to Benjamin S. Roberts, U. S. Army, February 27, 1866. U. S. Patent No. 52,887.

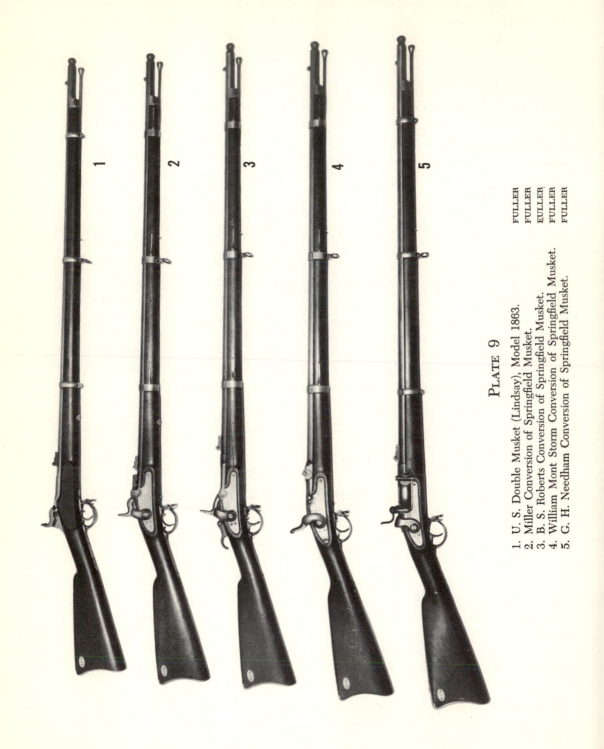

PLATE 9

1. U. S. Double Musket (Lindsay), Model 1863.   FULLER
2. Miller Conversion of Springfield Musket.   FULLER
3. B. S. Roberts Conversion of Springfield Musket. FULLER
4. William Mont Storm Conversion of Springfield Musket. FULLER
5. G. H. Needham Conversion of Springfield Musket. FULLER

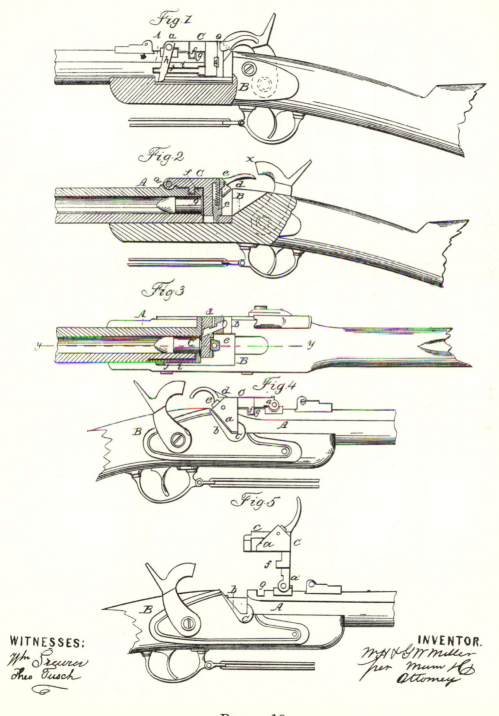

Fig.1

Fig.2

Fig.3

Fig.4

Fig.5

WITNESSES:

INVENTOR.

PLATE 10

W. H. & G. W. Miller Patent Application.   FULLER and U. S. ORDNANCE DEPT.

W. M. STORM.
Breech-Loading Fire-Arm.

No. 15,307.

Patented July 8, 1856.

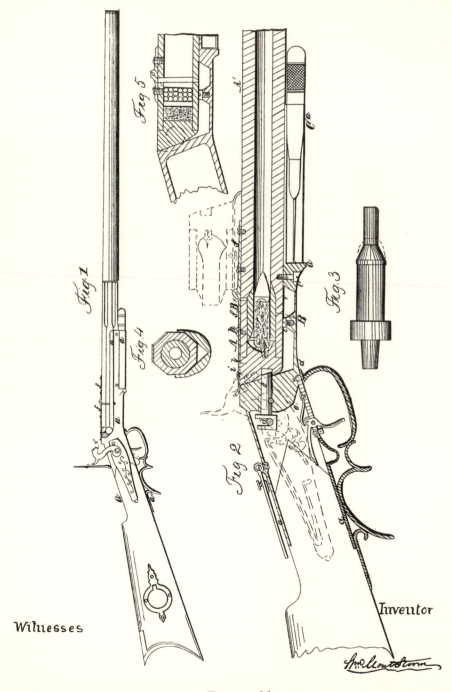

Fig. 1   Fig. 5   Fig. 4   Fig. 2   Fig. 3

Witnesses

Inventor

PLATE 11

W. M. Storm Patent Application.   FULLER and U. S. ORDNANCE DEPT.

Figure 4 is Mont Storm conversion of the Springfield Musket, based upon a patent issued to William Mont Storm, July 8, 1856. U. S. Patent No. 15,307.

Figure 5 is the Needham Conversion of the Springfield Musket, issued to J. and G. H. Needham, May 21, 1867. U. S. Patent No. 64,999.

Reproductions of Patent Applications. Plate 10 is a reproduction of the Miller patent application; Plate 11 is the W. Mont Storm application, which, with many others, were granted by the Patent Office. They represent only a few of the many methods of converting Springfield flintlock, muzzle-loaders into percussion, breech-loading shoulder arms.

In the West, both to the north and the south, Indian affairs were going badly. Hostiles were on the war path; they never had quite settled down since before the Civil War, since they distrusted the white men's promises. Now the buffalo were being slaughtered in untold numbers. This in effect took the food from their mouths, clothes from their backs and roofs from over their heads and spelled their destruction as a free-roving people. Yet they were putting up a desperate and a brilliantly savage fight.

By 1878, Apache warriors in New Mexico and Arizona, under the wise leadership of Geronimo, had been terrorizing ranchers and ambushing cavalry for six long years. Although in the north, Sitting Bull and Crazy Horse were at last defeated, the burning memory of the Custer massacre on the Little Big Horn, his Seventh Cavalry making their last stand with single-shot carbines against the bloody toll of Sioux' magazine rifles, was still a bitter, rankling memory.

The Ordnance Board was convened in Washington to examine magazine rifles—the kind of shoulder arm that was breech-loading, repeating and with cartridges fed from the magazine. Twenty-nine different makes were tested and only one was accepted. That was . . .

U. S. Rifle, Model 1878, Hotchkiss, also known as the Hotchkiss Military Magazine Rifle, Model 1879. This was a caliber .45 breechloader; center fire; 26.688-inch barrel; a 45.5-inch stock; total length 48.625 inches. The tubular magazine in the butt of the stock, loaded through a trap in the butt plate, receives 5 cartridges. With one in the chamber, the rifle then has a capacity of 6 loads. It was manufactured at the Springfield Armory, except for the actions, and was also produced under contract by Winchester. Apparently the Army received about 500 from 1879 to 1880, and strangely enough the U. S. Navy received 3,500 from 1879 to 1881, although the records are open to dispute. Plate 12 is an Army Ordnance drawing that shows a cross-section of the action, including butt, and also nomenclature.

[75]

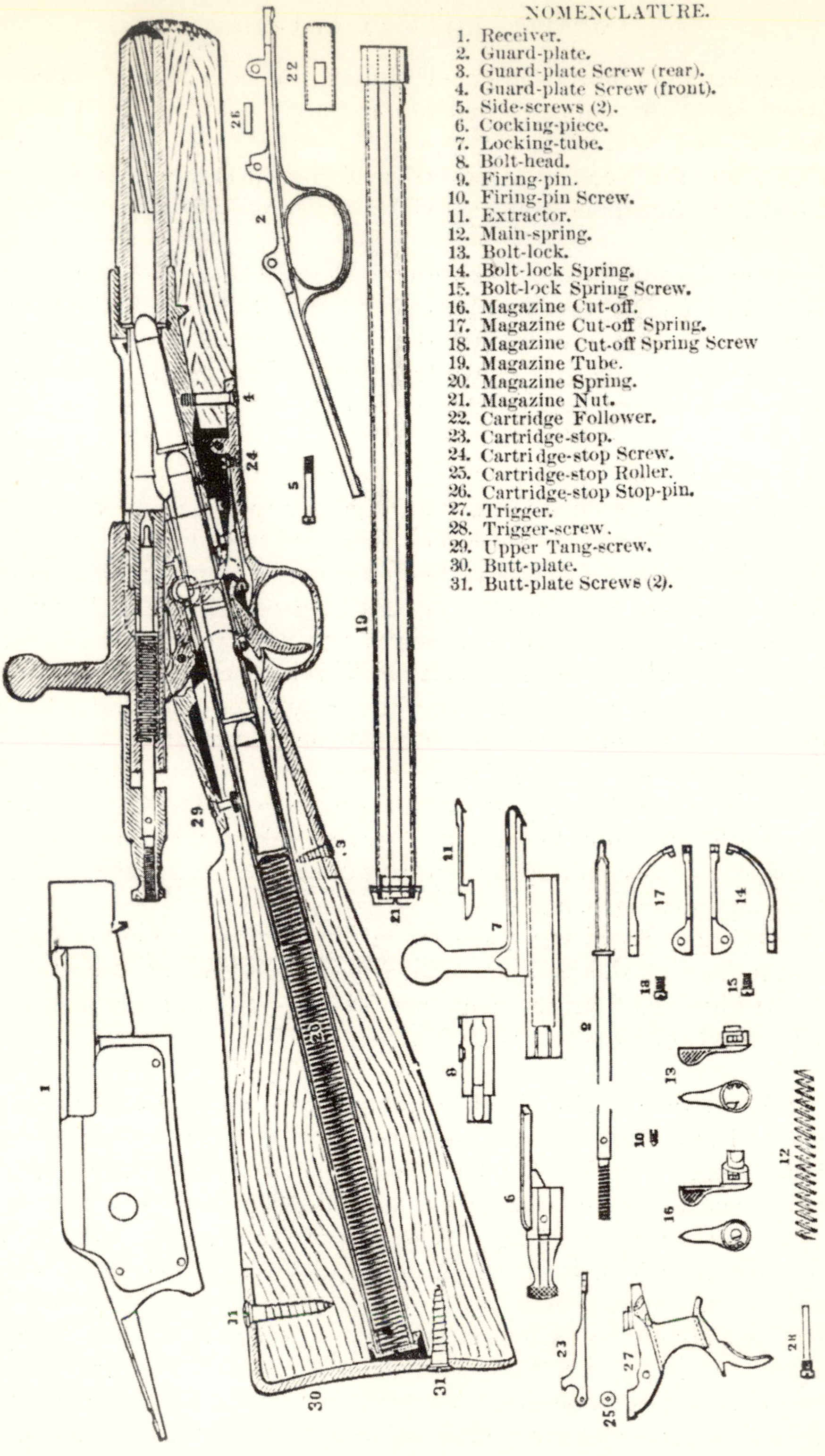

NOMENCLATURE.

1. Receiver.
2. Guard-plate.
3. Guard-plate Screw (rear).
4. Guard-plate Screw (front).
5. Side-screws (2).
6. Cocking-piece.
7. Locking-tube.
8. Bolt-head.
9. Firing-pin.
10. Firing-pin Screw.
11. Extractor.
12. Main-spring.
13. Bolt-lock.
14. Bolt-lock Spring.
15. Bolt-lock Spring Screw.
16. Magazine Cut-off.
17. Magazine Cut-off Spring.
18. Magazine Cut-off Spring Screw
19. Magazine Tube.
20. Magazine Spring.
21. Magazine Nut.
22. Cartridge Follower.
23. Cartridge-stop.
24. Cartridge-stop Screw.
25. Cartridge-stop Roller.
26. Cartridge-stop Stop-pin.
27. Trigger.
28. Trigger-screw.
29. Upper Tang-screw.
30. Butt-plate.
31. Butt-plate Screws (2).

PLATE 12

U. S. Rifle, Model 1878, Hotchkiss.   FULLER and U. S. ORDNANCE DEPT.

Even after the action of the Ordnance Board of 1878, most of the troops continued to be armed with single-shot rifles, so in 1882 another meeting of the board was held. It heard the claims of twenty inventors and tested 53 firearms, several of which were originated by the same inventor and fundamentally similar in design. Out of this 1882 Ordnance Board meeting came an arm sometimes called the . . .

Model 1882 Lee Magazine Rifle, which was the preference of that board. However, in his report to Secretary of War Robert T. Lincoln, Brigadier General S. V. Benet, Chief of Ordnance, said in part: "While the Lee gun is entitled to the first place, the comparative merits of the three guns put them nearly on a par in point of excellence."

The three to which he referred were the Hotchkiss, manufactured largely by Winchester; the Model 1882 Lee, manufactured by Remington, and the Chaffee-Reece Magazine Rifle, for which the Colt Patent Fire Arms Mfg. Co. made a bid, but which was actually manufactured in the Springfield Armory. Plate 13 is a sectional view of the Lee Magazine Rifle, with nomenclature of principal parts.

These three rifles were manufactured and then issued to troops for trial, while manufacturers, inventors, and—it is safe to say—at least some Army families—held their breath. Then came the big let-down. Reports from 149 Army companies showed a preference for the old Springfield single-shot rifle. This caused General Benet to write another report to the Secretary of War on December 15, 1885, that . . . "The Springfield rifle gives such general satisfaction to the Army that we can safely wait a reasonable time for further developments of magazine systems. . . ."

As a direct consequence of this report, development of a repeating rifle for U. S. martial use was delayed. The Army was safe and happy with their old single-shot rifles. Safe and happy—squarely in the sights of the Henry and the Spenser repeating rifles and carbines which, somehow or other, the Indians managed to get their hands on in quantity, and use with their usual deadly skill.

Eight years later, an Ordnance Board again convened in a long session —from December 16, 1890 to July 1, 1892—and at last selected the gun now known as . . .

U. S. Magazine Rifle, Model 1892, Krag-Jorgensen. This was a caliber .30 repeating rifle with a 30-inch barrel, a 46-inch stock. Its total length was 49.14 inches, and it operated by bolt action. On the whole, it was an improvement over the original Danish Krag-Jorgensen rifle. The magazine holds 5 cartridges and is under the receiver to the left. A magazine cut-off makes it possible to use it as a single-loader. This was the first U. S. rifle

NOMENCLATURE.

A. Receiver.	E. Thumb-Piece.	I. Trigger.	N. Magazine-spring.
B. Bolt.	F. Key-sleeve.	K. Magazine-catch.	O. Trigger-guard.
C. Firing-pin.	G. Extractor.	L. Sere-spring.	P. Stock.
D. Main-spring.	H. Sere.	M. Magazine.	R. Tang-screw.
		S. Guard-screw	

PLATE 13

U. S. Model 1882 Lee Magazine Rifle.   FULLER and U. S. ORDNANCE DEPT.

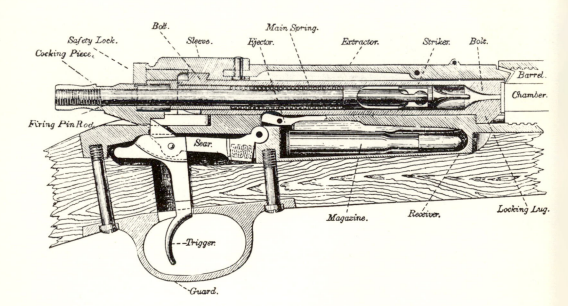

PLATE 14

U. S. Magazine Rifle, Model 1892, Krag-Jorgensen.   FULLER and U. S. ORDNANCE DEPT.

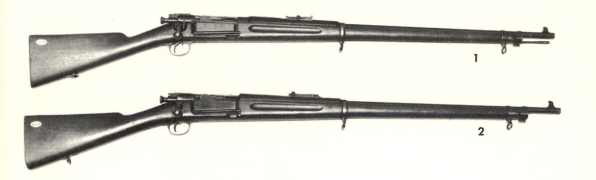

with the barrel top covered with wood to serve as a hand guard, and it was also the first U. S. martial rifle to use smokeless powder and a reduced-caliber cartridge. Eventually, all the 1892 models were converted to the Model 1896. Plate 14 is a sectional view of the action and shows nomenclature of important parts. Plate 15, figure 1 shows the gun.

The U. S. Magazine Rifle, Model 1896, Krag-Jorgensen. Although the Model 1892 was an important step in progress from the old single-shot rifles, after trial in the field it was decided that the length and weight of the rifle should be reduced. The thumb piece of the magazine cut-off was changed to cut off the magazine when it was down instead of up, as in the 1892 Model. The long cleaning rod carried beneath the barrel was replaced by one in three sections carried in a recess in the butt, accessible through a trap door in the butt plate. The rear sight was improved. The main characteristics of the Model 1896 then became: 30-inch barrel; 46.05-inch stock; total length 48.9 inches. It was also made in carbine and cadet models. This was, however, fundamentally the same rifle as the Model 1892. (Plate 15, figure 2.)

Judge David S. Terry, a Justice of the Supreme Court of the State of California, Stabbing S. A. Hopkins, a Member of the Second Committee of Vigilance. The man at the left of the picture is holding a pepperbox in his right hand.

V *Pepperboxes: Percussion and Cartridge*

BEFORE examining these once popular but now quaint-looking guns, we should glance at the device which, second only to the discovery of gunpowder, was the most important invention in all the history of firearms. This was a new ignition system called the percussion lock.

Whether or not the Reverend Alexander Forsyth salted his Scotch Presbyterian sermon with hellfire and brimstone, we do not know. Considering his absorption with the workings of the powerfully explosive fulminic acid, it might not be surprising if his kirk in Belhelvie, Aberdeenshire, did occasionally shake with the impact of his words, as the world of weapons was later to shake with the results of his experiments. His lock, for which he received a British patent in 1807, embraced the basic principle of the metallic cartridge we use today; it was responsible for the eventual success of breech-loading arms—replacing muzzle-loaders—and perhaps only less directly so for the magazine rifle, as well as almost all other firearm improvements of the present time.

It was not the first occasion that the percussion principle had been observed. Almost a century and a half before, Samuel Pepys, noted for his sharp and gossipy observations on English manners, morals and politics, set down in his famous diary on November 11, 1663:

> At noon to the Coffee House, where, with Dr. Allen, some good discourse about physick and chymistry. And among other things I telling him what Dribble, the German Doctor, do offer of an instrument to sink ships; he tells me that which is more strange, that something made of gold, which they call in chymestry Aurum Fulminans, a grain, I think he said, of it put into a silver spoon and fired, will give a blow like a musquet, and strike a hole through the silver spoon downwards, without the least force upwards; and this he can make a cheaper experiment of he says with iron prepared.

Later, too, other experiments had been made in applying fulminates to the ignition of guns, but the force of the explosion had always scattered the powder before it had a chance to ignite the main charge. Forsyth, however, at last managed to harness the force of that explosion by loading fulminate of mercury as a priming compound into a small metal bottle mounted on the outside of the gun where it would be struck by the falling hammer. The hammer hit a tiny plunger on the bottle, and this exploded the priming powder in the pan, which was now enclosed, on the outside of the gun. Then the flame from the explosion went through the touchhole and into the barrel to the main powder charge.

The lock was extremely effective, and in 1812 Forsyth formed his own company in London. His invention was a long step forward from the flintlock, for it was impervious to damp weather and heavy winds which damaged or dissipated the priming powder in the open pan of the old flintlock. At the same time, the new lock gave a quicker and more complete ignition to the whole powder charge without loss of power in escaping gases through the touchhole. Still, loose powder, even in an enclosed pan, did have disadvantages. To overcome them, the percussion system was to go through four stages of development before an efficient device was found.

The first step was in the introduction of the "pill lock," or "pellet lock," in which the detonating mixture was made into a pellet, and sometimes enclosed in paper, similar to that now used in toy cap pistols.

The second improvement was the "tape lock," an advanced form of pill lock, in which the detonator pellets were fastened to or enclosed by a long strip of paper or fabric, so that they could be successively fed into the firing position by the action of the lock. American authorities credit this to Dr. Maynard, a dentist in Washington, D. C., who received his first patent in 1845. It is the second step in the point of logical development, but third in point of time. The Maynard tape primer was used by the United States in 1851, on Sharps and other martial rifles. Thus, in the chapter on U. S. martial shoulder arms, in Fuller's descriptions, a good many rifles carried Maynard's name in parentheses as part of their classification.

Third was the "tube lock," patented by Joseph Manton in England in 1818, used mostly for fowling pieces or for dueling pistols, and having little to do with guns that were important in the West.

Fourth, and last, was the "cap lock," by which Forsyth improved on his original system by loading the fulminate into copper or brass caps, which we call primers today. The cap, to which was attached an anvil, or plunger, was placed on a nipple over the touchhole. When the hammer hit the plunger, it set off the cap containing the priming charge. The flame from the cap went through the touchhole and ignited the main powder charge. In modern cartridges, the priming mixture is built into the base (sometimes called the head) of the cartridge case.

Although English sportsmen readily accepted the Forsyth principle, the British Army held it dangerous. By 1835 other inventors had improved the original lock enough so that the percussion cap came into general use on private arms, and in 1836 it was officially accepted by the army; with the old Brown Bess muskets all converted to percussion by 1842. After much haggling by Parliament, the British government awarded Forsyth £5,000 sterling, paying the first installment to his widow on the day of his death, June 11, 1845.

In the United States, the government officially adopted the percussion system about 1842, although three years were to pass before it was to be in general use by sportsmen and in the manufacture of private arms.

The relation of the percussion system to breech-loading guns was mentioned before, and it brings out the following interesting sidelight in the development of firearms in the United States.

For many years before the Civil War, the value of breech-loading had been realized by ordnance officers, but the outbreak of that conflict prevented the change-over from muzzle-loading. This would have required designing and making new machinery and an extensive retooling of the government arsenals and the contract manufacturers, already under constant pressure to maintain and increase their arms production for the federal forces.

After the battle of Gettysburg, fought on the first three days of July, 1863, 37,574 arms were picked up from the battlefield and sent to Washington, D. C., for examination by ordnance experts. Of this number, 24,000 were found fully loaded. One fourth of these loaded guns had only one load in the barrel, but one half had two loads, and the remaining 6,000 arms had from three to ten loads in each gun.

Some of the muskets were loaded with the paper cartridges upside down so that the powder was not exposed to the ignition. One musket was found with twenty-three loads in the barrel, some right side up and some upside down. From all this evidence of the near-hysteria and excitement prevailing during the battle, the government authorities estimated that one third of the soldiers on each side were ineffective as fighting men. With a breech-loading arm, this multiple loading would be impossible; the soldier would have to fire one round before loading another into the chamber. Thus the end of the Civil War marked the end of the muzzle-loader, and it also marked the close of the percussion era, for it was the development of the metallic cartridge that made possible the sealing of the breech against loss of power from the escape of powder gas.

Thousands of men, released from the Union and Confederate armies, sought their fortunes in the new lands opened for settlement in the West. Many of them took with them the percussion muskets, rifles, and revolvers that they had carried through the war. These were used for hunting, for fighting the Indians, and to enforce the rude justice of the frontier. Few could afford the cartridge guns when they were first introduced, and they clung to the guns they knew, the firearms based on the invention of the Reverend Forsyth so many years before.

The Percussion Pepperbox, despite some of the claims of the early manufacturers, did not spring full-blown from the brow of some inventive genius. Its multibarrel principle dates back from the days of the primitive hand cannon, with two barrels placed side by side and a third on top. More advanced types have been made and used since 1600, through the various ignition systems used from that time (the firelock) up to the present cartridge period.

This hand gun that looks so quaint to us now is chiefly important as a historical bridge between the single-shot pistol and the revolver, and occupies a unique niche in the gallery of guns used in the Old West.

The gun was seldom if ever referred to by its manufacturers' or dealers' catalogues and advertisements as a pepperbox. Instead, it was called "a six-barrel self-cocking pistol," "a pocket pistol," "a patent rotary pistol," and other descriptive names, more or less apt. The word apparently came into general verbal use simply as a colorfully appealing colloquialism that caught the popular ear. A man who was facing a battery of six black, businesslike muzzles across a saloon card table, or during an interrupted romance in a velvet-draped room upstairs, might possibly have noted the similarity to the perforations in the top of an old-fashioned pepper shaker, but that is hard to imagine. More likely the man behind the gun, with the grim, drawling humor of the frontier, was the first to point out the likeness.

The pepperbox is not a revolver. Although both weapons are hand guns or pistols, the revolver is of a special kind. By definition, it has a cylinder containing chambers for holding cartridges. By revolving, the cylinder successively presents the cartridges in line with a single barrel through which the bullets are shot one at a time.

Since the pepperbox does not have a revolving cylinder containing chambers and a single barrel, but has three or more barrels revolving around a common axis, firing shots successively one at a time with a single hammer, or striker, the pepperbox is properly referred to as a pistol. Some arms authorities differ from time to time in their definitions of this weapon, favoring broader definitions which would include other varied types of multishot pistols and some oddities. For our purpose, however, since we are primarily interested in percussion and cartridge pepperboxes, we will restrict our definition to that included in the first sentence of this paragraph. Also, this is our understanding of what men and women used to mean when they spoke of pepperboxes.

Aside from the peculiarity about its name, there were a few other unusual features in the history of this pistol. Naturally, like almost all other firearms from the flintlock period on, the pepperbox was in wide popular use in the East and in the South from its introduction in 1837 to the close of the century. But it was bought, carried and used in great quantities in the West, especially from the days of the forty-niners. In the next few years it established itself as the fastest-shooting gun a man could own.

From 1849 to 1851 tens of thousands of citizens headed for the California gold camps. To make that trek—whether overland, by ship around the Horn, or via the Isthmus of Panama and thence to the Golden Gate by sail—without carrying a hand gun was courting disaster. The demand for pistols was greater than even the productive genius of Colt, now established in his Hartford factory, could meet—though a little earlier it was another story. Also, the pepperboxes were cheap—ten or fifteen dollars for a good specimen—whereas a Colt, during the early 1850's, bought in the East for $25 would fetch perhaps $200 on the Coast. No wonder the Colt revolver was hard to come by.

The pepperbox was a town, or more precisely, a city gun. It was usually of small caliber; few were of .41 caliber; most of them seemed to run from .28 to .36. It was not much good for outdoor work, for it was inaccurate at a range of more than a few feet; it had a heavy trigger pull, and it lacked proper sights. Also, the revolving of the barrels, whether accomplished by hand or mechanically, made aiming difficult.

To the mustached sports and the gay girls of the Barbary Coast, to the dive-keepers, saloonmen, gamblers, and a few of the more respectable gentry, these disadvantages meant nothing. Here was an "equalizer" that was miles ahead of the single-shot pistol; it made a nice big brother to the derringer—with which, by the way, it never really competed—and it was almost as easily concealed on your person. It was just the ticket to use on a well-heeled, rambunctious customer who became stubborn about sharing his wealth, or to convince that brassy-voiced strawberry blonde who'd just walked out with your man that she'd made a bad mistake. Sedate bankers and high-living speculators, railroad and mining tycoons, shady lawyers and respected lawmakers and strikingly beautiful adventuresses all seemed to find that the pepperbox gave them a needed sense of security; for it was a time and a place where almost everyone, at least part of the time, carried a pistol—and sometimes two or three. Not only in San Francisco, but in other Western cities, vibrant with the color and drama of the living frontier, the little multibarreled pistol found acceptance.

It was not popular, however, in the cattle country, the mining camps, or with stage drivers, express messengers and those who lived and worked largely under the big sky. They wanted a gun big enough and accurate enough to stop a man at fifty or more feet. And most of them carried a hidden derringer in town or city—"just in case."

Nor, one may well imagine, was the pepperbox endearing itself to the Yankee gunmaker, Samuel Colt.

Colt had obtained his very first patent on his revolver in England on December 18, 1835, and received his first U. S. patent, number 138, on February 25, 1836. It was followed by U. S. patent number 1304, dated August 29, 1839. These two American patents protected the design of the revolving arms that he manufactured at Paterson, New Jersey.

James E. Serven, in his monumental work, *Colt Firearms, 1836–1954*, said:

"Hot on the heels of Colt came Barton and Benjamin Darling with a revolving 'pepperbox' which they patented April 13, 1836. Allen followed in 1837, Nichols & Childs in 1838, and many others, including the ambitious Mighill Nutting.

"'Pepperbox' patents gave Colt his most serious competition, for these pistols sold at an average of $10 each, whereas Paterson pistols, we are told in old advertisements, retailed at $25 to $100, depending on type and decoration. Some were sold at a reduced bargain price of $16.

"John Ehlers, in an advertisement of 1845 featuring Colt's pistols, warned his readers: 'Great impositions have been lately practised on the public by representing and selling the six barrel or self cocking pistol as Colt's Patent Pistol.'"

Like the famed Kentucky rifle, pepperbox pistols cannot fall into the classification either of martial or of secondary-martial arms. Nevertheless, pepperboxes were owned, carried and used as personal weapons in every war and campaign from 1837 to the close of the Civil War by the federal armed forces, especially by commissioned officers.

Perhaps because they bore a superficial similarity in some respects to the true revolver, the classification of the pepperbox as a pistol was not at once agreed upon by all gun authorities. The weapons appear as both single- and double-action guns; in the single-action (abbreviated to S.A.) type, as with a S.A. revolver, the weapon is fired by first cocking the hammer and then pulling the trigger, a process that has to be repeated individually for each barrel fired. The double-action pepperbox, also like the revolver (abbreviated to D.A.), is fired simply by pulling the trigger, with the hammer cocking automatically with each pull of the trigger until all the barrels are fired.

Another feature shared by pepperbox and revolver is that in some of the early pepperboxes the barrels must be turned by hand—as with some of the early revolver cylinders. With others, especially in models made after the first or introductory years, the barrels revolve automatically, again as with the cylinders of various specimens of revolvers.

Benjamin and Barton Darling, gunsmiths of Bellingham, Massachusetts, obtained the first United States patent for a pepperbox April 13, 1836, and it was advertised by them as the "Darling Patent Rotary Pistol." The most important feature of their patent application was the claim that they originated the rotation of the cylinder by the cocking of the hammer. However, Samuel Colt's prior patent of February 25, 1836, also claimed mechanical rotation of the cylinder, and this patent by Colt was the apparent cause for the Darlings eventually to cease manufacture of their pepperbox.

One or more Darling pepperboxes were made in Bellingham, a few were made in Shrewsbury, Massachusetts, according to old records, and most of them were made in Woonsocket, Rhode Island, the third and final place of manufacture.

Benjamin Darling, the more vocal of the brothers, claimed all his life that he deserved credit for inventing the first revolver patented in the United States. Even if Colt is given credit by reason of the earlier patent date, the truth is that Elisha Haydon Collier, of Boston, Massachusetts, patented a flintlock revolver in England in November, 1818, and the same revolver was patented by Artemas Wheeler in the United States in June,

1818. Furthermore, there were far earlier inventions of revolvers in the Scandinavian countries. Consequently all arguments about which American invented the first pepperbox or the first revolver are academic.

Another well-known name in the manufacture of pepperboxes is that of Ethan Allen and his relatives, whose multibarreled hand guns were widely advertised and sold in the early days of the West.

Ethan Allen, apparently no relation to the Ethan Allen of Revolutionary War fame, was also a gunsmith in Bellingham, Massachusetts. Before the Darlings obtained their first patent, however, he moved to Grafton, Massachusetts, where he went into business with his brother-in-law, Charles Thurber, from 1837 to 1842; and then at Norwich, Connecticut, from 1842 to 1847. Except for a very few early specimens marked only with Allen's name, all these bore the name of Allen & Thurber. After 1847, new companies were formed by Allen and his relatives.

T. P. Wheelock, one of the officers of Allen & Wheelock, was a brother-in-law of Ethan Allen. After T. P. Wheelock died, two sons-in-law, Forehand and Wadsworth, came into the business with Ethan Allen.

The Allen pepperboxes made at Worcester, Massachusetts, from 1847 to 1865 were stamped at various times with the names of Allen & Thurber; Allen, Thurber & Co.; and Allen & Wheelock. After 1865, the name Ethan Allen & Co. was used and the company made about every type of firearm except pepperboxes. Apparently the year 1865 marked the high-water mark of percussion-pepperbox production, although the use of the weapons continued many years after manufacture ceased.

In addition to the percussion pepperboxes marked as described above, the various companies operated by Allen and his relatives made firearms for many distributors and retailers. These including J. G. Bolen, New York; J. Eaton; Lane & Read; A. W. Spies, who liked to see his name on the guns he sold, although he had to label them "A. W. Spies, Allen's Patent"; Tryon of Philadelphia; Warren & Steele; and Young & Smith. All these pepperboxes carried various marks, but nearly always "Allen's Patent" appeared somewhere on each gun in addition to whatever marks were ordered by the distributor or retailer.

One characteristic of the various Allen companies was that they had the faculty for hiring good men, if not for keeping them very long. There was, for example, George Leonard, Jr., who left Allen & Thurber to make pepperboxes under his own name, as did Alexander Stocking. Leonard obtained U. S. patent number 6723 on September 18, 1849, and another patent in 1850. His pepperboxes are characterized by a revolving hammer or striker, in contrast to the single hammer found on the Allen models and those resembling the Allen products.

A typical pepperbox was that made by the Robbins & Lawrence Company, under one of the Leonard patents. It is worth noting that while almost all other pepperboxes had smooth bores, the Robbins & Lawrence models had rifled barrels. The rifled barrels for a pepperbox were described, but not legally claimed, as an invention by Leonard in his 1850 patent.

The Robbins & Lawrence pepperboxes were usually marked "Leonard's Patent 1849" on the barrel group and also marked "Robbins & Lawrence Co., Windsor, Vt." Those known to have been used in the West were mostly caliber .31, 5-shot, with either 4.5-inch or 3.5-inch barrels, although a few were made caliber .28, with 3.25-inch barrels. The barrels are not separate but are drilled through a solid block which is round and fluted. Some are marked on the barrel group: "G. Leonard, Jr. Charlestown, Patented 1849."

Plate 1 is an illustration released by the Robbins & Lawrence Co., Windsor, Vermont, showing their "Leonard's Patent Revolving-Hammer Pistol" in several views. One is the left side view of the pepperbox cocked and ready to fire. Another is in a position for loading, and a third shows the barrels tipped forward for capping (insertion of primers), and the remainder of the pepperbox drawn to show the breech open and revealing the lock mechanism. In addition, there are drawings of the flask, the bullet mold, and the combination cleaning rod and capping device.

Bacon & Co., of Norwich, Connecticut, made the only single-action, underhammer percussion pepperbox manufactured and sold in quantity in the West. It is one of the very few with a cylinder which revolves clockwise. Since it has no top hammer, it is easy to aim, but is made without sights.

Blunt & Syms pepperboxes, next to those made by the various companies operated by the Allen relatives, were sold in the greatest number in the West because they were well made and marketed by people who understood merchandising their wares. This company was primarily engaged in the importation of firearms from Europe and selling them to wholesalers and retailers. There is some question about whether they made their own pepperboxes or not, but in the absence of evidence to the contrary, the assumption is that these were American-made arms.

The Manhattan Firearms Manufacturing Co., New York City, made percussion pepperboxes closely resembling the Allen specimens. The patent issued to Allen in 1837 expired in 1851, so anyone could use it thereafter. Allen also received a patent in 1845, but it was not worth copying for large-scale production, hence there is no reason to assume that the Manhattan pepperboxes were in any way infringements.

William Walker Marston obtained a pepperbox patent in 1855 and marketed his pepperboxes with marks such as "W. W. Marston, New York"; "W. W. Marston Armory, New York"; "W. W. Marston Phoenix Armory, New York City"; "W. W. Marston & Knox, New York 1854"; "Marston &

PLATE 1
Advertisement for Leonard's Revolving-Hammer Pistol, an early pepperbox.

Knox"; and "Sprague & Marston, New York," but they are all similar to the Allen guns.

Jacob Pecare and Josiah Smith, of New York, obtained a patent in 1849. Their main claim was a concealed trigger. The usual mark is "Pecare & Smith's Pat. 1849."

Jacob Post obtained a patent in 1849 for what he called the "J. Post Self Acting Pistol." In order to fire it, the trigger was squeezed and then released. It has several distinctive features but few were sold in the West because Post did not understand merchandising and advertising.

Plate 2 shows a group of percussion pepperboxes, representative of the type used in the West. From top to bottom: 1, Belgian. 2, Allen, caliber .36. 3, Allen, caliber .31. 4, Allen & Thurber made at Grafton, Mass., caliber .36. 5, 6, 7, and 8, Allen & Thurber made at Worcester, Mass. 9, Allen & Wheelock, caliber .36. 10, same company, caliber .31.

Plate 3 is another group of pepperboxes, all American-made. From top to bottom, left column: 1, 2, Blunt & Syms. 3, Darling, 4-barrel brass, caliber .30. 4, Darling 6-barrel, frame marked "J. Engh." 5, Darling 6-barrel, frame marked "A C S." 6, Leonard, caliber .31, 4-barrel. 7, Robbins & Lawrence, D.A., caliber .31, 5-barrel. 8, Manhattan. 9, Pecare & Smith, caliber .31.

Right column: 10, Pecare & Smith, caliber .28. 11, 12, Pecare & Smith, caliber .31. 13, Robbins & Lawrence, caliber .31. 14, Sprague & Marston. 15, Stocking & Co., caliber .31. 16, similar, caliber .41. 17, similar, caliber .28.

Plate 4, figure 1, Nicholson 7-barrel flintlock pepperbox, sometimes claimed as of American make, but probably made in England. Figure 2, English-made percussion, 1840. Maker not positively identified. This specimen is especially interesting as it is also a knife- or a dagger-pistol, sometimes classed with freaks and oddities. Figure 3, 18-barrel English percussion. Figure 4, more conventional English percussion. English pepperboxes were sold generally throughout the United States, usually by shops catering to persons able to pay prices higher than those asked for American arms.

Figures 5, 6, Japanese percussion. Figure 7, Korean percussion. Asiatic weapons, like those of the English, were sold extensively in the West.

Cartridge pepperboxes, despite their inaccuracy and lack of appeal for the Westerner who carried his holster gun for personal reasons, continued to thrive long after they had been superseded by the cartridge revolver. Although the handwriting was already on the wall, it had been put there by the bullets of only one major cartridge-revolver maker, instead of by many. That fact probably extended the productive life of the pepperbox by at least four years; possibly by many more. To appreciate that, however, we should glance briefly at the development of the self-contained metallic cartridge, that has its origin in Forsyth's far-reaching application of fulminates for firing the powder charge.

During the matchlock period of muzzle-loading and for some time thereafter, a cartridge was merely a charge of powder, wrapped in paper, linen, or animal skin and tied with string into a neat bundle. This was rammed into the gun barrel. The bullet, or ball, was separate and was loaded after the powder. Then gradually men began to combine powder charge and ball into a single package.

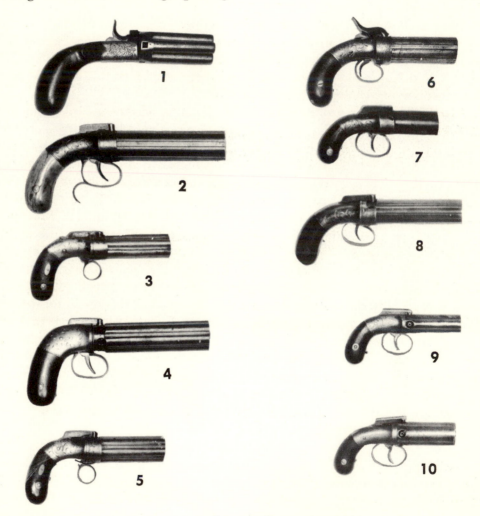

PLATE 2

A group of ten percussion derringers used in Old West. All but No. 1 of this group were made in the United States.   AUTHOR'S COLLECTION

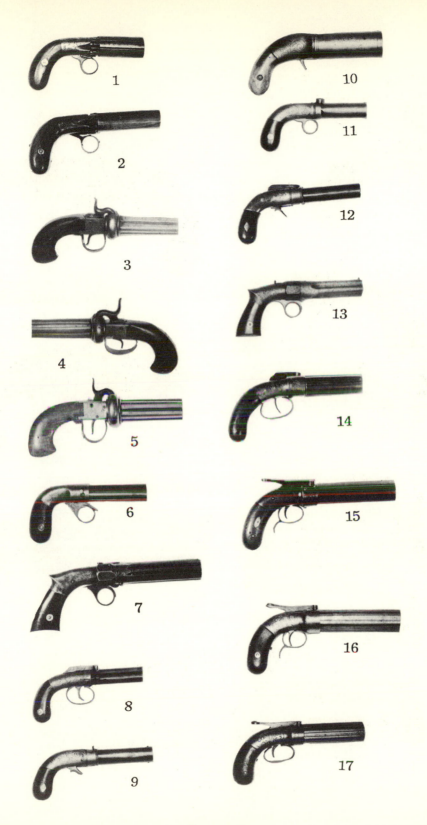

PLATE 3

A group of seventeen American-made percussion derringers.   AUTHOR'S COLLECTION

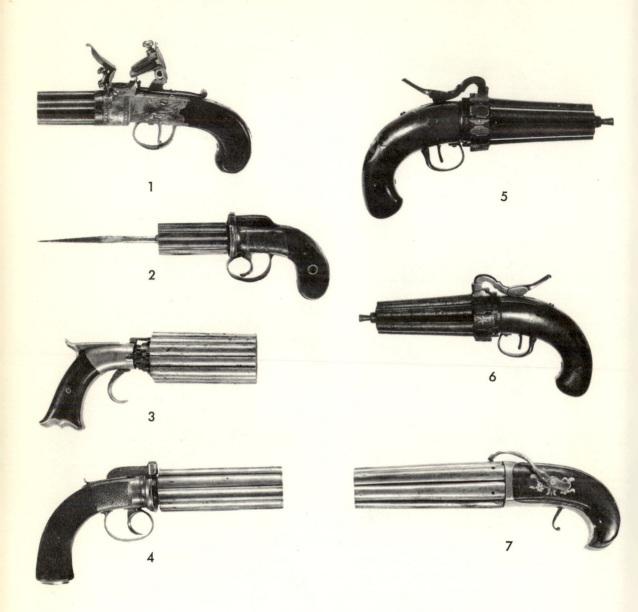

PLATE 4

1. Nicholson 7-Barrel Flintlock Pepperbox.
2. English-made Percussion Pepperbox, 1840.
3. English-made 18-Barrel Percussion Pepperbox.
4. Conventional English-made Percussion Pepperbox.
5, 6. Japanese Percussion Pepperboxes.
7. Korean-made Percussion Pepperbox.

The soldier, to load his smoothbore shoulder piece, tore open the cartridge, poured the powder down the barrel and rammed the ball in after it, with the paper and string forced down to form the wad. Later, during the percussion period, he found he could load more rapidly by biting off the end of the cartridge with his teeth, pouring most of the powder down the barrel, ramming down the ball, then placing the remainder of the powder into the priming pan.

The development of percussion ignition led to the invention of metallic cartridges containing everything except the primer. This was followed by the fully self-contained cartridge, but now the primer protruded from the base of the cartridge, making it awkward to carry and load. A variation of this is the French pin-fire cartridge, patented in 1847, which was used in a French revolver, Le Faucheaux, during the Civil War by both Union and Confederate troops.

The next big step was the introduction of the combustible cartridge, about 1850. It was the same string-tied package of powder and shot, but now the container was treated with niter to make it burn easily. One rather remarkable example of this was the Sharps Linen Cartridge for both sporting and martial arms, and especially for use in Sharps breech-loading rifles. This ammunition was to be advertised for sale as late as 1897, more than three decades into the self-contained metallic-cartridge era—a fact that would seem to award it the title of last leaf on its particular tree.

From the first, that ammunition was popular on the frontier. It was—with the Sharps rifle—just the right combination to bring down big game: bison, deer, bear. And man. Especially the last-named species.

The year is 1856; the place, Kansas Territory where a bitter civil war is raging over the slavery issue. This is a personal and an emotional quarrel, and no man dares to remain neutral. The crack of bushwhackers' guns—both those of the "Border Ruffians" and the Free Soilers—would sound in a heavier, more ominous echo five years later from Fort Sumter's cannon.

In Washington, President Pierce, in a special message to the Congress, spoke of "Bleeding Kansas." Senators made speeches, and so did that influential and popular orator, Reverend Henry Ward Beecher, who eloquently pleaded the antislavery cause from his Brooklyn pulpit, around the North and in England. Some citizens did more than talk.

A strange shipment of raw pine, coffin-like cases labeled "Bibles" arrived in Kansas from the East, consigned to one of the Free State leaders. Opening the boxes in the stillness of night in a lantern-lighted barn, there was no doubt but these "Beecher's Bibles"—gleaming caliber .50 Sharps rifles—would sound a convincing apostolic note to the proslavery element. Some of them probably found their way to the hands of the flaming-eyed, fanatical John Brown. Three years later, when that bloody-handed crusader was captured by federal troops—a detachment, incidentally, commanded by Col. Robert E. Lee—as he was attempting to capture the U. S. Arsenal at Harpers Ferry, 102 breech-loading Sharps were taken from him and his band.

So even before the Civil War, breech-loading arms were winning acceptance. While bitter strife raged in Kansas, in the East thousands of small-caliber rim-fire cartridge revolvers were being manufactured which would prepare the way for widespread public acceptance after the War. These would have a marked effect on the manufacture and sale of the cartridge pepperbox pistol.

The evolution of metallic cartridges followed generally the slow and uneven pattern of firearms history. It is by no means a straight-line progression, but is made up of various changes and refinements in various geographical areas, and frequently within the same period of time.

If the private citizen at the close of the Civil War welcomed the advent of the new, self-contained rim-fire (abbreviated to r.f.) cartridge and the guns that fired them, the government, as usual, was slow to evince its enthusiasm. However, more than ever before men were accustomed to using and owning guns. Also, the call of the West was strong to many returning soldiers. It seemed to promise, as it did in '49, a new hope for a golden fortune and a new excitement—if not in the mining camps of fifteen years before, then in the dramatically swift commercial development that kept pace with the western rails.

In establishing new town sites, in settling immigrants, in cattle-raising and feeding, in farming, in commerce of all sorts, the alert, ambitious man saw a chance to build for himself a great future. So once again the westward trek started. And, as always, a man needed a gun "out there." At least one firearm; usually more. A breech-loading cartridge rifle; maybe a shotgun. One of these new cartridge six-shot revolvers. Likely, too, an easily hidden derringer "hide-out" or "stingy gun," as they were called. Or a little multi-barreled pepperbox. A man couldn't tell what he'd be up against and any kind of gun might come in mighty handy.

Back in New England, the silence that was at Appomattox did not reach to the humming wheels and lathes of the arms factories in Hartford, Whitneyville, New London and New Haven, in Springfield, Massachusetts, or other bustling cities and towns. Exciting events were taking place inside those tall-stacked, red-brick buildings. Ideas born before the war were now really taking shape and being put into the kind of efficient production that brought a gleam to the eye of the practical Yankee gunmaker.

The citizens of Springfield, Massachusetts, in the year 1856, were probably as excited and concerned as anyone over the violent events in Kansas, but that year was to have a special significance for another reason. In the second floor of a small building on Market Street, above the stable occupying the ground floor, the world's first breech-loading revolver using metallic ammunition, as we understand that term today, was made by Smith & Wesson.

This was a caliber .22 r.f., with a nickel-plated brass frame, a round, blue-finished, rifled barrel, jointed to top of frame to top strap, and with an over-all length of 7 inches, a weight of 11 ounces. It was manufactured under patents for both revolver and the cartridge, and one specimen is marked with patent dates of April 3, 1855; July 5, 1859; and December 18, 1860. Thousands of these were carried as personal pocket weapons by officers and soldiers in the Civil War, even though the caliber was too small for official use.

Meanwhile, Rollin White, of Hartford, had obtained similar patents in 1855 and 1858, and shortly after the first Smith & Wesson revolver came on the market, he too began production in his own factory in Lowell, Massachusetts. White was not alone in trying to get in on the ground floor of the breech-loading, metallic-cartridge revolver business, for a good many other arms makers started to turn them out about that time. Smith & Wesson, however, instituted legal action against each rival for patent infringements and won judgments against them. Smith & Wesson, in 1860, acquired the Rollin White patent, and this move effectively prevented Samuel Colt and all other manufacturers from legally producing a revolver that had the cylinder chambers bored through, thus making them breech-loading arms. These patents, however, could not prevent the lawful manufacture of hand guns, other than revolvers, with the *barrels* bored through. Thus, of all the multishot hand guns, the pepperbox and the derringer were the only ones—besides the Smith & Wesson revolver—which could be legally manufactured and offered breech-loading for its cartridges.

Even though the Rollin White patent on the bored-through cylinder expired in 1869, thereby leaving the field open for Colt and other arms manufacturers to make their cartridge revolvers that loaded from the cylinder breech, the pepperbox and derringer had won a firm market from 1855. Long after most people had accepted cartridge revolvers, pepperboxes and derringers remained in demand—if not in actual manufacture—for many years, and were in use in Western cities up through 1900.

Remington multi-shot cartridge hand guns which were *not* revolvers include the "Remington Zig-Zag" and the "Remington-Elliot Ring Trigger" types. In this and in other texts by the author of this book, these Remington

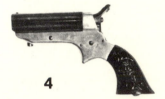

hand guns are classed as derringers. They are mentioned here only because some authors, collectors and historians erroneously group them with pepperboxes, which goes back to our original definition of a pepperbox and needs no more discussion. Actually, in 1862, one T. W. Moore, of New York City, advertised the Remington Zig-Zag hand gun, calling it "Elliot's Pocket Revolver," in *Frank Leslie's Illustrated Newspaper,* and in *Harper's Weekly.* Furthermore, the Elliot Arms Co., New York City, ran an advertisement in *Leslie's Illustrated Newspaper* for September 12, 1863, and called the Remington-Elliot cartridge derringers (or pepperboxes, or pocket pistols) "Elliot's New Repeaters," thus confounding the terminology.

The Sharps pepperboxes were the most widely sold and best liked of all cartridge pepperboxes. More of this make (including those marked Sharps & Hankins) were made and sold than all other makes, models and types of American-made cartridge pepperboxes put together, and they had a tremendous sale in the West. This has been overlooked by firearms historians and writers of the Old West because Christian Sharps is far more famous for his shoulder arms.

[98]

About 1863, Christian Sharps went into business with William Hankins to form Sharps & Hankins, a partnership organized to continue the manufacture of cartridge pepperboxes based upon the Sharps patent. A typical Sharps & Hankins cartridge pepperbox is caliber .32 r.f., 4-shot, with four 3.5-inch, round blued barrels marked "Address Sharps & Hankins, Philadelphia, Penna." This arm was also made in caliber .22 r.f.

Plate 5 shows cartridge pepperboxes.

The Sharps Cartridge Pepperbox, figure 4, is known to collectors as "Sharps Pepperbox No. 1." It is caliber .22 r.f., 4-shot, with 2.5-inch round barrels marked "C. Sharps Patent. 1859"; it has a spur trigger, and hard-rubber grips. This, and the other Sharps cartridge pepperboxes, are based upon a U. S. patent issued to Christian Sharps on January 25, 1859, for a "breech-loading repeating firearm." The drawing accompanying the patent application refers to his invention as a "revolver," and although it has been described by some people as a "derringer," we classify it as a pepperbox.

The Sharps Pepperbox No. 2 is caliber .30 r.f., and the Sharps pepperbox No. 3 is caliber .32 r.f., but the caliber differences are only superficial. There are variations in the mechanisms for opening the pepperbox for loading, and other deviations which are of interest only to highly specialized collectors of this type.

The Rupertus 8-shot Cartridge Pepperbox, illustrated in figure 3, is caliber .22 r.f., 8-shot, with 2.75-inch round, fluted barrels; walnut grips; brass frame; spur trigger; and a butt marked "Rupertus Pat. Pistol Mfg. Co. Philadelphia." The recoil plate revolves, exposing a loading gate. This arm was based on a patent issued to Jacob Rupertus, of Philadelphia, July 19, 1864. The same man made single-shot pistols, double-barrel pistols, and a 4-barrel derringer sometimes listed as a pepperbox.

In the next chapters we will find out a little more about the derringer, and about its originator, Henry Deringer Junior. Among many other things, he was one of the few men to have his name accepted as a common noun in our language—and perhaps the only one whose name is purposely misspelled in the dictionary.

Early American Gunsmith's Shop. LIBRARY OF CONGRESS

VI *Pocket-Sized Death: Development of the Famous Deringer*

OLD Henry Deringer knew guns. A man could tell that as soon as he stepped inside his little shop in Richmond, Virginia, during those final years of the 1790's. Neighbors and customers liked to see his painstaking care as he worked at the bench, the deft fingers fitting the jawed hammer to hold the flint, attaching the pan just so; the precise coordination of hand and eye as he aligned the sights on a rifled barrel. To some of his audience, watching this conscientious and skilled craftsman create from clumsy iron bars, rough blocks of seasoned maple, and heavy brass plate, the accurate graceful Kentucky rifles that bore his signature, it seemed like another miracle of birth. Man from common clay; a Kentucky—a *Deringer* Kentucky—almost alive from these crude raw materials!

Deringer's flintlocks were built to last, to shoot straight and true. They were fashioned by a man who loved his job and was proud of his calling. Kentucky rifle or pistol, when you called on either, you could trust it to answer.

Henry's son, named for him, was an apprentice in his shop and showed signs of soon being as fine a craftsman as his father. Young Henry, they said, had guns in his blood, and he came honestly by his heritage.

Few gunsmiths in America were better qualified than was this son of a gunmaking father. Appropriately enough, he was born in Easton, the heart of the Pennsylvania Kentucky-rifle country, in 1786. At that time the gun had already won its name, taken from the frontier wilderness where it was used, rather than from the commonwealth where it originated and continued to be made.

In 1806 the Deringers moved to Philadelphia where they continued to turn out the flintlock Kentuckies and pistols as well. At this date a change had come into the appearance of the rifle, as it was now used more as a sporting weapon than as a gun for its owner's survival. This was characterized by a thinner butt stock, the crescent shape of the butt plate becoming more pronounced, and generally carrying more inlay work than on the guns made before 1800.

At about the same time, the Deringers produced martial flintlock shoulder arms and hand guns under contract to the government. Descriptions of some of these guns will be found farther on in this chapter.

It was not until 1825 that the younger Deringer turned out the first of his heavy-calibered, short-barreled pistols that made firearm history and his name famous—if misspelled—throughout the world. He lived until 1868 and the age of 81, a wealthy and respected Philadelphian, and a few years after his death was the posthumous victor in a lawsuit he had brought for trade-mark infringement. The California Supreme Court's decision in Deringer vs. Plate was to become a landmark in that area of the law, just as his pistol was to become a landmark in the history of American firearms.

How do we try to find out just when and where in the frontier these guns were actually used? We hunt for facts.

We don't waste time in reading the literature of the Old West, for even the serious histories are not concerned with specific descriptions of fire-arms. The same is true of photographs, paintings and drawings of the fron-tier scene. No matter how authentic the artist may be in depicting details of dress and equipment of pioneer life he is usually content to show a weapon which at best may be identified either as a shoulder arm or a hand gun of the period, and that's about all. Since the names Colt, derringer, and Winchester have long been in common use to denote revolver, a small, large-calibered pistol, and a shoulder arm, respectively—as the name Stetson means any kind of five- or ten-gallon hat worn by Westerners—such a desig-nation becomes meaningless for our purpose.

One of the primary sources for the person interested in the study of fire-arms is in contemporary advertisements of the gunmaker, his agents and retailers. Generally this is unquestionable evidence that certain types of guns were actually made and sold. It answers the important questions of who, when, and where. But, as with almost everything else connected with firearms history, there are exceptions that at least are apt to ensnare the unwary, and at most form fascinating puzzles for the arms expert. For ex-ample, in old catalogues of some gunmakers, a description of a firearm may appear that never actually reached production, or so few of the model were made that it can scarcely be counted as being in commercial use.

Old records of firearms manufacturers during the percussion and early cartridge period are valuable, when available. However, because the meth-ods of identifying each model varied widely with each arms maker, and be-cause of the generally slipshod recording systems, these production lists demand the interpretation of experts.

Also highly important source material for the arms historian is found in court records of civil suits, especially in patent or copyright infringements, involving arms makers and/or dealers. As for martial arms, government ord-nance and commissary or quartermaster records usually supply accurate de-tailed descriptions of these weapons.

No one knows when or where some new and vastly important piece of information may be uncovered that will radically alter the picture of fire-arms history. Old records, long thought lost, may be discovered. Closer ex-amination of some weapon in relation to its time, its maker, or to other pieces, may completely change its classification. Such was the case with the Kentucky pistol, discussed in a previous chapter. An attempt to discover and classify precisely and accurately the various kinds of guns used in the Old West is an assignment not to be lightly undertaken.

In 1940, the author of this book wrote and privately published the first edition of *The Gun Collector's Handbook of Values*, and its preparation in-volved visiting many of the gun collectors and dealers on the West Coast. One result of this was the discovery that the greatest number and variety of

Henry Deringer, Junior's pocket pistols seemed to come from California homes. This observation was later confirmed in correspondence with outstanding collectors and dealers throughout the United States.

Also, in the case of Deringer vs. Plate referred to above—and which we shall further discuss in the next chapter—the record shows that it came to trial in the California District Court in San Francisco on January 8, 1868, when one William H. Brown, as witness for the gunmaker, testified under oath:

"I am a manufacturer and vendor of arms; been in the business over twenty years; knew Deringer of Philadelphia personally, and his reputation. He is a manufacturer of the Deringer pistol. I have known the pistol for twenty-five or thirty years. It stands in high repute. The reputation among the people of the genuine Deringer pistol is high. There is no other pistol of that character that I know; the public have sought after it. I sold the first on this Coast in 1849. I have sold pistols simulating the Deringer pistol here."

We may assume the truth of the testimony; at least there is nothing to contradict it in the early records of California. Yet it stands as a rather curious fact that none of the well-known books, periodicals or catalogues published in or about California in the early Gold Rush years mention Deringer's pocket pistol, or any of his pistols, even indirectly, earlier than the 1854 edition of the San Francisco Directory. Even then, the reference is about as indirect as one can imagine, as there is no mention of Deringer or his products by name. The volume does, however, list four San Francisco merchants who were known at the time to have been retailers of Deringer's pocket pistol. They were: Charles Curry, A. J. Plate, A. J. Taylor, and W. C. Allen. None of them was listed in the Directory for 1850, although Plate, who described himself as a "gunsmith," arrived in California in 1849. Taylor, listed as "gunsmith and shooting gallery," reached California in 1850; Curry, "fancy goods," in 1852, and Allen, "importer of watches and jewelry," in 1853.

An examination of the Philadelphia Directory, in various editions from 1837 to 1867, first lists Henry Deringer, Junior, as a pistol manufacturer as well as a rifle maker in the 1853 issue. Previous editions indicate that he made only shoulder arms.

H. H. Bancroft, in his *California Inter Pocula*, published in San Francisco in 1888, described a pistol duel between Colonel John Bankhead Magruder and Dr. William B. Osborn in San Diego in 1852. As the person challenged, Magruder had the right to name the weapons, and he is quoted as having specified "Derringer pistols across the dining-room table." Since neither was wounded, the account of the duel was probably exaggerated, or else the table was of incredibly heroic proportions. It is difficult to imagine two men facing each other with pistols across the width of the ordinary dining table without fatal results, especially since it's reasonable to assume that Bancroft had in mind the regulation-sized Deringer dueling pistols.

All available records indicate that California was the principal outlet for Deringer's pocket pistol, and that more dealers for this deadly little weapon were found in San Francisco than in any other city in the United States. However, this does not imply that other cities did not supply a ready market. Old newspapers and directories show that dealers advertised and sold the pocket Deringer in New York City; Washington, D. C.; in Louisville, Nashville and Memphis; in Shreveport and New Orleans.

Most Deringer pocket pistols bore only Deringer's markings, but a considerable number were marked to show that they were manufactured for particular dealers by Deringer. In the collections examined by the author of this book, those marked for San Francisco dealers exceed the number marked for Southern dealers. Nevertheless, there is a well-founded belief by arms historians that Deringer's pocket pistol was popular in Southern states, including those along the Mississippi River, before it became well known in California. Consistent with this belief is the conclusion that the pistol made its first widespread appearance in California during the early Gold Rush days, as part of the personal armament of adventurous Southerners. In that unsettled and often violent frontier, it seems probable that the hot-blooded sons of Dixie found ample opportunity to demonstrate dramatically the lethal efficiency of the tiny percussion Deringer pistol. Also, because it was a single-shot, muzzle-loading weapon, it was usually manufactured, sold and carried in matched pairs. This feature alone may have added a certain promotional value that led to the gun's acceptance by other gold seekers from every part of the United States as well as from many foreign countries.

Despite the dearth of direct documentary evidence until 1855–1856 that the Deringer pocket pistol was actually in general use in California, it seems reasonable to assume that it was. Certainly there is no indication to the contrary. Before the era of "vigilance committees" starting in 1851, settlers habitually carried personal firearms wherever they went, and most miners either in town or back in the diggin's would have considered themselves half-naked without a hand gun of the period and a Bowie knife stuck in their belts. But these weapons were both conspicuous and bulky, and percussion revolvers of large enough caliber to be effective were relatively heavy. It is clear that men in the camps of the canyons and creeks, as well as those of the mushrooming canvas-and-clapboard cities, formed a market ripe for a small, lightweight, yet deadly pistol.

The advantages of the Deringer pocket pistol—as well as its many imitators—were both obvious and unique. Unlike most percussion hand guns of effective caliber, it was small enough and light enough to be well concealed in the trousers' waistband, hidden in a coat or shirt sleeve, tucked inside a boot, carried in a hat, or placed in a lady's muff, corset, or garter.

For a man in a tight spot, with an armed enemy only a few feet away, a pair of single-shot Deringer pistols was more effective than the multishot pepperbox. You either got your man at the first or second shot—if, indeed, you were given the chance to fire twice—or you got a fast funeral. That heavy-calibered little gun was a man-stopper at short range, an effective surprise weapon, an "equalizer" with which many a gold-camp David permanently tamed the muscle-bulging, belligerent Goliaths of the frontier. Included in a man's personal arsenal, the pistol was carried either as a principal weapon or as a reserve to be used when revolver, pepperbox or Bowie knife failed.

Advertisements of merchants carrying guns appearing in California publications, from the year 1856 onward, indicate that the Deringer pistol was a staple item in the sales of many firearms dealers. Along with the products of Colt, Wesson, Bacon, and other hand-gun makers, "Derringers," "Deringers," and "Derringer pistols" are offered for sale. As early as 1855, in the Memphis (Tennessee) Directory, F. F. Clark & Co. advertise "Pistols—in great variety, including colts of all sizes, and the genuine Derringer." The misspelling of the Deringer name by inserting the extra "r" is not at all unusual, although in view of its later usage, coupling the word "genuine" with the double-r "Derringer" seems a curious paradox. The use of the small "c" in "colts" instead of the proper capital letter appears to bear out a later belief, quoted below, that the misspelling of the Deringer name was due to carelessness rather than intent. It was an almost universal oversight, especially in referring to his famous pistol, and finally was to become the correct name for the type of small-sized, large-calibered pistol of which Deringer's derringer—or the Philadelphia derringer—was the prototype.

> der'rin·ger, *n.* [After its American inventor.] A short-barreled pocket pistol of large caliber.
>
> —*Webster's Collegiate Dictionary*, Fifth Edition.

Henry Deringer, Senior, came from Germany and settled in America before the Revolutionary War. He left in his native land two variations of his surname, which was apparently derived from Thuringer, meaning a person born in Thuringia, formerly a semi-autonomous state in central Germany. It is doubtful if Deringer, Senior, gave the matter any thought, or that his son considered the origin of his name of any great importance. For, as the nineteenth century grew older, an increasing number of advertisements in magazines, newspapers and catalogues throughout the country misspelled his name with the extra "r" in referring to Henry Deringer, Junior. Significantly, there is no record that Deringer protested this misspelling.

When the author of this book wrote the first edition of *Gun Collecting*, and in its earlier revisions, he stated—quite mistakenly—that the double-r version of the name was spelled that way purposely by gunsmiths producing imitations of the genuine Philadelphia derringer in a rather transparent attempt to escape lawsuits for infringement on patents held by the Philadelphia gunmaker. Subsequently, however, two startlingly odd facts were revealed: There was simply no patent on the design of the pocket pistol—and no copyright covering the marking. Anybody and everybody legally could try to produce the same weapon, and—apparently—use the same markings. And almost every gunsmith—with variations described farther on in this chapter—did just that. During the 1860's the demand for both the original Deringer derringers as well as derringers produced by reputable imitators, among them Colt, Remington, Smith & Wesson and others, seemed to exceed the supply. Apparently it was a situation unparalleled in the history of this highly competitive business of manufacturing and selling guns.

John E. Parsons, one of the country's most reliable and outstanding firearms historians, in his book, *Henry Deringer's Pocket Pistol* (Wm. Morrow & Co., New York, 1952), said:

"It seems probable . . . that trial reporters or editors on first recording the name did not actually examine the stamping on the gun, but followed their own inclination as to the proper spelling. Such usage soon became standard, so much so in fact that Deringer's own agents, Clark, Allen, Taylor, and Curry adopted it."

Instead of calling the pocket pistol made by Henry Deringer, Junior, simply a Deringer (without the double-r), gun authorities prefer to use the dictionary noun, "derringer," as properly meaning that type of gun. Therefore we use the term "Deringer derringer" or sometimes "Philadelphia derringer." To this author, the first form seems preferable, if only because it acknowledges, by use of his correctly spelled name, the genius of a fine gunsmith, the famed pistol he designed and made, and a new word with which he enriched our language.

Henry Deringer, Junior, like his famous and younger contemporary, Samuel Colt, firmly established himself in business by producing martial arms under contract to the United States government. In other important respects, as we shall indicate later, they seemed to approach their gunmaking from almost opposite angles. Because most gun historians have neglected discussion of any Deringer arm but his celebrated pocket pistol, we may explore briefly this phase of Deringer production and describe some of

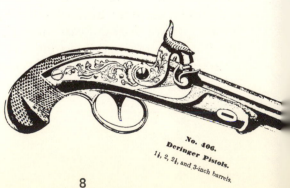

ADVERTISEMENTS FOR DERINGER'S PISTOLS

These are of interest to the gun collector because they are reliable indications of the distribution and use of early western firearms.

1. F. H. Clark & Co. advertisement, Memphis *Directory,* 1855, states that they sell "Pistols in great variety including colts of all sizes and the genuine Derringer, indicating that Colt revolvers and the genuine Deringers were popular in the southern states in 1855.

2. W. C. Allen & Co.'s advertisement in the *Daily Alta California,* 1856, lists Derringer pistols as well as jewelry and silver.

3. W. C. Allen & Co., in the *Daily Evening Bulletin,* San Francisco, 1856, had "Deringer Pistols direct from the manufacturer."

4. The Sportsmen's Emporium, in the *Fireman's Journal and Military Gazette,* San Francisco, 1856, advertises Wessons, Sharps, and Minnie Rifles, Colts and Marriette Revolvers, Derringer, and Bacon's Pistols.

5. Charles Curry, in the San Francisco *Daily Evening Pathfinder,* 1856, advertised Colts and Derringers.

6. In the *San Francisco Directory,* 1858, Curry advertised "Leman's, Wesson's, Wurflein's and Sharp's Rifles. All sizes Colt's Revolvers and Derringer Pistols."

7. D. O'Donnell, gun manufacturer, openly advertised in the *New York City Directory,* 1860, that he was an "Imitation Deringer Pistol Manufacturer."

8. A page from the 1864 catalogue of Schuyler, Hartley & Graham, New York City gun dealers, advertised Deringer pistols available in four different barrel lengths.

the martial shoulder arms and pistols that he made for the United States armed forces.

Between the beginning of the War of 1812 and the close of the Mexican War in 1848, Henry Deringer Junior supplied more than twenty thousand arms, both flintlock and percussion, to the federal government. About five thousand of these were muskets and rifles made for Indians to use in hunting, principally as a result of a series of treaties completed during the administration of Andrew Jackson. The nations of the Cherokee, Chocktaw, Chickasaw and Creek were to leave their ancestral homes in Alabama, Georgia and Mississippi and move to allocated lands reserved for them in Arkansas Territory.

For example, we know that in the Treaty of Dancing Rabbit Creek between the United States and the Choctaw Indians, each warrior was to be given "a rifle, moulds, wipers and ammunition." Henry Deringer Junior received $12.50 for each rifle he made, some of which were flintlock and others percussion. Records still on file in Washington, D. C., show that in 1833, Deringer wrote to the commissary general of the Army: "I can assure you that a better set of rifles the Indians never got, and as good as any that were sent to the United States arsenal."

This statement, along with other evidence, that shows Deringer's pride in the workmanship of his product becomes especially interesting in the light of events that were to occur during the twilight years of his life, as we shall see in the next chapter.

Deringer Flintlock Martial Firearms

U. S. Pistol, Model 1807–1808, caliber .52, 10-inch, round, pin-fastened barrel. Total length 16.5 inches. Weight 2 lbs. 10 oz. Full stock, walnut. Brass trigger guard, butt cap and thimbles. Iron pan with fence. Flat double-necked hammer. Bevel-edged flat lock plate. Hickory ramrod. Lock marked "H. Deringer Phila." Barrel marked "M."

U. S. Rifle Contract Model 1814, caliber .54, flintlock; rifled, 33.312-inch, part-round, part-octagonal barrel; marked on top flat at breech with the maker's name and city; marked on left flat at breech with one or more proof marks and sometimes other letters. It has stud band retainers and finger grips in rear of the trigger guard. There is an oval iron patch box in the stock, which was later carried over to the U. S. Rifle, Model 1817. It has a brass-head, steel ramrod. This was made by Henry Deringer, Jr., in Philadelphia under a contract dated November 23, 1814. It is an extremely rare collector's piece.

[110]

U. S. Rifle, Model 1817, "The Common Rifle," made and marked by Henry Deringer, Jr. It is caliber .54, flintlock, rifled 36-inch barrel, 48-inch stock. Total length 51.5 inches. Lock plate 5.5 inches long and 1.18 inches wide. Trigger guard 9 inches long with round ends. Weight with bayonet 10.25 lbs. Three bands. The lock is like that of the Model 1816 musket but smaller. All parts are iron except the pan, which is brass. Oval-shaped patch box in right of butt with iron cover. The model made at the U. S. Armory at Harpers Ferry differs from those made by contractors such as Deringer, in having a bayonet lug on the barrel and a front sight on the top band, in addition to having the distinctive markings of the U. S. Armory. Highly desirable, but less valuable than above piece.

U. S. Musket, Model 1821 (also called **Model 1822** by some historians), was made by Deringer and other contractors after 1821. The contract for this weapon was dated December 31, 1821, although work did not start until 1822, hence the confusion regarding the model year for identification.

This musket is caliber .69; flintlock; smoothbore; barrel 42 inches long with bayonet lug on top. Black walnut stock 54 inches long, made without a comb. All iron mountings. Double band carries knife-blade front sight. Total length from muzzle to butt 57.64 inches, with fixed bayonet 73.64 inches. Weight without bayonet, 10 lbs., ¼ oz.

There is no official record that justifies the designation of the Model 1821 (1822) as a distinct model. Authors, collectors and dealers fell into the habit of treating this as an official separate model through a misinterpretation of the War Department's efforts to collect and classify muskets. This is indicated by correspondence initiated by the War Department in 1842 and continued until at least 1848, wherein arms of the third class were to include arbitrarily those made from 1812 to 1820, and arms of the second class were to include arms made from 1821 to 1831.

In addition to the above description, collectors agree that this model was also made with a brass pan without a fence, and without a swivel lug. Muskets of this description were made in huge quantities by the Harpers Ferry and the Springfield Arsenals, and in large numbers by private contractors, probably including Henry Deringer Junior.

U. S. Martial Percussion Pistols, besides being manufactured by the United States arsenals, were also produced by the following private contractors: Henry Aston; the reorganized firm of H. Aston & Co.; Ira N. Johnson, all of Middletown, Connecticut; William Glaze & Co., operating as the Palmetto Armory, Columbia, South Carolina; N. P. Ames, Springfield, Massachusetts; and Henry Deringer Junior, Philadelphia, Pennsylvania. These weapons bear the model years of 1842, 1843, and 1855.

The Deringer models so closely resemble the **U. S. Pistol, Model 1843,**

Army, made by N. P. Ames, that we shall describe that weapon, which was made in greater quantities and serves as a comparison piece for the Deringer models. Details are: Caliber .54; 6-inch, smoothbore; round, browned barrel without sights, marked "USR" (United States Mounted Rifles), "RP," and "P," with the date. Three-quarter, 10.625-inch walnut stock extending to the swivel ramrod. Total length 11.625 inches. Brass mountings. Case-hardened box lock, with hammer inside lock plate. Rounded, countersunk, brass butt plate. Flat lock plate 4.3 inches long and 1.25 inches wide, marked "N. P. AMES," "Springfield Mass" and "USR" with date. Trigger guard 4.75 inches wide with square ends. One band. Brass-blade front sight. No rear sight. The Navy Model made by N. P. Ames is the same but marked "USN" in place of "USR."

U. S. Pistol, Model 1843, Deringer, Army, caliber .54, smoothbore, is identical with the N. P. Ames pistol, except that the lock plate is marked "US DERINGER PHILADELa." There may be a "USR" behind the hammer, but it is usually absent. Barrel may be unmarked, marked either "RP," or "DERINGER PHILADELa RP." Brass-blade front sight. No rear sight. A variation of this model is the same pistol but having a rifled barrel and both front and rear sights.

The Deringer Navy Model is a smoothbore, marked "USN," with the date 1847 behind the hammer.

Deringer Dueling Pistols were made during the flintlock and percussion periods, and possibly during the early cartridge period. In both flintlock and percussion forms, these pistols answered the generally accepted requirements for dueling weapons as described in a previous chapter. The dueling flintlocks were usually stocked to the muzzle of their 9- or 10-inch barrels, although later models often had three-quarter or half stocks. The maximum allowable trigger pull was 3 pounds, and the barrel was almost always octagonal in shape, smoothbore, 0.5-inch in diameter, or what we call caliber .50. Sights had to be fixed. These were provided for target practice only, for the dueling code prohibited the principals from taking deliberate aim. That is, the opponents faced each other at a prescribed distance, usually with loaded and often cocked pistols held at their sides, until the signal or command to aim and fire was given by the seconds.

Hair triggers were invented so that it would be possible to fire by a pressure on the trigger so light that it would not disturb the aim. A small, powerful spring was first compressed or "set" by pressing the trigger forward. Years later, triggers were made so that they could be "set" by means of a button.

The unfortunate custom of some collectors and dealers to classify almost any unknown or unidentified pistol as a "dueler" in order to raise its value can be avoided if these facts are remembered. As dueling pistols were not the property of poor men, they were carefully made, usually with checkering, engraving, inlay work and other forms of ornamentation, although some were entirely lacking in decoration but unmistakably showed the skill of their maker.

These pistols were almost always made and sold in matched pairs, and in a case which itself was in harmony with the fine quality of the pistols. Finally, certain gunmakers, both in Europe and the United States, were famous for their superb dueling pistols, although they did not always place their names or other identifying marks on their products for fear of becoming involved in prosecution after dueling was prohibited by law in most countries.

A dueling pistol made by Henry Deringer Junior is described in the August 10, 1872, issue of the *Army and Navy Journal* as having ". . . a barrel nine inches in length, rarely chambered for less than a .41 projectile, and, if rifled, finished in this respect with the extreme perfection then obtainable. These qualities, for the possession of which the fame of the maker soon gave his wares a guarantee, insured the dueling weapon almost a monopoly of patronage in an era distinguished for its 'little unpleasantnesses.' In these encounters, too often eventuating fatally to one or the other party, the Deringer rifle was sometimes used, but generally the 9-inch pistol."

A careless or too hasty reading of this quotation might result in some disastrous conclusion-jumping if one infers that the pistol described was made in 1872. However, noticing at the end of the first quoted sentence, the words "then obtainable," the use of the past tense in the rest of the passage, and the general wording, we may be safe in concluding that the quotation refers to a pistol made a good many years before the issue date of the magazine. Besides that, by 1872, the practice of dueling was falling into disuse, both because of enforcement of laws against it, and because men were coming to regard it as an extremely silly way to attempt to settle an argument or avenge an insult. Vituperously crusading editors were still being horsewhipped; individuals shot, stabbed, or beat others to death on occasion, just as personal "shooting matches" were held between two enemies; but all this was quite remote from the "code duello" with its rigid etiquette and its handsome and expensive armament.

Also interesting in the quoted passage is mention of the Deringer shoulder arm as a dueling weapon. In Philip Hone's Diary, which that observant former New York mayor wrote from 1828–1851, he mentions a duel between two members of Congress, William J. Graves of Kentucky and Jonathan Cilley of Maine, in which Deringer percussion rifles were used. Cilley, although he had the reputation for being the better marksman, was killed.

[113]

Here is Henry Deringer Junior's own description of the famous weapon that he designed and made:

"It is a single-barrel pistol with a back-action percussion lock, patent breech, wide bore, and a walnut stock. It varies in length from 1½ to 6 inches for the ordinary pistol, and from 6 to 9 inches for the dueling pistol. It is commonly mounted with German silver. The barrels used are all rifled. The locks vary in proportion to the length of the barrels. On the lock plates and breech of such pistol the words DERINGER PHILADEL^A are stamped, the stamps being the same which have been used from the first manufacture of these pistols and by which they are known everywhere."

In his last statement, however, the facts seem to indicate that Deringer was mistaken. An examination of the detailed descriptions of Deringer's derringers found in *The Gun Collector's Handbook of Values* shows that Deringer used more than one abbreviation for Philadelphia, and sometimes spelled it out in full.

Here, we have arranged a group of 15 specimens of Deringer's derringers which we'll refer to as Plate 1, and after each description you will find the identifying number of the individual derringer in this group:

Caliber .48; 3.5-inch round, flat-top barrel marked "Deringer Philadel," with short rib underneath for brass-tipped hickory ramrod. Total length 7.625 inches. Walnut stock with German silver tip. Engraved German silver guard. Cap box in butt. Back-action lock, engraved and marked like barrel. Figure 1.

Caliber .41; 4-inch, round barrel marked "Mand. for F. H. Clarke & Co., Memphis Tenn. Agents." Lock marked "Deringer Philadel." Figure 2.

Caliber .46; 4.25-inch round barrel with octagon breech. Back-action lock. Walnut stock, checkered grip. German silver mounting. Spur trigger enclosed in a German silver housing. Usual marks. Figure 3.

Caliber .48; 3.25-inch, round, flat-top barrel marked "Phila." Walnut stock, checkered grip. German silver stock tip, trigger guard, inlay in butt, side plate, and wedge escutcheons. Trigger guard and butt inlay engraved. Back-action lock engraved. Walnut ramrod. German silver tip, with slotted steel ferrule on small end. Short iron rib under barrel. Lock marked "Derringer" (double-r). Browned finish. Figure 4.

Caliber .44; 2.5-inch, round, flat-top barrel marked "Deringer Philadel." and "Made for A. J. Plate San Francisco." Back-action lock, engraved and marked "Deringer Philadel." Walnut stock. German silver guard and mountings. Figure 5.

[114]

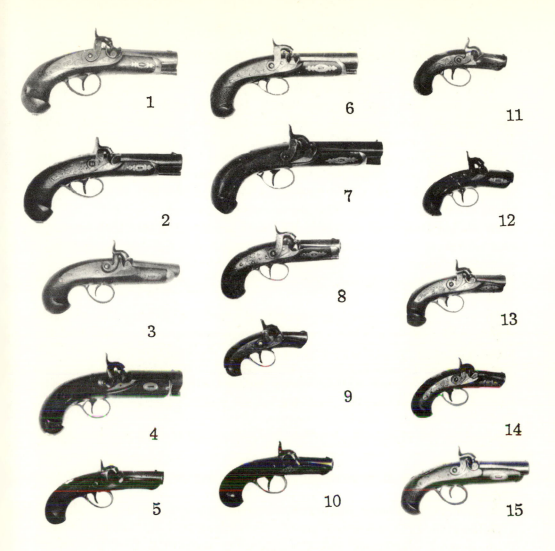

PLATE 1. Henry Deringer, Jr.'s Derringers.

1. Caliber .48, marked "Deringer, Philadel."
2. Caliber .41, Philadelphia.
3. Caliber .46, round barrel with octagon breech.
4. Caliber .48, round, flat-top barrel, marked "Phila."
5. Caliber .44, marked "Made for A. J. Plate San Francisco."
6. Caliber .43, marked "Deringer Philadela. Manud. for Hyde & Goodrich Agents N. Orleans."
7. Caliber .43, "Mand for Hyde & Goodrich Agents N. O."

8. Caliber .43, "Mand. for A. J. Taylor & Co. San Franco. Cala."
9. Caliber .41, marked "N. Curry & Bro. San Franco Cala. Agents."
10. Caliber .41, "C. Curry San Franco Cala."
11. Caliber .41, marked "Deringer Philadel."
12. Caliber .41, "Mand. for E. H. Clarke & Co. Memphis Tenn."
13. Caliber .40, marked "Deringer Philadela."
14 and 15. Caliber .40, "N. Curry & Bro. San Franco. Cala. Agents."

Caliber .43; 3.5-inch, round, flat-top barrel marked "Deringer Philadela. Manud. for Hyde & Goodrich Agents N. Orleans." Lock marked "Deringer Philadela." Walnut stock with German silver tip. German silver guard and escutcheons. Back-action lock, engraved. Cap box in butt. Short iron rib under barrel for brass-tipped hickory ramrod. Two gold bands inlaid at breech. Figure 6.

Caliber .43; 4-inch, flat-top, round barrel marked "Mand for Hyde & Goodrich Agents N.O." Lock marked "Deringer Philadela." Walnut stock. Checkered grip. German silver tip. German silver mountings; engraved guard. Short iron rib under barrel for ebony ramrod. Figure 7.

Caliber .41; 2.5-inch, round, flat-top barrel marked "Deringer Philadela. Mand. for A. J. Taylor & Co. San Franco. Cala." Walnut stock. German silver tip. Back-action lock marked "Deringer Philadela." Guard and all mountings German silver, engraved. Hickory ramrod under barrel. Cap box in butt. Figure 8.

Caliber .41; 1.75-inch round, flat-top barrel marked "Deringer Philadel" and "N. Curry & Bro. San Franco Cala. Agents." Total length 4.25 inches. Walnut stock. Cap box in butt. German silver guard and mounts. Back-action lock marked "Deringer Philadel." Figure 9.

Caliber .41; 2.125-inch, round, flat-top barrel marked "Deringer Philadel. C. Curry San Franco Cala." Engraved back-action lock marked "Deringer Philadel." German silver guard and mountings. Figure 10.

Caliber .41; 1.75-inch, round, flat-top barrel marked "Deringer Philadel." Back-action lock marked like barrel. Total length 4.375 inches. Walnut stock. German silver guard and mountings. Cap box in butt. Figure 11.

Caliber .41; 4-inch flat-top barrel marked "Deringer Philadel. Mand for E. H. Clarke & Co. Memphis Tenn." Total length 8 inches. Walnut stock, checkered grip and German silver tip. All mountings engraved German silver. Cap box in butt. Wooden ramrod. Lock marked "Deringer Philadel." Figure 12.

Caliber .40; 1.75-inch, round flat-top barrel marked "Deringer Philadela." Engraved, back-action lock marked the same. Full-length walnut stock, checkered grip. German silver guard and mountings. Figure 13.

Caliber .40; 2-inch, round, flat-top barrel marked "Deringer Philadel. N. Curry & Bro. San Franco. Cala. Agents." Walnut stock. German silver mountings. Lock marked "Deringer Philadel." Figures 14 and 15.

Caliber .41 percussion Deringer with a 1⅜-inch barrel, a total length of five inches, and nickel-silver inlays and trim. Plate 2, figure 1.

Caliber .43 percussion Deringer with a 3-inch barrel, a total length of 7 inches, and a trap in the butt plate. Plate 2, figure 2.

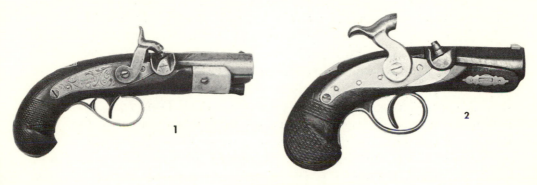

PLATE 2

1. A Deringer, caliber .41, 1⅜-inch barrel.   EVERETT SAGGUS
2. A Deringer, caliber .43, with 3-inch barrel.   EVERETT SAGGUS

Deringer Vest-Pocket Pistol, caliber .28, single-shot; 1.5-inch round barrel marked by letter "P" within a wreath. This was Henry Deringer's registered mark. Blued metal finish. Fancy engraving on trigger guard, lock, and hammer. Brass-post front sight. Indented rear sight. Total length 4 inches. Polished hardwood stock to within ¼ inch of muzzle. Bird's-head handles. Barrel fastened to stock with a pin. This was designed for a gambler or for a lady to carry in a muff or purse.

Deringer Pocket Pistol, Lincoln Murder Model. The Deringer derringer pistol with which John Wilkes Booth murdered President Abraham Lincoln is in the possession of the United States government—and it will stay there. About five hundred fools and liars claim they have the identical pistol used to kill one of the three greatest Presidents in our history. Quite often dealers advertise that they have this pistol. The reader is advised to be careful in dealing with such persons, and it is recommended that they refer the matter to the nearest district attorney for prosecution. The genuine pistol is caliber .44 with a 2.5-inch barrel marked "Deringer, Philadelphia." The total length is 6 inches. It has a polished hardwood stock and forearm; bird's-head-shaped butt. The wood is checkered. However, many guns were made exactly like this.

Henry Deringer not only knew guns as well as his father; he also knew his market. The famous little pocket pistol carried its own built-in appeal to the people of the Western frontier. When the demand outstripped the number he could conscientiously produce without sacrificing the quality and accuracy always associated with his name, Deringer let other gunmakers take up the slack. This they proceeded to do right from the first, with a celerity that pointed to the increasing use of machines in their New England factories. More guns could be made in less time, with less handwork.

Meanwhile, especially in California and in the booming Golden Gate city, those small, large-bore guns were being sold, advertised, and put to deadly use. For a while, at least four reputable gun-dealers were proud to handle the "original" Deringer pistol—with Deringer spelled in almost any way that hit their fancy. Double-r or single, capital D or small, no matter how it was printed, the name sounded the same when you asked the storekeeper for that little gun; there was no mistake then about what weapon you wanted to buy. As these guns were carried and used, they were talked about by name; newspaper stories mentioned them—no matter how you spelled it, people knew just what kind of pistol was meant—and in a country where almost everyone went armed, that was important.

In the next chapter we will look briefly at some of the San Francisco outlets for the Deringer pistol, and meet some of the people who used them during those early days. More important, however, we will discuss some of the many imitations of the Deringer derringer—and find that while Henry Deringer Junior tolerated and perhaps even welcomed well-made imitations of his pocket pistol, he could put up a tough and effective fight against counterfeiters of his product.

Saturday Night on San Francisco's Barbary Coast. CALIFORNIA STATE LIBRARY

VII *The Voice of the Derringer: Imitations, Counterfeits and Competitors of Deringer's Pocket Pistol*

It has always been a practice with a large proportion of the citizens to carry loaded firearms or other deadly weapons concealed about their persons, this being, as it were, a part of their ordinary dress; while occasionally the rest of the inhabitants are compelled also to arm themselves like their neighbors.

—*From* The Annals of San Francisco,
New York, 1854.

In the pre-Vigilance Committee era of California, thou-sands of these pistols found a ready market in that new domain, "the sharp crack of the Deringer" being heard in the land much more frequently than the voice of the turtle.

—From The Army & Navy Journal,
August 10, 1872.

SAN FRANCISCO during the 1850's was still the lusty, lustful, brawling offspring of the first frantic stampede of '49. By the end of that year, California's population had boomed by a hundred thousand, and by no means all of those who came to the city at once headed with pick and shovel and pan back into the hills. Many immigrants stayed and set up in business. Others, divining a rich vein of gold that might be got without the sweating drudgery of physical labor, just stayed.

By 1851, the annual output of gold had reached an impressive $55 million. No longer did the bearded boys from the diggin's have to choose each other as partners for floor-shaking jigs, reels and polkas. From saloons, dance houses and variety halls came high-pitched feminine laughter, screams of merriment or anger, or a female voice giving someone a real muleskinner's cussing-out. The ladies—God bless 'em!—had arrived!

There was only one thing wrong—there were not enough of them.

Particularly, there weren't enough young and pretty ones to go 'round—not counting, of course, Indians. In a woman-starved, gun-carrying country, that fact—plus many more contributory causes—spelled the kind of trouble that led to violence, and the kind of violence that led most men to carry more than one hand gun. Despite lack of solid evidence, it seems reasonable to suppose that derringers were in use at that early time in California.

The wording of one gun-dealer's catalogue—that of J. H. Johnston, published as late as 1883, but offering for sale a number of percussion, muzzle-loading derringers (almost twenty years after the breech-loading cartridge system had been in general use), is worth attention:

"The shooting power of these celebrated weapons is well known to nearly every Southerner and many of the old frontiersmen; and this, with their deadly accuracy, make them most desirable for 'sure work.'" They were offered at "$5.50 a pair, or $3.00 each, molds included, post paid, fully warranted." Doubtless a good buy, even for a pocket pistol perhaps thirty-five years old, especially when Johnston also points out that "the price of these pistols has been until lately $15 to $20 a pair."

Twenty-eight years before that catalogue appeared, one San Francisco citizen found the derringer—or perhaps Deringer's derringer—excellently adapted for "sure work." He was Charles Cora, a gambler, who had quarreled with General W. H. Richardson, United States marshal for the Northern District of California. Or November 18, 1855, Cora stood at the bar of the Blue Bird Saloon when Richardson entered and headed for the gambler with the apparent intention of fulfilling his previous threat to slap the man's face. Cora drew his derringer and shot Richardson through the heart, thus helping to precipitate the Second Vigilance Committee's cleansing of the city the following year, when Cora was hanged for the murder.

General Richardson was a highly respected citizen, and the killing got full coverage in the newspapers of the day. Testimony at the trial discloses some interesting details regarding the use of derringers and the habits of those who carried them.

A. J. Taylor, who started selling firearms in San Francisco in 1850 and expanded his business, testified:

"I am a gunsmith. I carry on a shooting gallery. I met Cora coming out of my gallery on the day of the killing. I had seen Cora frequently at my house before for the purpose of having his pistols loaded, and shooting once in a while. He had a pair of Derringers."

Since Taylor was one of the four well-recognized dealers in Deringer's derringer, it seems likely that Cora used the genuine Philadelphia article. If the idea of going to a firearms man to have pistols loaded seems strange to us today, it is necessary to remember that with each pair of Deringer pocket pistols, a bullet mold for that individual pair was supplied. Even when the caliber was approximately the same, bullets cast from one mold would not necessarily fit guns supplied with another, just as parts of one model would not necessarily fit corresponding parts of another individual gun, although of the same model and caliber. A man thoroughly familiar with firearms would have little trouble in fashioning the bullets to fit any derringer of the same caliber, but many citizens, having neither time nor talent to cast, then hand-shape the bullets for these muzzle-loaders, went to places like Taylor's establishment to have their pistols loaded. And, while there, why not take advantage of Taylor's shooting gallery for practice? That was a common habit, even though the customers practiced with pistols that were never meant to be fired at a range of more than a few feet. However, it was probably the facility with which the shooter could unlimber his derringer and get into action that counted, rather than the number of bull's-eyes scored.

A good many of Taylor's customers were prominent and respectable men, but seemed homicide-prone, and Taylor himself spent a good deal of his time giving testimony on the witness stand. This certainly did not injure his gun-loading business or the sale of his Deringer pocket pistols.

Thus, in February 1857, Thomas S. King, editor of the *Daily Evening Bulletin*, after defending himself against assault, said: "I drew a small Derringer pistol, two of which I carried." He told the court that he had had them loaded at Taylor's gallery.

Once again, in May of the same year, Taylor stated in court that he had "loaded a Derringer pistol" for one Ned McGowan, accused of being an accessory in the murder of the crusading editor, James King, of William.

In a pamphlet published after McGowan's acquittal, that doughty individual was quoted as saying that during one period of his career he went about with a loaded derringer pistol in each coat pocket, another pair in his trousers, and—better be safe than sorry!—his belt bulging with a six-shot revolver and a Bowie knife. Such a formidable arsenal seems better adapted to a man of Bluebeard's ferocity than to a private citizen, but in the dangerous and violent decade of 1850–1860, multiple armament of that kind was not unusual equipment for many San Franciscans, both the law-abiding and the denizens of ferocious Sydney-Town or their flashier brothers of the tenderloin.

Most arms experts believe that Deringer pocket pistols bearing the marks DERINGER PHILADEL[A] on the breech and lock, and MAN[D] FOR A. J. TAYLOR & CO. SAN FRANC[O] CAL[A] on the barrel were made and sold between 1852, when Taylor really began to prosper, and 1858, the year of his death. This period of time is probably correct, but variations in the reference to Taylor on the barrel are reported on several specimens.

Second of the four recognized Deringer retailers was W. C. Allen, who was well established in 1853 as a watch importer and jeweler at 136 Montgomery Street. The sale of firearms, however, was apparently less important to him than was his other business, and it was not until the Second Vigilance Committee was organized in 1856 that he, in common with other gun dealers, started to advertise his Deringer pistols in the newspapers. And, as usual, in mentioning Deringer's product, he left the r's fall where they would.

Most collectors who specialize in the genuine Deringer pocket pistols, and further specialize in those with the marks of dealers or agents, believe that the W. C. Allen specimens were made by Deringer and sold in San Francisco during the same period. They are stamped on the barrel: MAN[D] FOR W. C. ALLEN & CO. SAN FRANC[O] CAL[A], and also bear the regular Deringer marks.

These are undoubtedly the rarest specimens of all genuine Deringer pistols bearing the marks of a San Francisco agent or dealer, and are at least as valuable as the others in this group.

Charles Curry, another important genuine Deringer dealer and agent, came to San Francisco from Philadelphia in 1852. Although he did not know Henry Deringer Junior personally, there seem to be more genuine Deringer pocket pistols bearing one of the Curry marks in present-day collections than those of any other agent or dealer. With the others, he seemed not to have advertised firearms until 1856, when he offers, among other things, "Derringer Pistols" for sale. In 1858, in an advertisement in the San Francisco Directory for that year, Curry refers to his shop as a "gun ware-house" at 87 Battery Street, and later, in the *Daily Alta California*, Curry says: "N.B.—C. Curry is the only authorized Agent for Derringer's Pistols in California."

The genuine Deringer pistols marked for Charles Curry were stamped: C. CURRY SAN FRANC° CAL^A in addition to the regular Deringer marks. Apparently these were made and sold from 1856 until Charles Curry died in 1863. His business was thereafter conducted by his two brothers, Nathaniel and John Curry, who called themselves Nathl. Curry & Bro., and also N. Curry & Bro., selling genuine Deringer pistols marked N. CURRY & BR° SAN FRANC° CAL^A until the market for muzzle-loading, percussion, single-shot pistols began to drop sharply with the advent of breech-loading cartridge weapons.

A. J. Plate, the last on the list of prominent Deringer dealers, is so placed because in one sense he is the most interesting to gun historians of the West, since he was one of the relatively few counterfeiters, or forgers, of the original Deringer pistol. That there is a vast difference between a counterfeiter and an imitator should be obvious, but to Adolphus Joseph Plate, of Prussia, who came to New York in 1830 where he set up as a cabinet and furniture-maker, the sharp line that distinguished the counterfeit from the imitation seemed to grow dim with the years.

With thousands of others, Plate was early infected with the gold fever. Late in 1849 he arrived in California with some of the first Argonauts to seek his fortune in the gulches and hills. Apparently, however, he failed to strike either vein or pay dirt, for in the spring of 1850, we see him with other merchants on the waterfront, selling firearms and ammunition, his place of business probably a tent with a rough plank as a counter, supported by two boxes or sawhorses across the entrance. Apparently he found this more profitable than his prospecting in the gold fields, for the San Francisco Directories of 1852 and 1854 both carry his business card in which he lists himself as gunsmith.

This term should not be taken too seriously. In modern usage, a gunsmith is considered one skilled in the repair of arms and even the manufacture of parts, but throughout the history of firearms the word "gunsmith" has been used very loosely to include manufacturers, repairers, salesmen and owners of gun shops. Actually, an all-around master gunsmith should be at the same time a first-class general machinist and a master wood-worker. Obviously, there are very few in the United States who can claim these qualifications. A. J. Plate evidently was a skilled woodworker and it is possible that he transferred some of his ability to metalworking, but all the evidence indicates that in San Francisco he was primarily a merchant, a skilled salesman.

It is not, however, until 1861 that Plate mentions that he sells "Derringer Pistols," both as wholesaler and retailer, but thereafter his advertisements mention, among other weapons, "Deringer and Dueling Pistols" (1863 San Francisco Business Directory), although whether the correct spelling here is a matter of luck or intent is not evident.

During the period when Plate was the authorized legitimate dealer for the genuine Deringer pocket pistol, these weapons were marked on the bar-rel with the usual stamping: MADE FOR A. J. PLATE, SAN FRANCISCO, CAL^A. These were sold to Plate by Deringer through the New York City firm of Folsom & Stevens, who sent him 54 pairs, starting in 1858 and con-tinuing until the order was completed.

But Adolph J. Plate was unhappy. A diligent salesman, unwilling to miss an order either from other firms that he supplied as wholesaler and jobber, or as a retailer, he simply could not get as many genuine Deringer pocket pistols as he could sell. Like many another businessman the thought of the profits just out of reach irritated him. A remedy for this situation was indi-cated, and that remedy was not difficult to find. He had only to turn to one of his employees, one Charles Schlotterbeck, who had arrived in 1850 from Philadelphia and in 1860 took a job with Plate. This was a name that Henry Deringer Junior knew well and for the past year had had no cause to regard with affection.

Back in Philadelphia in 1859, five of Henry Deringer's employees left him to form their own firearms concern, among them Henry Schlotterbeck and his brother Frederick, and set up shop under the simplified version of that name, Slotter & Co. Perhaps the aspiring entrepreneurs felt keenly that the full profit potential of the Deringer pocket pistol was far from being re-alized, thus limiting their opportunities for advancement; perhaps they heeded echoes of the mass-production machinery already installed and busy in New England arms factories. Or perhaps Charles Schlotterbeck had writ-ten from San Francisco of the growing pile of unfilled orders for Deringer pocket pistols that was roweling A. J. Plate's disposition. Whatever the mo-tives, Slotter & Co. at 400 Lynd Street, Philadelphia, proceeded to manu-facture—apparently still by hand—almost exact duplicates of Henry Derin-ger's prize product.

Undoubtedly the Schlotterbecks knew—for it was no secret, in any event

—that there were no patents covering any feature of the Deringer pocket pistol. Therefore they believed that they were well within their legal rights to turn out copies, just as close as they could make them, of the original.

The derringer situation was a curious one and deserves some comment. Other arms makers were doing the same, but there were differences and in some instances improvements on the original. With the outright imitators, there was no attempt to deceive the public into thinking that these guns were the genuine Deringer product; they were merely the same *type* of pistol, fashioned to answer a popular demand. Slotter & Co., however, decided to go them all one better and turned out pistols not only mechanically extremely close to the genuine article, but with Deringer's mark on lock and breech exactly as it was stamped on the original.

The forgeries were profitable; they must have been. Or at least, Slotter & Co. foresaw a good profit in the immediate future from their product. The strange part of the whole affair was that their counterfeits were thoroughly good guns, but of course they weren't true Deringer pistols. Had these five Deringer-trained mechanics gone into hasty production and turned out a cheap and shoddy weapon for fast profits, their forgeries might have been more understandable. Indeed some of them, as the descriptions of the Slotter derringers point out, had barrels bored out of solid steel, instead of using the wrought iron of the original Deringer arm. This practice was followed often during the percussion period by many of Deringer's legitimate imitators, as they regarded the steel barrel safer than one of wrought iron—which, of course, it was.

With the new concern well into production, Frederick Schlotterbeck decided he could afford to take a few months off and journey to San Francisco. There he would visit his brother Charles. Not surprisingly, while there, he met Charles's boss, A. J. Plate; even less surprisingly, they had long conversations about their common vocation and business, the manufacture and sale of firearms, and especially of the derringer pocket pistol. It was still in 1860 when the West Coast began to receive shipments of almost identical copies of the true Deringer weapon—not only with all the Deringer marks, but with the additional legend: MADE FOR A. J. PLATE, SAN FRANCISCO—an exact copy of the stamping done at the Philadelphia Deringer factory for guns that Plate had customarily ordered.

At the trial of the suit for copyright infringement against Plate, filed on November 10, 1863, Henry Deringer said through depositions presented by his California attorneys, that his suspicions were aroused when Plate and other West Coast outlets decreased their orders for his pocket pistol:

"I sent agents to New York and elsewhere to try to find out who was counterfeiting my goods, and offered a hundred dollars reward for information, but could get no evidence against the guilty parties.

"After a time I learned that the defendant was selling these counterfeits, and I procured two pairs from his store, one pair of which I attached to my former deposition in this case."

Now seventy-six years old, Henry Deringer had but five more years to live, and would not be able to rejoice in the final decision of his case. He was probably too feeble to make the taxing trip from Philadelphia to San Francisco.

Plate, sometime during or after 1860, purchased 428 pairs of counterfeit Deringer pistols from Slotter & Co., and sold them in San Francisco at various times up to 1866. Some, he said, bore the Slotter & Co. mark, but he admitted that about three-quarters of them carried marks almost identical to those that Deringer had made for him in 1858. Also, like any enterprising businessman, Plate wanted to investigate and explore both sources and markets. Charles Schlotterbeck made some counterfeit Deringer pistols for him, which Plate sold both to individuals and retailers in California. R. Liddle & Co., and Wilson & Evans were two of the concerns that bought from Plate—but they also bought directly from Slotter in Philadelphia, realizing it was cheaper to deal direct, by the dozen or more, than to work through a middleman. Plate was now too busy to worry about such picayune matters, even if he had known about them. He was industriously cultivating a market that extended from the Comstock Lode's booming Virginia City to Seattle, and beyond into British Columbia. Gone now was Adolphus Plate's ulcerous irritation at thought of orders for a product he could not supply. He could give 'em what they wanted, and he did—selling a small, large-caliber gun that looked and performed like the genuine Deringer pistol, and even stamped with Deringer's own mark—if you didn't look too closely. The only difference was that the weapons Plate sold were simply not the real, honest-to-God Deringer pocket pistols which, in many instances, they were represented to be. And if no one else got mad about it, one old Philadelphia gunsmith did.

Derringer asked for fifteen thousand dollars for damages suffered through trade-mark infringement. Plate's lawyers answered that a California law, since April 3, 1863, had required registration of trade-marks. Deringer, they maintained, had not complied with this; therefore he had no cause for action.

Nathaniel Curry, one of the surviving brothers of Charles Curry, one of the pioneer retailers of the true Deringer, said: "I have known Henry Deringer personally since June, 1856, and have seen him often since. . . . He is a very old man, and so appears. I saw him in the winter of 1858 maybe ten or fifteen times."

Parenthetically, this statement is interesting as it seems to cast light on the business relations between Deringer and the Currys. An advertisement in 1864, inserted in a San Francisco business directory by "Nathl. Curry & Bro, Successors to Chas. Curry," states:

"N.B.—N. Curry & Bro are the only authorized Agents for Deringer Pistols in California, and none are genuine except marked CURRY, AGENT, on the barrels."

The District Court awarded Deringer damages of $1,770, and issued a permanent injunction against Plate's using Deringer's trade-mark. Plate thereupon appealed.

Besides making history in trade-mark law, records of the case helped to solve one of the mysteries that for years had puzzled arms collectors, dealers and historians in this general field.

Among the most interesting counterfeits which were undoubtedly made by Slotter & Co. are those stamped with the name J. DERINGER, and J. DERINGER PHILADEL[A] on the barrel, and also on the lock and breech. Some of those marked in this manner on the lock and breech carried the stamp SLOTTER & Co PHIL[A] on the barrel. Deviations from the genuine Deringer pistol were like those described later in this chapter for the Slotter & Co. counterfeits.

Who was this J. Deringer?

There was a John H. Deringer, a younger brother of Henry Junior who described himself as a "gunmaker" in his will, but there was no reason for him to counterfeit his brother's pistols and no evidence that he ever did. However, in records of the case against Plate, there is the following statement:

"Philadelphia, January 13, 1866. Co-partnership. I have this day formed a partnership with Slotter & Co. for the manufacture of Pistols and Fire-arms at No. 400 Lynd Street. (signed) John Deringer."

This seems obviously a scheme on the part of Slotter & Co. to justify their use of the name Deringer on their pistols. Note the date of the statement, and remember that Deringer's case had been in litigation for three years in San Francisco, and before the decision on the appeal would be reached another two years would pass. Just as significant if not more so, was the fact that the above John Deringer—apparently no known relation to the gunsmith—had been a tailor, and apparently unacquainted with the first thing about the manufacture of firearms. There is an ancient axiom of law which translates as "The act (thing) speaks for itself." Apparently the Slotter Company's attempt to get Plate off the hook by this device came— at the very least—a little late in the day. However, it did succeed in solving one of the puzzles, at once annoying and fascinating, that seem an integral part of gun collecting.

In 1867 one of Slotter & Company's published advertisements in Philadelphia includes the statement: "We are also the makers of the J. Derringer Pistol."

Again we see the conventional discrepancy in the spelling. However, although the pistols bearing the mark of J. DERINGER did not carry a facsimile of the genuine Deringer stamping, the use of the name and its correct form of spelling justifies classifying these pistols with the other counterfeits.

Definite proof that Henry Deringer was unable—and apparently did not care to attempt—to satisfy the market for his pocket pistol is found in his depositions, dated July 12, 1866:

"The aggregate sales of my said pistols for the last ten years marked DERINGER PHILADEL[A] amounted to 5280 pairs. I am unable to give the numbers sold each year, my books not being kept in such a way as to separate the sales for each year." And: "I have manufactured and sold, within the last five years, 1280 pairs only of said pistols . . ."

The summary at the top of the report of this history-making case, encompassing the California Supreme Court's decision, reads:

"Trade-Mark—Measure of Damages. In an action to recover damages for a violation of plaintiff's trade-mark, the profits actually realized by defendants of the spurious article under the simulated trade-mark, is a proper measure of damages, but the recovery of the plaintiff is not limited to the amount of such profits."

As one of the famous decisions of patent law, this case has been cited up to the present time in litigation involving many times the amount of money asked for by the Philadelphia gunmaker. Aside from the use of his name as a common noun in the language, the decision in Deringer vs. Plate serves to commemorate the craftsman whose hands, heart and brain went into the fashioning of each pair of the pistols stamped with his genuine mark. In all the history of firearms no gun has been so widely imitated—or actually counterfeited.

Because Deringer pistol collectors regard both imitations and counterfeits almost as highly as they do the originals, here are detailed descriptions of some of the more famous specimens of the derringer:

F. R. J. Bitterlich & Co., caliber .42; rifled, 2.875-inch octagon barrel marked "F. R. Bitterlich & Co. Nashville, Tenn." Back-action lock marked like barrel. Walnut stock. Square butt with German silver inlay. German silver guard. Plate 1, figure 1.

Same, caliber .44 or .45; 4.25-inch round barrel with octagon breech, marked as above. Walnut stock extending nearly the full length. Back-action lock, engraved, and marked as above on some specimens. Spur trigger. Made without trigger guard. Figures 2 and 3.

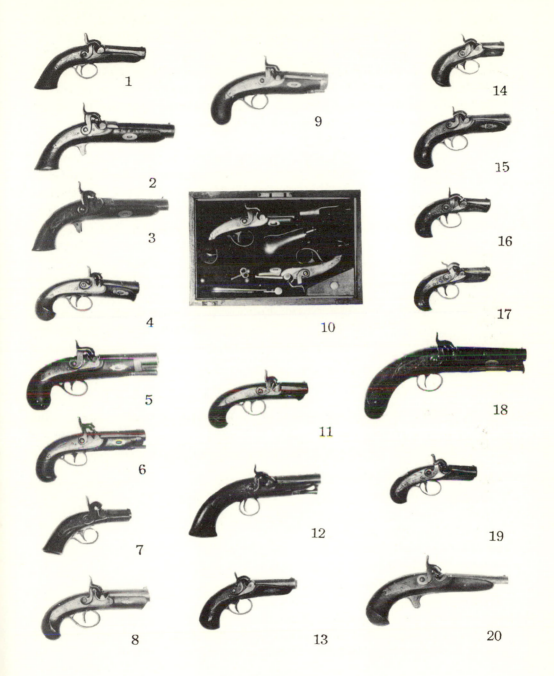

Plate 1

Derringers made by Henry Deringer, Jr.'s competitors, imitators, and counterfeiters.

Bruff, caliber .41; 2.5-inch, flat-top, round barrel marked "R. P. Bruff N.Y. Cast Steel." Back-action lock. Full-length walnut stock. Figure 4.

R. Constable, caliber .43; 3.5-inch, round, wedge-fastened, flat-top barrel marked "R. Constable." Hickory ramrod. Walnut stock. German silver tip. Back-action engraved lock. Engraved iron guard. Short rib under barrel for hickory ramrod. Figure 5.

Dimick, caliber .47; 3-inch, round, flat-top barrel marked "H. E. Dimmick & Co., St. Louis, Mo." Engraved back-action lock marked "H. E. Dimick & Co." Fine burl walnut stock, silver tipped. Engraved iron guard. Not shown.

Same, but with barrel marked "H. E. Dimick." Back-action lock engraved with American eagle. Walnut stock, checkered grip. German silver guard and wedge escutcheons, engraved. Browned finish. Not shown.

G. Erichson, caliber .41; 3.25-inch, flat-top barrel marked "G. Erichson Houston." Lock marked like barrel. Full-length walnut stock with white metal tip and checkered grip. Plain German silver mountings. Wooden ramrod. Front and rear sights. This is regarded as a Texan imitation of a Deringer derringer. Figure 6.

J. E. Evans, caliber .50; 2-inch, round, flat-top barrel marked "J. E. Evans Philada." Walnut stock, checkered grip. German silver trigger guard, side plate, and shield inlaid in back of grip. Engraved back-action lock. Hammer and lock casehardened in colors. Browned barrel. Also made in caliber .36. Figure 7.

Glassick, caliber .40; 3.75-inch octagon barrel marked "F. Glassick & Co. Memphis, Tenn." Back-action lock. Sheathed spur trigger. Walnut stock almost to muzzle. Not shown.

Grubb, caliber .40, single-shot; 3.5-inch octagon barrel. Walnut stock. Resembles Deringer derringers, but grip more closely approximates a square shape. Not shown.

Hawes & Waggoner, caliber .41; 3-inch, round, flat-top barrel marked "Hawes & Waggoner." Resembles Deringer derringers. Figure 8.

Krider, caliber .43; 3.25-inch, round, flat-top barrel marked "Krider Phila." Back-action lock marked "Krider." German silver mountings. Walnut stock, checkered grip. Also made caliber .40 with 2.25-inch barrel. Figure 9.

Same, cased presentation pair, caliber .40; 2.187-inch, round, flat-top rifled barrel, marked "Philadelphia." Back-action lock marked "Krider." Gold and silver name plates. Mahogany case with accessories. The pair described was presented to M. S. Latham, governor of California, later U. S. Senator. Figure 10.

Lins, caliber .50, 2-inch barrel. Total length 5.75 inches. Marked "A. Frederick Lins, Phila. Pa." Also made with a 6-inch barrel and a total length of 9.75 inches—very long for a derringer. Not shown.

J. P. Lower, caliber .43; rifled, 2-inch, round, flat-top barrel marked "Philada." Back-action lock engraved and marked "J. P. Lower." Walnut stock, checkered grip. German silver guard, engraved. Either made by Lower in Denver or by Deringer in Philadelphia for Lower as distributor. Figure 11.

Schneider & Co., caliber .40; 3.75-inch octagon barrel marked "Schneider & Co. Memphis, Tenn." Spur trigger. Back-action lock. Walnut stock. Checkered grip. Not shown.

Schneider & Glassick, caliber .45; 3-inch octagon barrel, marked "Schneider & Glassick, Memphis, Tenn." Otherwise like Schneider Derringer above. Not shown.

Simpson, caliber .55; 3.25-inch, round, Damascus steel barrel with grooved top, marked "R. J. Simpson, New York." Steel-mounted. Engraved. Back-action lock. Walnut stock almost to muzzle. Checkered fishtail grip. Steel-tip hickory ramrod. Figure 12.

Slotter & Co., a few specimens of which are described below, usually vary from calibers .31, through .41, .44, and .46 to about .50. There is little variation in marking except that some carry the names of the same agents that were marked on genuine Deringer derringers. Like them, the usual barrel length varies from 1.5 to 5 inches. The longer barrels and larger calibers usually are valued higher, but a combination of a very short barrel and a very large caliber raises the value.

Slotter & Co., caliber .50; 3-inch, round, flat-top barrel marked "Slotter & Co. Phila. Steel." Back-action lock marked "Slotter & Co. Phila." Walnut stock nearly to muzzle. German silver guard, escutcheons, butt inlay, and name plate, all engraved. Figure 13.

Same, caliber .46; 2-inch, round, flat-top barrel marked "Slotter & Co.

Phila." Back-action lock marked as barrel. Total length 4.5 inches. Full-length walnut stock. German silver guard and mountings. Figure 14.

Same, caliber .44; 3-inch, round, flat-top barrel marked "Slotter & Co. Phila. Made for R. Liddle & Co. San Franco Cala." Back-action lock marked "Slotter & Co. Phila." Walnut stock. German silver guard and mountings, engraved. Cap box in butt. Figure 15.

Same, caliber .44; 2-inch, round, flat-top barrel marked "Slotter & Co. Phila. Made for A. J. Plate, San Francisco." Back-action lock marked "Slotter & Co. Phila." Walnut stock. German silver guard and mountings. Figure 16.

Same, caliber .41; 2-inch, round, flat-top barrel marked "Slotter & Co. Phila." German silver guard and mountings. Engraved. Back-action lock marked like barrel. Figure 17.

Same, Large, caliber .40, 5.625-inch, round, flat-top barrel. Total length 10 inches. Usual marks. Not shown.

Tryon, caliber .47; 4-inch, octagon, twist-steel barrel marked "E. K. Tryon Philada." Walnut stock. Checkered grip. Swivel iron ramrod. Engraved iron guard and thimble. Back-action lock, elaborately engraved. Figure 18.

Same, caliber .41; 4.625-inch, round, flat-top barrel marked "Philadelphia." Back-action lock, engraved, marked "Tryon." Total length 8.625 inches. Walnut stock. German silver tip. Cap box in butt. Engraved iron guard. Rib under barrel with one thimble. Ivory ramrod. Figure 19.

A. Wurfflein, caliber .22; 4-inch, nickel-plated, round, flat-top barrel. Walnut stock nearly full-length. Spur trigger. Back-action lock marked "Wurfflein Phila." Also made with conventional derringer trigger. 2.125-inch, round, flat-top barrel. Figure 20.

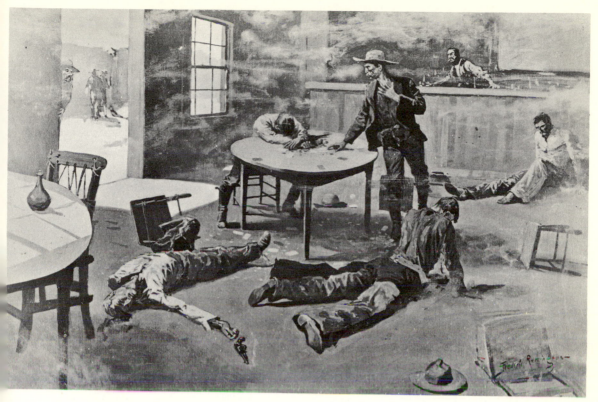

A Misdeal. From a painting by Frederic Remington. DENVER PUBLIC
LIBRARY WESTERN COLLECTION

VIII *Twilight of the Derringer: Breech=loading Cartridge Types; the Derringer in Transition*

IF the year 1860 was one of vast portent for the United States, it was also to have its effect on the little heavy-calibered hand gun that won so high a place in the personal armament of citizens in the new, turbulent towns and cities of the West. The doom of the true Deringer pistol, its imitations and counterfeits, had already been sealed by the increasingly rapid development and manufacture of breech-loading, metallic cartridge arms. Its eclipse was forecast by the pounding hoofs of the Pony Express as, on November 13 of that fateful year, a rider clattered up before the Wells Fargo office in Sacramento with the news of Lincoln's election—a record-breaking relay run of six days and seventeen hours from the western railroad terminus of St. Joe, 2,000 miles to the east on the banks of the muddy Missouri.

The Pony Express, with its seventy-five lightweight riders who often carried a brace of derringers, was to carry news of the fall of Sumter and Lincoln's call for volunteers before it was struck down by the lightning of the telegraph in 1861, while the breech-loading metallic-cartridge weapons were finding increasing favor among Westerners. Although the voice of the true derringer would not be stilled for years—it was to resound savagely the night of April 14, 1865, in Ford's Theater in Washington, when John Wilkes Booth fired a fatal .44 caliber ball into President Lincoln—the little weapon "most desireable for 'sure work'" was being replaced by the more convenient, swifter-action guns. The early ambition of all gun-makers, to produce an effective multishot weapon, was being realized in the pepperbox pistol, in the multibarreled derringer types, and in the development of the true revolver. The fact that, from the first, the original Deringer pistols were made to be sold in pairs with a bullet mold to supply ammunition for each pair, provided the average purchaser with two heavy-calibered shots. As late as 1867, Tryon Brothers & Co., of Philadelphia, described their "Superior Derringer Pattern Pistol" with the statement, "Each pair is accompanied with a Bullet Mould for slug and round bullets, a Loading and Cleaning Rod, Powder Flask and Covers, and contained in a neat paper box." (See Plate 1.)

It is worth noticing at this time that all double or multibarreled short, light, large-caliber pistols, whether or not designated as derringers by their manufacturers, were almost never advertised to be sold in pairs. The implication is clear enough: Why bother with two single-shot pistols when this one weapon, or others like it, gave you the same advantage? Thus, among many other indications, these straws showed the direction of the public favor for the type of hand gun people wanted. The time was ripe and the demand was growing for multishot, breech-loading cartridge pistols.

The prospering firm of Wilson & Evans, with shops in both San Francisco and Sacramento, advertised that they were "Gun-Makers, Importers & Dealers in Colt's Rifles and Pistols, Sharps Rifles, Gun Materials, Powder, Shot, Caps, Wads, etc." Their advertisements appearing in the San Francisco Business Directory and Mercantile Guide for 1864 were quaintly written, as if by some admiring friend—a windy, glowing eulogy on the many busi-

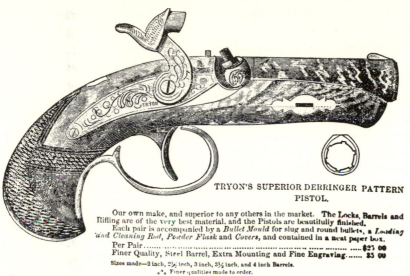

TRYON'S SUPERIOR DERRINGER PATTERN PISTOL.

Our own make, and superior to any others in the market. The Locks, Barrels and Rifling are of the very best material, and the Pistols are beautifully finished.
Each pair is accompanied by a *Bullet Mould* for slug and round bullets, a *Loading and Cleaning Rod, Powder Flask* and *Covers*, and contained in a neat paper box.
Per Pair.......... ....$25 00
Finer Quality, Steel Barrel, Extra Mounting and Fine Engraving...... $5 00
Sizes made—2 inch, 2½ inch, 3 inch, 3½ inch, and 4 inch Barrels.
** Finer qualities made to order.

PLATE 1

ness virtues of the concern and its products. To gun collectors and historians, however, the real meat of the notice is in this significant sentence:

"Their stock of Cartridges and Gun Materials is unsurpassed by any in the Trade. . . . They are also constantly manufacturing Wilson and Evans Improvement on the Deringer Pistol. . . ."

Here we have, in the same advertisement, equipment and ammunition for both cap-and-ball and metallic cartridge types of guns offered for sale. This is typical of the transition period between the two firing systems, and was to continue for some years, long after the manufacture of percussion weapons had given way to more modern improved products. But cap-and-ball arms were still being used, if not made; and they formed a market—even though a diminishing one—for tools and supplies used in that type of gun. The same advertisement also demonstrates the impossibility of attempting to classify guns generally in neat little chronological pigeon-holes.

Both members of this firm seemed fully aware of the changes in firearm fashions that were taking place. John R. Evans said that from the beginning of 1862, there had been a "general falling off of sales of pistols. . . . Each year has shown a decrease on the previous year in sales. Since 1860 a number of new and improved pistols have come upon the market of the world, and especially California. There has been introduced the Sharp [sic] pistol, Smith and Weston [sic], the breech-loading Deringer, the Remington Deringer and others. Since 1860 there has been a general run for breech-loaders. They have since that time been the most popular pistol of the

[135]

day. The laws of California against carrying concealed weapons have also caused sales to fall off."

H. H. Wilson, senior partner of the firm, said, "We had orders for various kinds of pistols—the 'Moore Derringer,' the 'Slotter Deringer,' and other kinds of Deringers, and we bought all these kinds. Moore's Deringer has the word 'Deringer' on it, I think. It is a breech-loader. Colt's pistol barrels are of steel."

Here again, as with the Evans quotation, we have some rather weird variations in spelling of gunmakers' names; whether it was due to printers' oversights or to carelessness of the gun-dealers, we're not sure. Since this was a time of rugged individualism in spelling as much as in anything else, no one seemed to take seriously such inconsistencies, although it does not ease the task of firearms historians.

The recognized prototype of the breech-loading cartridge derringer, probably the one referred to in the above quotation, was made according to the patent granted February 19, 1861, to Daniel Moore, of Moore's Patent Fire Arms Co., Brooklyn, New York. Moore obtained another patent on February 24, 1863, but this covered only the ornamental features of the all-metal handle. Some of the Moore derringers are marked with both patent dates, and some of the very early specimens are marked "Patent Applied For" on the top of the barrel.

Although Moore also made revolvers at about the same period, they never attained much popularity in the West because of the competition of the Colt and other well-known makes. Descriptions of the Moore revolvers may be found in the present author's *Gun Collector's Handbook of Values*, from which comes this description of . . .

Moore's Derringer, caliber .38. 2.25-inch, round, flat-top barrel marked "Moore's Pat. F. A. Co., Brooklyn, N.Y." on top, and "D. Moore's Pat. Feb. 24, 1863," on under side. Brass frame. No ejector. Not shown.

Same, but Caliber .41.

The Moore company was either sold to or reincorporated as the National Arms Co., also of Brooklyn, about 1865, and their cartridge derringers were based on the Moore patents. They are described in the author's above-quoted *Handbook of Values*, with this note regarding the markings:

National Arms Co. weapons are also found marked "D. Moore, Brooklyn, N.Y.," or "Moore Fire Arms Co., N. Y." Also, the later model "D. Moore" is found with the marks of the National Arms Co. Apparently this switching of marks does not have much effect on values.

National Derringer, caliber .41 r.f.; 2.25-inch flat-top barrel marked "National Arms Co. Brooklyn N. Y." Spur trigger. Engraved brass frame.

Same, silver plated. Ivory grips.

The National Fire Arms Manufacturing Co. apparently did not have a much longer life than Moore's company, for sometime between 1870 and 1872, the Colt Patent Firearms Manufacturing Co. acquired National. The transaction turned over to Colt all patents, machinery, tools, arms in process of manufacture and other stock. Edwin Stevens, one of the most highly skilled employees of National, was hired by Colt, along with other craftsmen of the former company. And Colt proceeded to turn to the production of cartridge derringers.

With the Colt revolver in its various styles and calibers already a favorite weapon for all-around use from the High Plains cattle country, along the stage routes and in the wild mining camps, it was not surprising that the Colt Derringer would find a welcome. Almost everyone, it seemed—both men and women—had use for such a compact, convenient little pistol, and it sold in large numbers in the West of that time. There were many localities where the tranquilizing influence of both the .45 revolver and the pocket pistol were needed, and the name of Colt on a hand gun, like that of Deringer, stood for an accurate, dependable weapon. The rest was up to the person using it.

One authority on Colt firearms, Arthur L. Ulrich, for years secretary and historian of the Colt company, discussed the classification of Colt derringers made in the 1870's into three types, with the third again subclassified into another three varieties, in his booklet called *A Century of Achievement:*

"The first Deringers introduced by Colt's and National were short, all-metal, single-barreled pistols, using .41 caliber, rim-fire cartridges. A second type, known as the No. 2 Deringer, using the same-caliber cartridge and with wood stocks was later produced by both Colt's and National, which was followed by the third Deringer, often referred to as the New Type Deringer. These third [No. 3] Deringers were introduced by Colt's in the late seventies and were furnished with two types of stocks. They used .41 caliber rim-fire cartridges and were manufactured until about 1912 when the models were discontinued."

Types No. 1 and No. 2 definitely reflect the Moore and the National designs, but Type No. 3, with its own three variations, is pure Colt—a distinct and original product of the famous arms maker. James E. Serven, the great authority on Colts, believes it's possible that the Colt factory produced

Type No. 3 actually before they started to bring out Types No. 1 and 2. The subdivisions of the Type 3 Colt derringer are discussed in the descriptions of those guns, below.

In his book, *Colt Firearms 1836–1954,* Serven classifies the Colt cartridge derringer as Colt No. 1 National derringer (all-metal construction); Colt No. 2 National derringer (iron construction with detachable stocks); and the Colt Thuer derringer (generally called the Third Model, or No. 3) which was equipped with the novelty of an automatic cartridge shell extractor. This was invented by F. A. Thuer, and it ejects the shell when the barrel is pivoted to the right. Serven also states that "unlike the Colt National derringers, the frames of the Thuer models were of bronze," and he points out many other identifying details.

As suggested by Serven, using the breech mechanism as a means of classifying the various makes and types of cartridge derringers is all right, so long as there are other identifying details to supplement it. While it's interesting to note that both the Moore and the National derringers had the barrel rotate downward to load the cartridges—as did some other makes of this gun—we will find that in certain borderline cases of hand guns that are not derringers, yet have long been so classified by most collectors and historians, this method of classification appears at the least superficial.

Plate 2, a page from Colt's 1888 catalogue, should give a general idea of what the Colt derringer looked like. It shows Colt's "New Deringer," and below the two versions of the National, one with the wood stock, and the second in the all-metal model.

The following descriptions of Colt cartridge derringers are from the author's *Handbook of Values,* quoted before:

Colt No. 1 Derringer, caliber .41 r.f., single-shot; 2.5-inch oval, flat-top barrel with a button on the right for lock, and sometimes marked "Colt's P & F. A. Mfg. Co. No. 1 Hartford Ct. U.S.A." Knife-blade ejector. Curved all-metal butt. Engraved all-metal frame. Total length 4.25 inches. Weight 9 oz. Spur trigger. Barrels on some specimens are marked "Colt's Pt. F. A. Mfg. Co., Hartford, Ct. U.S.A. No. 1." Originally made by the National Arms Co., this model was made from 1870 to about 1890 by Colt.

Colt No. 2 Derringer, caliber .41 r.f., single-shot; 2.5-inch, oval, flat-top barrel with button on right for lock, sometimes marked "Colt's P & F.A. Mfg. Co., Hartford. Ct. U.S.A. No. 2," or "Colt's Pt. F.A. Mfg. Co. Hartford, Ct. U.S.A. No. 2." Knife-blade ejector. Bird's-head walnut grips. Engraved iron frame, nickel plated. Spur trigger. Total length 5.25 inches. Weight 9 oz. Originally made by National Arms Co., but made by Colt from 1870 to about 1890. Barrel swings left to load. The same model was also made with plain ivory grips.

PLATE 2

A page from Colt's 1888 catalogue, showing Colt Deringers, including the National Deringer.   AUTHOR'S COLLECTION

Colt No. 3 Derringer, Type No. 1, caliber .41 r.f., single-shot; 2.5-inch round barrel with snap-type latch, marked simply "Colt's." Spring-type ejector. Bird's-head walnut grips. Nickel-plated brass frame. Spur trigger. Total length 4.5 inches. Weight 7 oz. Made only by Colt, from about 1875. Barrel swings right to load. The distinguishing feature of this Type No. 1 is the very straight-up or high hammer spur. This model and type also was made with engraved frame and ivory grips.

Same, Type No. 2, with walnut grips and nickel-plated frame. Production started sometime after 1875. The distinguishing feature is the tipped-back, or back-curving, hammer spur.

Same, Type No. 3, with walnut grips and nickel-plated frame. Production started sometime after 1875. Discontinued in 1912. The distinguishing feature is the butt, which is larger and has a smaller curvature.

The Remington Cartridge Derringer may vary somewhat in the design of the breech mechanism, according to the different models. In several of

[139]

the single-shot models the barrel is fixed, but the breech block rolls or rotates. However, an exception is found in the double-barreled Remington derringer, with its barrels superposed and hinged to the top of a stationary breech block. When the barrels swing up, the fired cartridge cases are extracted and the live cartridges loaded. This procedure is sometimes referred to as "tipping up to load."

The following descriptions of the various types of the Remington derringer are from the author's *Handbook of Values:*

Remington Zigzag Derringer, caliber .22 r.f.; 6-shot, D.A., 3.25-inch fluted barrels, with rib in each flute. Ring trigger. Barrels revolved by stud engaging angular grooves in barrel, similar to principle of modern Webley-Fosbury automatic revolver. Loaded through hole in recoil plate. Frame marked "Manufactured by Remington. Ilion N.Y."

Remington Vest-Pocket Derringer, caliber .41 r.f.; 4-inch round-octagon barrel. Spur trigger. Rolling-block action but breechblock is split and hammer rises in center. Marked "Remingtons Ilion N.Y. Patd. Oct. 1, 1861 Nov. 15, 1862." Also made in calibers .38 r.f., .32 r.f., and .22 r.f., with barrels varying in length between 3.25 inches and 4 inches.

Remington First Model, Double-Barrel Derringer, caliber .41-long r.f.; 3-inch round superposed barrels. All-metal grips. Spur trigger. High hammer spur. Extractors operated by two arms extending down sides of barrels. When barrels swing up, fired cases are extracted.

Remington Presentation Double-Barrel Derringer, caliber .41 r.f.; 3-inch, round superposed barrels. Spur trigger. Barrels swing up to load. No provision made in this model for extractor. Elaborate engraving. Pearl grips.

Remington-Elliot Ring-Trigger Derringer, caliber .22 r.f.; 5-shot, D.A.; 3-inch round fluted barrels. Nickel plated. Barrels tip up to load. This model also was made in caliber .30 r.f., 4-shot, D.A.; 3.5-inch round fluted barrels; and the same in caliber .32.

Remington-Elliot Single-Shot Derringer, caliber .41 r.f., S.A.; 2.5-inch round barrel marked "Derringer." Spur trigger, walnut grips, iron frame. Total length 5 inches. Blued finish. Barrel unscrews for loading. Hammer acts as breechblock and falls past center so that force of cartridge case, expanding when fired, tends to hold block tighter. Brass-blade front sight. Notched rear sight. May have bone handles on some specimens. Marked "Remingtons, Ilion, N.Y. Elliot Pat. Aug. 27, 1867."

As opposed to the Remington double-barrel, the breech mechanism of the Starr derringer has a barrel that tips down to load, which is sometimes called a "top-break action." The same type of breech action is also found on the Ballard derringer. The Starr models began to appear in 1865, but after a few years were displaced from the Western market by the superior qualities of other derringers, especially the Sharps.

The following descriptions of the Starr derringers are from the *Handbook of Gun Values:*

Starr Derringer, caliber .38 r.f.; single-shot, 2.875-inch round barrel. Brass frame, button trigger, side hammer. Frame marked "Starr's Pats. May 10, 1864."

Same, but caliber .41 r.f.

Starr 4-Shot Button-Trigger Derringer, caliber .41 r.f., 2.75-inch round barrel. Brass frame, button trigger, side hammer. Top-break action. Frame marked as above.

Same, but caliber .32 r.f.

The Ballard Derringer, a contemporary of the Starr, also had a tip-down barrel. It was sold and carried in the West, but like the Starr, it was eventually driven off the market by better weapons. Here is its description:

Ballard Derringer, caliber .41 r.f.; 2.75-inch, round-octagon barrel usually marked "Ballard's" on top and "Ballard's Worcester Mass.," or "C. H. Ballard & Co. Worcester Mass.," with patent dates in either case, although "Ballard" is the only mark on some. Total length, 4.75 inches; weight 8 oz. Spur trigger, bronze frame. Also made with an iron frame, but iron frame specimens are exceedingly rare.

The Allen Cartridge Derringer was the first pistol of its type with a side-swinging barrel, and was patented by Ethan Allen—of pepperbox fame—on March 7, 1865. Typical specimens are described as follows:

Allen Cartridge Derringer, caliber .41 r.f., single-shot; 2.5-inch round-octagon barrel marked "E. Allen & Co. Worcester Mass. Allen's Pat. Mch 7, 1865." Resembles Colt No. 3 derringer. Also made in caliber .32 r.f. with a 3.25-inch round-octagon barrel.

Same, but with octagon barrel marked as above. Spur trigger. Iron frame.

The Southerner Derringers get their name from the word "Southerner" stamped on the barrel, but this was a trade name obviously concocted to appeal to the people of the Southern states, especially those bordering on the Gulf of Mexico and along the Mississippi River.

Charles H. Ballard, for whom the Ballard derringer was named, was issued a patent on April 9, 1867, for a few features of two derringers described below:

Merrimack Arms & Mfg. Co. Southerner Derringer, caliber .41 r.f., single-shot; 2.5-inch octagon barrel marked "Southerner." Total length 5 inches. Weight 8 oz. Some specimens marked on frame "Merrimack Arms & Mfg. Co., Newburyport, Mass. Patented April 9, 1867." Side swing, sheath trigger, square walnut grips. Frame may be either brass or iron.

Brown Mfg. Co. Southerner Derringer (also called a pocket pistol), caliber .41 r.f., single-shot; 2.5-inch octagon barrel marked "Southerner." Left side of frame marked "Brown Mfg. Co. Newburyport, Mass. Pat. Apr. 9, 1867." Total length 5 inches. Weight 8 oz. Sheath trigger, center hammer, brass or iron frame. Side-swing.

The Marlin Derringer: John M. Marlin obtained a patent for a derringer mechanism on April 5, 1870, that was somewhat similar to that of Charles H. Ballard covering features of the Southerner derringers. The most easily recognized feature of the Marlin is the side-swing barrel also found on the Allen, the Southerner and the Colt derringers. However, in discussing patents, it is well to know that a patent drawing may portray an entire derringer, but the specific claims made by the applicant may pertain to one or more comparatively minor features. For example, the tip-down breech mechanism of the Ballard derringer was based on a patent issued to Louis T. Fairbanks, June 22, 1869.

John M. Marlin made both single-shot pistols and revolvers. The usual barrel marking was "J.M.Marlin, New Haven Ct." together with a trade name on some specimens, such as "Victor" in the case of one of his single-shot cartridge pistols.

Marlin XL Derringer, caliber .41 r.f.; 2.5-inch, half-octagon barrel. Total length 4.75 inches. Bird's-head grip, nickel-plated frame. Marked "X.L. Derringer."

The bright nickel-plated frame kept the Marlin derringer from obtaining much popularity in the West, although it was bought and carried by men and women in the 1870's and a few were still in use until about 1900.

In striving for an accurate classification of firearms, there are some areas where the collector and historian have to proceed at half-speed; for the waters are tricky, filled with uncharted contradictions and conflicting possibilities. Considering the many forms and models of the cartridge derringer and related pistols, this situation seems especially apparent. There are some types and makes, among them the double-barreled pistols of the American Arms Co., Boston, Massachusetts, the Frank Wesson two-shot pistols and several others which have thus far evaded a generally agreed-upon definite designation. It is true that they fail to meet the traditional requirements to place them safely within the derringer category, yet for many years a great number of collectors and historians have persisted in classifying them as derringers, since they do have some of the features of that pistol.

Here we will acknowledge the power of tradition—mistaken though it may be—and include these very doubtful borderline guns with the other derringers we have been discussing. Also there is the additional fact that they have, in all cases, been in wide use throughout the historical West during the period we're observing.

The American Arms Co.-Wheeler Double-Barrel Pistol, advertised in Boston in 1868, was not offered or referred to by the manufacturer as a derringer. The patents granted to Henry F. Wheeler on October 31, 1865, and on June 19, 1866, apply to the breech mechanism for extracting cartridge shells, for combining the two barrels so that one could be of one caliber and the second barrel of another caliber, as well as other features.

Here are the descriptions:

American Arms Co.-Wheeler Double-Barrel Pistol, caliber .41 r.f.; 2.625-inch superposed barrels. Walnut grips, spur trigger, brass frame. Rifled in solid block. Marked "American Arms Co. Boston Mass. Wheeler's Pat Oct 31, 1865. June 19, 1866."

American Arms Co. Double-Barrel Pistol, caliber .32 r.f.; 2.5-inch superposed barrels. Spur trigger. Bird's-head butt, walnut grips, brass frame. Marked "American Arms Co., Boston, Mass. Pat. Oct. 31, 1865, June 19, 1866."

American Arms Co.-Wheeler Double-Barrel Pistol, two 3-inch superposed barrels, one caliber .22 and one caliber .32 r.f., rifled in solid block marked "American Arms Co. Boston Mass. Wheeler's Pat Oct. 31, 1865. June 19, 1866."

The Frank Wesson 2-Shot Pistol, like the Wheeler double-barrel pistol described above, has a breech mechanism involving rotating double barrels. Before going on to the most interesting of the Wesson products we'll look briefly at the two models of this transitional pistol which, with others, was forming the bridge between the true single-shot hand gun and the genuine cartridge revolver:

Frank Wesson 2-Shot Vest-Pocket Pistol, caliber .22 r.f.; 2-inch, round, superposed barrels marked "Frank Wesson Worcester Mass. Pt. Dec.15/68." Total length 3.75 inches. Walnut grips. Spur trigger. Brass frame. Ring hammer. Barrels revolve by hand.

Frank Wesson 2-Shot Superposed Pistol, caliber .22 r.f., 2-shot; 2.5-inch octagon barrels marked "Frank Wesson, Worcester, Mass. Pat. Dec. 15, 1868." Spur trigger. Walnut grips. Also made in calibers .32 and .41 r.f.

As an arms maker, Frank Wesson did not lack imagination, and on July 20, 1869, he obtained a patent for attaching a knife or dirk to his already patented pistol, and to provide a sheath or scabbard for the dirk between the barrels. In his circular advertising his new weapon, he referred to it as a "Double Shot Pocket Pistol with Extension Dirk Knife," and indicated that it was made in three sizes: calibers .41, .32, and .22, all r.f., but the present author has never seen a specimen of the .22 r.f., and none has ever been reported to him.

This "Ladies' Friend" was apparently designed to be bought by women endowed both with a highly incandescent allure for men, and also a temperament which, to say the least, was volatile and explosive. Such ladies were not noted for cool-headed marksmanship, although—despite the song —many a man was gotten with a gun. In any event, if both shots missed, the outraged damsel could try her luck with the dagger. Perhaps the female customers believed that was the most appealing feature. Whatever they thought, the weapon was popular during the 1870's and later with the glittering girls of the frontier sporting world.

This little weapon was a triple threat in more ways than one, and might be classified in any of three categories. It is basically a firearm, so it may be considered as much a derringer as the Wesson two-shot pistol. It could also come under the heading of a combination weapon, which it certainly is; or it could easily be placed among the large group of freaks and oddities which includes sword-guns, knuckle-duster pistols and other unusual arms. Here is its description:

Frank Wesson Dagger Pistol, caliber .41 r.f.; 2-shot; 3-inch octagon superposed barrels marked "Frank Wesson Worcester Mass. Pat. Dec. 15, 1868, July 20, 1869." Brass frame, spur trigger. Also made in caliber .32 r.f., and possibly in caliber .22 r.f.

The same firm much later produced the Frank Wesson Pocket Rifle but this could by no stretch of the imagination be classified as a derringer. It was made with barrel lengths from 10 to 20 inches and came equipped with a detachable metal skeleton stock. It was primarily designed as a sporting weapon, listed originally as the Sportsman's Jewel and sometimes referred to as a bicycle rifle. It was not in wide use during the frontier days, however.

Plate 3 shows a group of characteristic cartridge derringers, identified as follows (Author's collection.):

Figure 1 is the Allen cartridge derringer, caliber .41, r.f., single-shot; which resembles the Colt No. 3 derringer. No. 2 is a similar Allen cartridge derringer, caliber .41, single-shot, and like the other has a 2.5-inch octagon barrel.

Figure 3 is the National Derringer, caliber .41 r.f., with a 2.5-inch flat-top barrel marked "National Arms Co. Brooklyn N.Y.," silver-plated, with ivory grips.

Figure 4 is the Reid Revolver, sometimes erroneously called a derringer, and listed here only to correct the common mistake. It is caliber .41 r.f., 5-shot, with a 2.75-inch octagon barrel marked "Reid's Derringer," which may explain the general misclassification of this weapon. This is a good example of one type of firearm merging into another without any definite time and place of change.

Figure 5 is the Remington Zigzag Derringer, caliber .41 with a 4-inch round-octagon barrel. No. 6 is the Remington Vest-Pocket Derringer, caliber .41 r.f., with a 4-inch round-octagon barrel. No. 7 is the Remington First Model, Double-barrel Derringer, caliber .41-long r.f., with two superposed round, 3-inch barrels.

Figure 8 is the Remington-Elliot Ring-Trigger Derringer, caliber .22 r.f., 5-shot, D.A., with 3-inch, round, fluted barrels which tip up to load. Figure 9 is the Remington-Elliot Single-Shot Derringer, caliber .41 r.f., S.A., with a 2.5-inch round barrel, marked "Derringer," which is unscrewed for loading. The hammer acts as a breechblock and falls past center so that the force of the cartridge case when expanding tends to hold the block tighter.

Figure 10 is the Rupertus 4-Barrel Derringer, caliber .30 r.f., 4-shot, with 3-inch round barrels. The frame is marked on the side "Rupertus Patent Pistol Mfg. Co. Phila. 1863."

Figure 11 is a Sharps Presentation Derringer, caliber .30 r.f., 4-shot, with 3-inch round barrels, a silver-plated frame marked "C. Sharps Patent 1859," and ivory grips with a Roman soldier carved on the left.

Figure 12 is the Starr Derringer, caliber .38 r.f., single-shot, with a 2.875-inch round barrel, a brass frame, a button trigger, a side hammer, and a

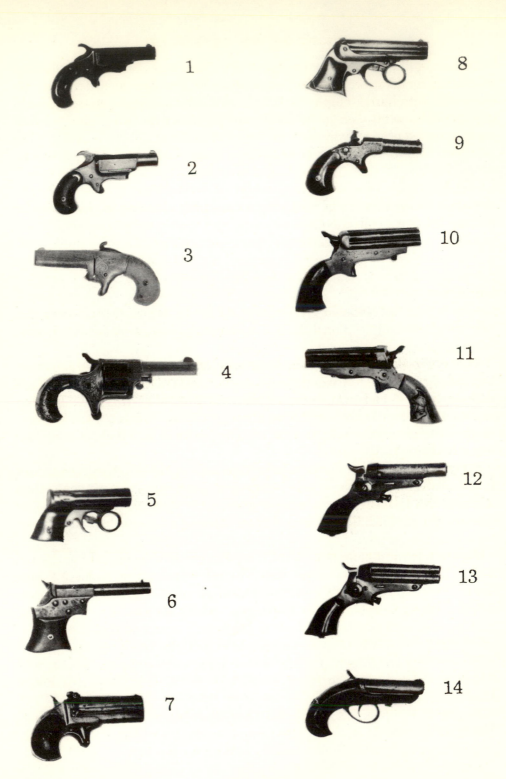

PLATE 3

frame marked "Starr's Pats. May 10, 1864." This was also made in caliber .41 r.f. Figure 13 is the Starr 4-Shot Button-Trigger Derringer, caliber .41 r.f., with 2.75-inch round barrels, brass frame, button trigger, side hammer, and top-break action, with the frame marked as in No. 12. This also was made in caliber .32 r.f.

Figure 14 is the Williamson Derringer, caliber .41 r.f., with a 2.5-inch, round, flat-top barrel marked "Williamson's Pat. Oct. 2, 1866, New York," a total length of 5 inches, and a weight of 6 oz. When it was originally placed on the market it was sold with an auxiliary chamber so that it could be used for percussion fire because cartridges were not yet universally accepted.

It seems appropriate, before leaving this account of the derringers—which, by the way, makes no pretense of being the complete Deringer (and derringer) story—that one last mention should be made of Henry Deringer Junior, even though posthumously.

After his death in 1868, his estate went to three sons and six daughters. A grandson of one of the daughters, I. Jones Clark, manufactured cartridge firearms under the name of Deringer Rifle and Pistol Works, in Philadelphia, turning out a breech-loading rifle and tip-up revolvers, similar to the early Smith & Wesson calibers .22 and .32 r.f. The business, however, did not last long into the cartridge period.

Typical Deringer revolvers are described below, because they were used to some extent in the West, and because gun hobbyists should know that —despite the fact that these were legitimately "Deringer" weapons—they were *not* the product of the late and great Henry Junior:

Deringer Revolver, caliber .32 r.f., 5-shot; 3.5-inch, round, ribbed barrel marked "Deringer Philada" and also "Manuf'd at the Deringer Rifle and Pistol Works, Phila. Pa." Spur trigger, engraved frame, walnut grips. Nickel-plated. The same revolver was made as a caliber .22 r.f.

Deringer Revolver, caliber .22 r.f., S.A., 7-shot; 3-inch, round, ribbed barrel marked "Deringer, Philadelphia" on top, and on the left marked "Manuf'd at the Deringer Rifle and Pistol Works. Philadelphia." Stud-type trigger. Nickel finish, fancy engraving. Total length, 6.75 inches. Nickel front sight, notched-frame rear sight. Bird's-head polished hardwood handles. Breaks upward to load.

IX

Captain Walker's Gun=Hunt: Early Colt Revolvers

Nine men out of ten in this city [Washington, D.C.] do not know what a Colt Pistol is and although I have explained the difference between yours and the six-barrel Pop Gun, that is in such general use, a thousand times, they are still ignorant on the subject. . . .
　　　　　　　　—Samuel H. Walker to Samuel Colt,
　　　　　　　　1847.

STRANGELY enough, this man whose name is so closely associated with the high dramatic moments of frontier history was no buckskin pioneer, trail-blazing mountain man, town-taming lawman or saddle-warped cattle baron. The drumbeat that Samuel Colt was to follow echoed neither from the shining mountains nor boundless seas of grass, but rather from the swift rivers of the Atlantic seaboard that supplied power to the stone and brick boxlike factories of his native New England.

Like many Yankees, Sam Colt had an innate love of tinkering with mechanical things and a purposeful curiosity about the "natural sciences" —physics, chemistry, electricity. His precocity, probably to the annoyance of neighboring farmers, took the form of experiments involving frightening explosions, stifling stinks, and a certain personal satisfaction of knowledge gained. At the ripe age of eleven he was making gunpowder; at twelve he constructed a galvanic battery, waterproofed wires which he ran under the surface of a pond, attached a charge to the bottom of a small raft, and blew it "sky-high" by remote control. The echoes of this boyish prank were to reverberate through the years and far beyond the outraged locality of

Ware, Massachusetts. That experiment was stored in Sam's memory. It is doubtful, however, that he recognized its significance in that year of 1826. Nor is it probable that he would have heeded an item making its initial bow in hardware and jewelry stores around the country, and which was to play an important part in Sam Colt's business future—the new, midget-sized pocket pistol made by Henry Deringer Junior, in Philadelphia.

With other trail-breakers, Jedediah Smith was scouting the Pacific Northwest, and in his own area Colt was also an explorer. While most of the old mountain men and hunters clung to their romantic dream of an unending demand for beaver and other peltry which they could supply from an inexhaustible storehouse of almost a million square miles of barely charted wilderness, Sam Colt, too, held to his dream. But his shining vision was, characteristically, very specific and immensely practical: the traditional gunsmith's classic urge to design a successful repeating firearm, preferably one that would function without manual help. The seed of that dream was planted early in young Sam's imagination.

Already he had solved the principle of the flintlock firing mechanism from tinkering with an old horse pistol that his grandfather, a veteran of the Revolution, had given him. The old soldier's tales of that conflict thrilled Sam, but above all his favorite story concerned the double-barreled rifle of one Tim Murphy. This was exciting—a gun you could shoot twice without having to reload! The boy became thoughtful, and when Sam pondered, action followed. He could, he decided, improve on the original—a trait that was to help pattern his career throughout his life. If two barrels were good, obviously four would be that much better.

Tying four gun barrels together, he attached a single lock at the breech, and revolved them so that each would be fired in turn. The contraption seemed to be successful, until he charged each barrel—and all of them fired at once in a blazing roar that seemed to shake the Connecticut hills.

For a while then, experiments were subordinated to farm chores and school, but memory of those four gun barrels kept nudging and nagging him like a sore tooth. The revolving mechanism needed a control of some sort. If he could only figure some device that would do it. . . .

A few years later, Sam was to find his solution not in the machine complex of a Hartford or New Haven factory but far from home, aboard the brig *Carlo*, Calcutta bound, on which he had signed as seaman at the age of sixteen. Watching the steersman at the vessel's wheel, he noticed that whichever way the wheel turned, right or left, a spoke came directly in line with a clutch that held it fast. Here it was—the idea that had been eluding him for so long. From a discarded tackle block he carved a working model —the prototype of the first practical revolving gun with automatic revolution and locking cylinder, operated by cocking the hammer.

The sea voyage lasted a year; when Colt returned, he had no money to hire a gunsmith to make models of his invention, so he turned out two models, himself, in 1831, with the help of an ordinary mechanic. One failed to fire at all and the other exploded with the first shot. Most men would have quit after this experience, but Colt was more determined than ever. For a year he helped his father in his factory, spending most of his spare time in chemical experiments, and then, at the age of eighteen, he toured the country under the name of "Dr. Coult," giving lectures in chemistry accompanied by demonstrations of the effect of laughing gas.

In 1832, Colt sent a description of his basic idea to the United States Patent Office. In 1833 he constructed, with money saved from his lecture trips, both a pistol and a rifle on the principle for which he obtained French and English patents in 1835, when he visited Europe. On his return to the United States, he received his first American patent, February 25, 1836. On March 5, he formed the Patent Arms Manufacturing Co., at Paterson, New Jersey, at the foot of the falls of the Passaic River where he could obtain water power to run the machinery.

Here at Paterson were made the famous revolvers, revolving rifles, and revolving shotguns so highly regarded by gun collectors.

At about the time that Colt was starting to produce his first Paterson guns, school geographies still showed, spreading eastward and south of the Sierras, an area of vast emptiness forbiddingly labeled "The Great American Desert." Despite the activities of the early mountain men, the trappers and explorers, this mythical barrier effectively blocked emigration and commerce. The Colt revolver was to play an important role in exploding that imaginary rampart, and the effect of this weapon in opening the frontier wilderness to settlement would be considered roughly comparable to the later extermination of the great buffalo herds and the westward push of the steel rails.

It is quite probable that Samuel Colt never realized that he was turning out firearms destined to revolutionize frontier warfare. More likely he was attending to the business of getting government orders for his products. The ambition so long ago implanted by tales of Tim Murphy's double-barreled rifle, the dream that had kept growing throughout the long sea voyage, his lecture tour as "Dr. Coult," and his struggles to perfect a successful pilot model, all were now being realized. Government contracts were traditionally the lifeblood of the arms business, and having achieved his primary goal, Sam Colt was determined to secure it and go on from there.

The first orders soon found their way to the factory on the Passaic. Texans wanted arms for their fight to free themselves from Mexican rule. Especially they wanted the new "patent revolving pistol," for a single mounted Texan, armed with the repeating hand gun, was worth a squad or more of

Mexican soldiers with their single-shot muskets, or even a platoon of lancers. The revolver and the man on horseback were natural affinities.

The United States equipped Mounted Rifles and Dragoons with the gun for use in the Seminole War in Florida, where the Colts stood up well in their baptism of fire. They were especially needed to offset one favorite tactic of the Seminoles against troops armed with single-shot pistols and shoulder arms, a trick that had resulted in distressingly heavy casualties for United States forces. The Seminoles would first draw the soldiers' fire, then immediately swoop down on them before the troops had a chance to reload, thus massacring entire units. Now, thanks to the Colt's multifire power, the dark picture was reversed and victory, although without formal surrender, was assured in 1842.

Texas had gained its freedom from Mexico in 1836 and the new republic was organizing a force of seasoned frontiersmen called the Texas Rangers. These veterans knew the work that the Colt could do, and the Paterson pistol, in pocket, belt, and holster sizes, had proved so popular that they had been termed loosely the Texas model. For years the legend gained currency that Captain Sam Walker came to Paterson to confer with Colt and make suggestions for improving the model to better adapt it to Ranger use. However, there is no proof that Walker came up at that time, as he certainly did later, to Whitneyville to assist in designing the 1847 model.

Colt did turn out at Paterson a heavier revolver than the caliber .34, five-shot pistol in the six-shot, caliber .44 gun. This has been termed the "Original Walker," the "First Walker" and the "Paterson Walker," and has been the subject of more disputes among advanced Colt collectors than any other gun in the history of the avocation. Some authorities believe that none of this heavy model was made commercially; others claim that three hundred were produced between 1839 and 1841. A few specimens of this model are in existence, but their authenticity as the "First Walker" remains in doubt. Indeed there may be no justification for such a classification.

History, which had favored Colt from 1836 to 1839, now seemed to turn from him. The Seminole troubles were about over; the Rangers were equipped, and in general the market for martial arms, at least in America, seemed sadly meager. Sales fell off, bad financial management of the company—completely beyond Colt's control—an economic depression, a government order that failed to materialize, and dissension among the officers of the Paterson company all combined to bring failure to the business in 1841 and a complete, permanent shutdown in 1842.

Disheartened, Samuel Colt spent the next five years in continuing his experiments with the galvanic battery where he had left off after the explosion of the raft, and he developed his waterproof cable to the extent that he was able to present the United States with a submarine mine for harbor defense.

Congress showed its appreciation by appropriating $20,000 for further experiments. The boyhood pranks were now recognized as scientific achievements. That was all right, but Colt appreciated most the newspaper headlines which made him known nationally, for quite another purpose. They gave him a prestige he needed for the sale of his revolvers.

The outbreak of the Mexican War gave him a chance to capitalize on his publicity. Texas Rangers joined the forces of General Zachary Taylor, taking with them their own mounts and equipment, including the already famous Colt revolver. The Texans were brave fighters with any equipment, but General Taylor was particularly impressed by their ability to deliver a withering fire from their revolvers that sent the Mexican line reeling back, time after time. Determined to have the latest weapons for his men, Taylor sent an order for a thousand Colt revolvers, while the government combed secondhand shops and bought up all those available. And Samuel Colt was back in the business of making arms.

Or he would be, if he could only find one of his guns to use as a model, for he had kept none. Extensive newspaper advertisements for any of his early revolvers failed to produce a single one. Then it was that General Zachary Taylor sent Captain Sam Walker up from Texas to speed the manufacture of Colt's guns. At one point, Walker stopped off in the national capital to promote the gun that he liked and had so impressed Taylor. From there, he wrote the letter to Colt, part of which is quoted at the beginning of this chapter. While important legislators and Cabinet members were fully aware of the virtues of the pepperbox—which had almost none of the requirements for an effective martial multishot hand gun—Walker at first seemed to be crying in the wilderness, although before the first order for Colt's revolver was completed, a second government contract was approved for a like number.

Unable to buy one of his own guns—according to legend he had advertised for the caliber .44 six-shooter that came with an attached lever for ramming the bullet into the cylinder chambers, and with a fixed trigger guard, the now controversial "Original Walker"—he sought a solution. And found it.

According to legend, Colt designed another model from memory, and possibly with Walker's help. This seems credible, for Colt's genius was a dedicated one, and Walker was doubtlessly at Colt's shoulder, functioning as what would later be known as government expediter. Characteristically, Colt improved on the former model by simplifying it—the best possible kind of improvement to meet a rush order for a precision mechanism. Also he was alert to the rapid progress made in New England's machine-tool industry since he had left Paterson where many operations had to be done by hand.

These factories for making tools to make other tools—such as locks, rifles and revolvers, watches and clocks, for example—were run by men schooled in precision metalwork, in gunsmithing, watchmaking, locksmithing, and the like. They had Sam Colt's kind of imagination and knew where they were heading: elimination of hand labor, increased precision in making minutely complicated parts interchangeable in any one model of the finished product; automation, and straight-line manufacture. Interestingly enough, many of the jigs and dies, presses, planers, profilers and other machines are —more than a hundred years later—still in use.

At Whitneyville outside New Haven, the son of the inventor of the cotton gin was turning out Harpers Ferry percussion rifles for the government. Colt went to the Whitney Arms Company and, with Whitney and his tool-makers, designed new machine tools for making the revolvers to fill his contract, with the new machine tools to pass into Colt's possession on the completion of the first government order. Colt had regained full ownership of his patents after the failure of his Paterson firm, and Whitney knew it. He urged Colt to form a partnership, but Colt, probably still smarting from the Paterson misadventure, wanted no part of such an arrangement. He'd keep his own counsel and steer his own course. And, as a further precaution, he placed orders for making some of his revolver parts with various other plants.

The factory he set up at Hartford in 1848 to complete the second contract was the most advanced application of the great drive toward mass production seen up to that time. It must have delighted Samuel Colt's passion for orderly and economical mechanical production, though it is doubtful if Henry Deringer Junior would have been warmly impressed with the Colt theory that pointed so clearly to the operation of the huge industrial plants of today. Deringer's annual production was, at a rough average, five hundred pairs of his pocket pistols; in 1863 Colt made on government order 136,579 of his revolvers for martial use, not counting shoulder arms.

Although in 1846 and the few years following, Colt may not have realized it, the Paterson debacle was paying off in something more than a bitterly learned lesson. That was a second harvest on the five or six thousand revolvers he had turned out from 1836 to 1842. By '46 most of those guns had come, by a sort of natural-selection process, to the area where they were most needed—the Western frontier. As the eminent historian Walter Prescott Webb has long pointed out, Colt was the first to supply the weapon for the frontiersman to combat the Plains Indian on equal or superior terms. Each of those guns—with the Colt stamping on them—was doing an eloquent job of missionary work. By 1849, with newspaper and magazine filled with accounts of the Argonauts' overland trek, with articles on the gold fields, with books and catalogues filled with detailed advice to prospective Western emigrants, mention of the advantages of the Colt re-volvers was not lacking. It was all excellent publicity, and orders flowed back to Hartford.

Each year was marked by the issuance of new models—which by no means supplanted the manufacture of former popular types. In 1851 Colt embarked on a European junket, visiting rulers and others high in govern-ment circles, especially those who might be interested in placing orders for his patent revolver for martial use. In England, he laid plans for opening his London factory, which manufactured guns from 1853 to 1857, and the Navy and Pocket models made there are stamped on the barrel "Address:— Col. Colt. London." (He had been made a lieutenant colonel in the Con-necticut State Militia.)

He returned to Hartford laden with orders from nations preparing for the Crimean War, and turned his attention to operation of the London factory, a project beset with unsuspected difficulties. It would have been more in line with Colt's idea of commercial diplomacy if he could have had ma-chines made in England or Europe to manufacture his guns, and English or European mechanics to turn them out. No machines of sufficient accuracy could be made, and he had to import them from the United States. Nor could mechanics be found properly skilled in precision work who could operate them. The trade guilds, having weathered the Industrial Revolu-tion in England's north-country mill towns some years before, were any-thing but sympathetic to this Yankee who wanted to start the trouble all over again, with the vast machine installation that only threw honest work-men out of their jobs. The guilds were backed by public officials. Colt was stymied, but as usual, not for long. Despite these difficulties—Samuel Colt had never lacked assurance or persuasiveness—production went ahead. The London factory furnished the viceroy of Egypt with five thousand of his revolvers, and supplied two hundred thousand to the British government for the Crimean War.

Back at Hartford in 1855, Colt obtained a charter for his company under the name: Colt's Patent Fire Arms Manufacturing Company. There he estab-lished the world's largest private armory, and developed a new revolver called the Root Side Hammer Model, or the Model 1855.

Samuel Colt was one of the few industrialists who foresaw the coming of the Civil War in time to prepare for it. He enlarged his factory, installed additional machinery, and made his estimates for production, based—with astounding accuracy—on a million Union soldiers fighting for a period of five years. He early realized the conflict for what it was—a crucial life-and-death struggle for survival of the Union—and drove himself mercilessly. Now all thoughts of profit or loss—and of his personal health—were for-gotten in his effort to produce the needed arms. His death on January 10,

1862, at the age of forty-eight was attributed to overwork. He was buried with full military honors after lying in state for three days. To the beat of muffled drums, troops with reversed arms followed the casket between the long double lines of employees of the company he had founded.

The list of models, calibers, and sizes of revolvers, rifles, carbines, and shotguns made by Colt is a long one. No one, not even an authority on Colt arms like Arthur L. Ulrich, could say *exactly* how many were made because Samuel Colt was constantly experimenting with new ideas, launching new models, and improving on the older types. He was probably too busy as an inventor, manufacturer, and salesman-de luxe to stop long enough to record every gun turned out by his factory. To make matters more complicated, a great fire destroyed most of the Colt documents in 1864. Instead of discouraging collectors, this lack of certainty adds to the enjoyment of specializing in Colts, for some new variation is found each year, thus adding to our store of knowledge.

In order to identify Colt revolvers with successive periods of Western history of the percussion era, it will be convenient to divide the weapons into four main groups:

(1) Those made at Paterson, New Jersey, from 1836 to 1841, frequently called "Paterson pistols," even when they were being manufactured, and marked "Patent Arms M'g. Co. Paterson, N.J. Colt's Pt." on the barrel, sometimes with minor variations.

(2) The Colt Army Revolver, Model 1847, often called the Whitneyville Walker, based on recommendation made to Colt by Walker. Also referred to as the Colt-Walker Model 1847, it was manufactured at the plant of the Whitney Arms Company at Whitneyville, Connecticut.

(3) The Colt Army Revolver, Model 1848, made at the new Colt plant at Hartford, present home of the Colt company.

(4) Colt percussion revolvers assembled or made in London, England, and simply called Colt London Models—and which also found their way into the American frontier West.

Paterson Colt Revolvers were made with revolving cylinders, all with five chambers, so these were five-shot revolvers. They were described in early Colt advertisements as Pocket Pistols, Belt Pistols, and Holster Pistols. Although the word "pistol" is a loose term, Samuel Colt used it himself because "pistol" meant a hand gun to the people of that time and the word "revolver" did not have any meaning when Colt was getting started, although the phrase "revolving pistol" later came into use.

[156]

Pocket pistols are normally in calibers .28, .31, or .34, and their barrel lengths are usually 2.5, 3, 3.5, 4, 4.5, or 4.75 inches, although a few variations are found. Belt pistols are normally either in calibers .31 or .34, and the barrel lengths range between 4 and 6 inches, although a few, especially in cased sets, were made with an extra 12-inch barrel, although the barrel on the pistol itself was of normal length. Holster pistols are all caliber .36 and the barrel lengths are 4, 4.5, 5, 5.5, 6, 7.5, 9, and 12 inches, although most known specimens are either 7.5 or 9 inches.

The concealed folding trigger—without a trigger guard—which snaps out when the pistol is brought to full cock is an outstanding characteristic of the Paterson Colt, although it was retained after the factory at Paterson closed, and it was used until 1847 by Colt on revolvers not made at Paterson.

The Hartford Models, starting with the Colt Army Revolver, Model 1848, mark the beginning of a new era in the history of Colt firearms manufacture. Here all Colt arms were made, except those in the London factory up to 1857. An interesting sidelight on the markings of many Colts, both percussion and cartridge types, lies in fact that they were stamped "Address Col Saml Colt New York City," or with other indications that the weapons were made in New York. This erroneous address was used merely because Colt believed that potential customers—and perhaps especially foreign government officials—would be more favorably impressed by a New York City address than by the correct one of Hartford, Connecticut.

The Hartford percussion models often were guns of many aliases. For example, one of the famous early revolvers is . . .

The Colt Army Revolver, Model 1848, also known by six other names: the Improved Holster Pistol, the Old Model Holster Pistol, the Old Model Army Pistol, Model of 1848 Holster Pistol, the Dragoon Colt, and the No. 1 Dragoon. Aside from being classified as a U. S. martial percussion revolver, it was popular throughout the West even long after cartridge revolvers came into common use.

It is caliber .44, 6-shot, S.A.; 7.5-inch round barrel, semioctagonal at rear, and rifled with seven grooves. The total length is 14 inches and the weight is 4 lbs. 1 oz. Superficially, this Model 1848 appears to resemble the Whitneyville Walker Model 1847, but the Model 1848 has a shorter cylinder and barrel, weighs less, and has a better catch spring for the loading lever.

Authorities specializing in Colt percussion revolvers recognize three principal variations, or types, especially in classifying the larger models, such as the Dragoons:

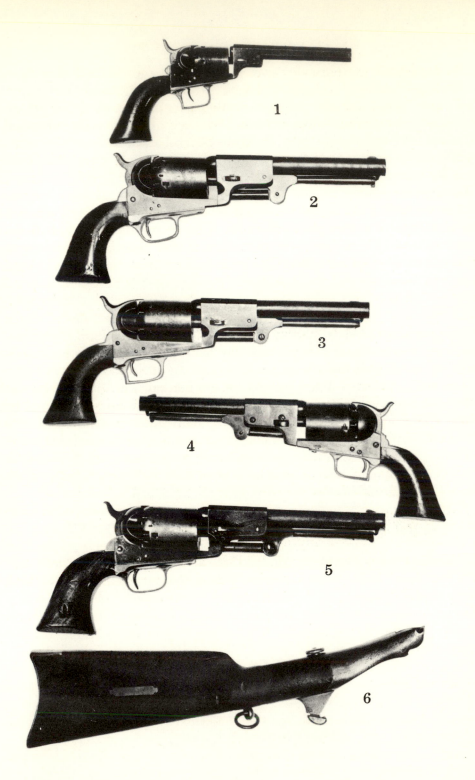

PLATE 1

(1) Square-back trigger guard, rounded cylinder-stop recesses, and vertical loading-lever latch, illustrated by figures 3 and 4 of Plate 1.

(2) Trigger guard usually oval but sometimes square-backed, as before. Rectangular cylinder-stop recesses. Loading lever is usually horizontal instead of vertical. Illustrated by figure 5 of Plate 1.

(3) Has a two-leaf rear sight and is cut for shoulder stock. A shoulder stock is illustrated by figure 6 of Plate 1.

There were several express companies, and also several pony express companies, from 1849 onward carrying valuable cargo from San Francisco and Los Angeles eastward. Large in the saga of the historic West is the name of Wells Fargo, and several models of the percussion Colts were known as the Wells Fargo Model, as some of them were bought and issued to express messengers of that company. However, it should not be assumed that the Colt revolvers were the only guns used by the pioneer transportation companies. Stagecoach drivers, the guards or messengers as well as the pony express riders were all highly individual in their choices of armament, and there was no hard-and-fast rule that they had to carry Colts if they preferred some other make.

It seems probable that the heavy Colt Army Revolver, Model 1848, also called the Dragoon as well as other titles, described above, was carried by some express guards, stage drivers, and even some pony express riders. Although it's doubtful if the famed pony express riders of Russell, Majors & Wadell, a specially selected group of hardy young men, all lightweight, burdened themselves with so heavy a gun on their swift relays between St. Joe, Missouri, and the Coast in 1859–1860.

Wells Fargo, after its organization in 1852, purchased a number of Colts for use of their messengers, as shown in Plate 2, figures 1 and 2, supplied by the Wells Fargo Bank in San Francisco. These are specimens of the Colt Old Model Pocket Pistol, Model 1848, as described by Wells Fargo and, with the Model 1849 Pocket Revolver, were frequently known as the Wells Fargo Model.

PLATE 1. Colt Old Model Pocket Pistol; Army Revolver, Model 1848; and Shoulder Stock for Model 1848.

1. Old Model Pocket Pistol, also called Baby Dragoon, etc.; 5-inch octagon barrel, square-back trigger guard, oval cylinder stops, and made without a loading lever.
2. Army Revolver, Model 1848, also known as the Dragoon Colt, etc.; oval trigger guard, vertical loading-lever latch, usual Dragoon markings, but with English proof marks on barrel and cylinder.
3. Army Revolver, Model 1848, with square-back trigger guard and rounded cylinder-stop recesses.
4. Army Revolver, Model 1848, with square-back trigger guard and vertical loading-lever latch.
5. Army Revolver, Model 1848, with oval trigger guard and rectangular cylinder stops.
6. Shoulder Stock for Army Revolver, Model 1848.

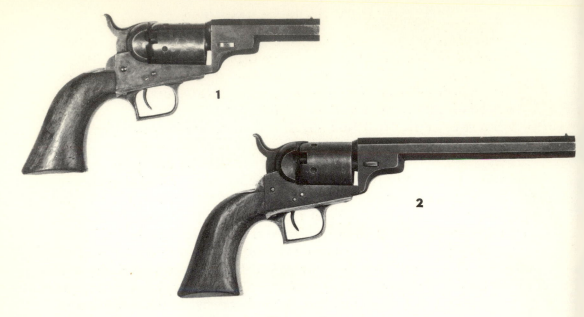

PLATE 2

Colt Old Model Pocket Pistols, Model 1948.   WELLS FARGO BANK

The Colt Old Model Pocket Pistol (also called Model of 1848 Pocket Pistol, Baby Dragoon, Model 1848 Baby Dragoon, and Model 1848 Pocket Revolver), was caliber .31, 5-shot, with 3-inch octagon barrel, total length 8 inches, weight about 1 lb. 4 oz. In addition to the 3-inch barrel, it was made with 4-, 5-, and 6-inch barrels.

PLATE 3. Colt Model 1849 Pocket Revolver.

1. Model 1849 Pocket Revolver, caliber .31, 5-shot, 3-inch octagon barrel, silver-plated guard and straps. Rectangular cylinder stops. Round-back trigger guard. Made without loading lever. Sometimes called the Wells Fargo Model.
2. Model 1849, caliber .31, 5-shot, 6-inch octagon barrel. Brass guard and straps. Trigger guard has square back.
3. Model 1849, caliber .31, 5-shot, 6-inch octagon barrel engraved "Saml. Colt." Silver-plated oval trigger guard and straps. All metal parts elaborately decorated. Blued barrel and cylinder. Frame case-hardened in natural colors.
4. Model 1849, caliber .31, 5-shot, 6-inch octagon barrel. Silver-plated oval guard and straps. English proof marks on barrel and cylinder.
5. Model 1849, caliber .31, 5-shot, 6-inch octagon barrel. All metal parts are elaborately engraved and inlaid with gold mark-

ings, figures of animals, floral patterns, and borders.
6. Model 1849, caliber .31, 5-shot, 5-inch octagon barrel, one-piece ivory grips, and engraved metal parts.
7. Model 1849, caliber .31, 5-shot, 4-inch octagon barrel, with one-piece ivory grips and engraved metal parts. Guard and straps silver-plated.
8. Model 1849, caliber .31, 5-shot, 5-inch octagon barrel, with one-piece ivory grips. Silver-plated engraved guard and straps. Engraved barrel, cylinder, and frame. Blued finish.
9. Model 1849, caliber .31, 5-shot, 5-inch octagon barrel. Square-back, brass trigger guard. Made with loading lever.
10. Model 1849, caliber .31, 5-shot, 5-inch octagon barrel. Same details as figure 8, above.
11. Model 1849, caliber .31, 5-shot, 4-inch octagon barrel. British proof marks. Cased with accessories.

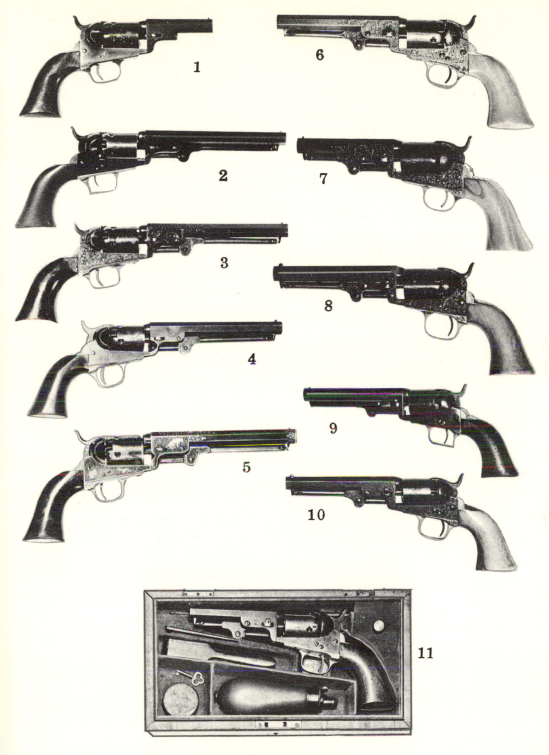

PLATE 3

The true Model 1848 has a square-back brass trigger guard, no loading lever or latch, and no bearing wheel (roll) on the hammer. One safety pin is between the chambers. The back strap is made of brass. The cylinder stops may be either round or oval. The straight, round cylinder may be engraved with the scene of a stagecoach holdup, although some have a battle between Indians and soldiers.

The Colt Model 1849 Pocket Revolver (also called Improved Pocket Pistol, Old Model Pocket Pistol, and Model of 1849 Pocket Pistol), was made in barrel lengths from 4 to 6 inches, but the one sometimes called the Wells Fargo Model is caliber .31, 5-shot, with 3-inch octagon barrel, round-back trigger guard, and made without loading lever. The cylinder stops are rectangular and the guard and straps are often found silver-plated. This is illustrated by figure 1 of Plate 3.

Other specimens of this model are shown in slight variations explained in the captions for figures 2 to 11.

Colt Pocket Model of 1850. Historians and collectors specializing in Colt percussion revolvers are not in agreement as to whether a Model 1850 was ever produced by Colt. A more detailed discussion is given in the author's above-mentioned *Handbook of Values*, but on the few occasions when the Model 1850 is mentioned in Western historical literature, it is probable that the writer meant the Colt Old Model Pocket Pistol, Model 1848, or the Model 1849 Pocket Revolver.

Colt Model 1851 Navy Revolver. In all Western literature and history referring to the pre-Civil War period, the phrase "Colt Navy Revolver," if accurately used, meant the Colt Model 1851 Percussion Revolver (also called Old Model Belt Pistol, Old Model Navy Pistol, Model of 1851 Navy,

PLATE 4. Colt Model 1851 Navy Revolver and Colt Flasks.

1. Model 1851 Navy Revolver with ivory grips, butt stamped "U.S.N."
2. Model 1851 Navy Revolver with walnut grips and square-back trigger guard. Silver-plated trigger guard and straps.
3. Model 1851 Navy Revolver, Belgian-made with "Colt Brevete" on the barrel and Liège proof marks.
4. Colt Rifle Powder Flask.
5. Model 1851 Navy Revolver with square-back trigger guard and the wedge screw under the wedge instead of above. Known to collectors as the first type or model of the Model 1851.
6. Colt Pistol Powder Flask.
7. Model 1851 Navy Revolver, London Model. Barrel marked "Address Col. Colt London." English proof marks on barrel and cylinder.
8. Model 1851 Navy Revolver with one-piece ivory grips carved with Mexican eagle in high relief on left grip and silver-plated frame.
9. Model 1851 Navy Revolver, probably made by Confederates during Civil War. Dragoon-type barrel. Bronze frame, guard, and straps.
10. Colt Pistol Powder Flask.
11. Model 1851 Navy Revolver, London Model, cased pair with accessories.

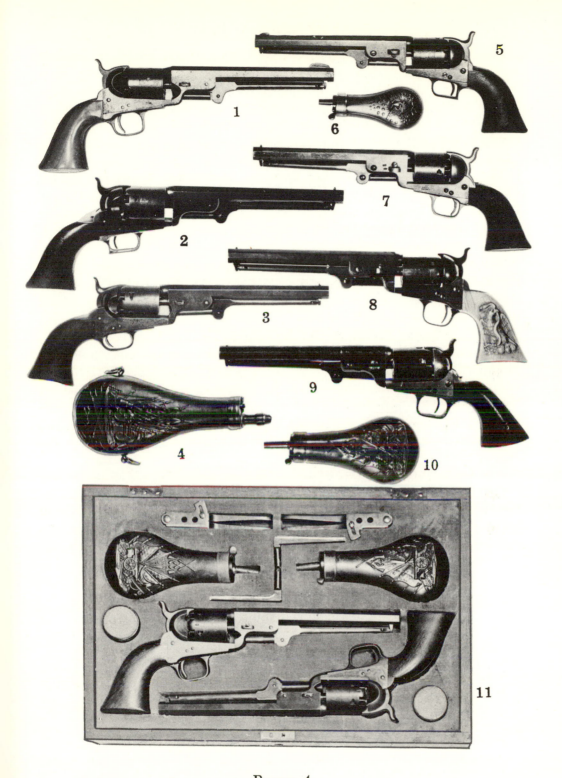

PLATE 4

and Model of 1851 Navy Pistol). It is caliber .36, 6-shot, S.A., with a 7.5-inch octagon barrel, a total length of 13 inches, and a weight of 2 lbs. 10 oz.

Plate 4 comprises eleven specimens of the Colt Model 1851 Navy Revolver, with variations as explained under the number of each.

The Colt Police Pocket Pistol (also called the Old Model Pistol, and sometimes erroneously termed the "Wells Fargo Colt"), is simply the Model 1849 Pocket Pistol without a loading lever, or ramrod. It was made for express messengers and law officers who could load in advance and were not expected to reload quickly on duty. This modification was probably made between 1851 and 1860.

The Colt Pocket Model 1853 never existed. This name is sometimes mistakenly given to the New Model Pocket Pistol of Navy Caliber, described later in this chapter.

Colt New Model Pocket Pistol (also called Model of 1855 Pocket Pistol, Side Hammer Colt; Root's Patent Pistol; and erroneously as Colt Pocket Model 1855 Side Hammer Revolver), was not sold to the public before 1857, and was probably made from 1857 to 1872. Collectors and dealers often list this as caliber .28, but the Colt factory experts insist that it should be caliber .265. It is a 5-shot revolver with a 3.5-inch straight octagon barrel, the total length is 8 inches, and the weight is 1 lb. 1 oz.

The Colt Army Revolver, Model 1860 (also called New Model Holster Pistol, New Model Army Pistol, and Round-barreled Army Pistol), is a U. S. martial percussion revolver, caliber .44, 6-shot, S.A.; with an 8-inch round barrel. The total length is 14 inches and the weight is 2 lbs. 11 oz. When the revolver is attached to a shoulder stock the total length is 26.5 inches and the weight is then 5 lbs.

PLATE 5. Colt New Model Pocket Pistol of Navy Caliber, New Model Pocket Pistol; and Army Revolver, Model 1860.

1. New Model Pocket Pistol of Navy Caliber with 6.5-inch barrel.
2. New Model Pocket Pistol of Navy Caliber with 5.5-inch barrel.
3. New Model Pocket Pistol, also called Model of 1855 Pocket Pistol, etc., with 4.5-inch round barrel and full-fluted cylinder.
4. New Model Pocket Pistol with 3.5-inch round barrel, round cylinder engraved with stagecoach holdup scene, and a screw in the cylinder.
5. New Model Pocket Pistol with 4.5-inch round barrel and a full-fluted cylinder.
6. Army Revolver, Model 1860, with 7.5-inch round barrel and full-fluted cylinder.
7. Army Revolver, Model 1860, with 7.5-inch round barrel, full-fluted cylinder, and studs screwed into sides of frame for shoulder stock support.
8. Army Revolver, Model 1860, with 8-inch round barrel, straight cylinder, left ivory grip carved with Mexican eagle in high relief within an oval, all metal parts engraved, except rammer, and nickel-plated.

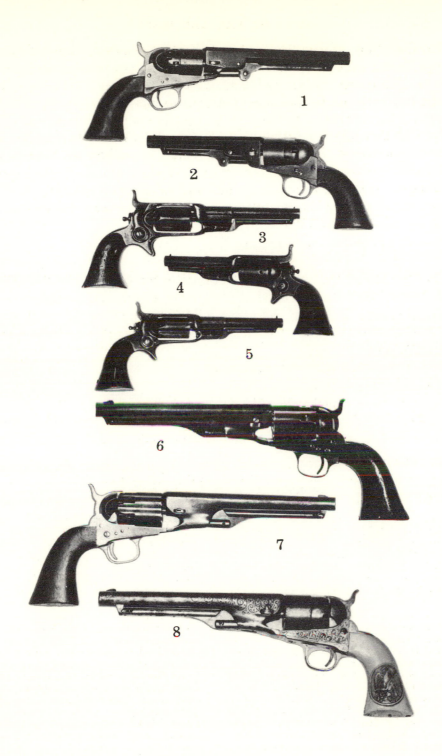

PLATE 5

The Colt New Model Pocket Pistol of Navy Caliber (also called the Pocket Navy Revolver, and the Pocket Navy Pistol), was made from 1860 or 1861 to 1872. It was made with the grips and frame of the Colt Model 1849 Pocket Revolver, but the frame was cut out to make room for the rebated cylinder. This is caliber .36, 5-shot, S.A.; usually made with a 4.5-inch, 5.5-inch, or 6.5-inch barrel; total length 9.5 inches, weight 1 lb. 9 oz. for the 4.5-inch octagon barrel. The "Navy Caliber" refers to caliber .36. Plate 5, figures 1 & 2.

Other revolvers illustrated by Plate 5 and explained by the captions below the numbers, are specimens of the New Model Pocket Pistol and the Army Revolver, Model 1860.

Plate 6, figures 1–5, inclusive, are . . .

The Colt Model 1861 Navy Revolver (also called New Model Belt Pistol, New Model Navy Pistol, Model of 1861 Navy Pistol, and Round-barreled Navy), is caliber .36, 6-shot, S.A.; with a 7.5-inch round barrel, total length 13 inches, and weight 2 lbs. 9 oz. and sometimes 2 lbs. 10 oz. This is a U. S. martial revolver.

And figures 6–10, inclusive, are named . . .

The Colt New Model Police Pistol (also called Model of 1862 Pocket Pistol, Officers' Model Pocket Pistol, 1862 Belt Model, and New Model Police Pistol with Creeping Lever Ramrod), is caliber .36, 5-shot, S.A.; with 6.5-

PLATE 6. Colt Model 1861 Navy Revolver and Colt New Model Police Pistol.

1. Model 1861 Navy Revolver, service issue.
2. Model 1861 Navy Revolver with checkered, one-piece ivory grips, and all metal parts silver-plated except screws, which are black.
3. Model 1861 Navy Revolver with ivory grips and silver-plated guard and straps.
4. Model 1861 Navy Revolver with one-piece ivory grips with Mexican eagle carved in high relief on left grip. All metal parts elaborately engraved. Silver-plated guard and straps. Low blade front sight.
5. Model 1861 Navy Revolver with ivory grips with Mexican eagle carved in high relief inside a scalloped border on left grip. Silver-plated guard and straps. All metal parts finely engraved.
6. New Model Police Pistol, also called Model of 1862 Pocket Pistol, Officers' Model Pocket Pistol, 1862 Belt Model, and New Model Police with Creeping-Lever Ramrod. The specimen illustrated conforms to the description in the text.

7. New Model Police Pistol with 4.5-inch round barrel, genuine elephant-ivory grips carved with man's head in high relief on left grip and all metal parts elaborately engraved.
8. New Model Police Pistol with 5.5-inch round barrel, ivory grips, and all metal parts except the cylinder and loading lever engraved. Rear sight removed from hammer; open sight set into barrel in front of cylinder.
9. New Model Police Pistol with 4.5-inch round barrel, one-piece ivory grips carved with American eagle and shield in relief on left grip. Engraved, silver-plated guard and straps. Engraved frame, barrel cylinder, and hammer. Blade front sight.
10. New Model Police Pistol with 4.5-inch round barrel, ivory grips with Mexican eagle carved in high relief on right side, and nickel-plated barrel, frame, and cylinder; hammer polished bright.

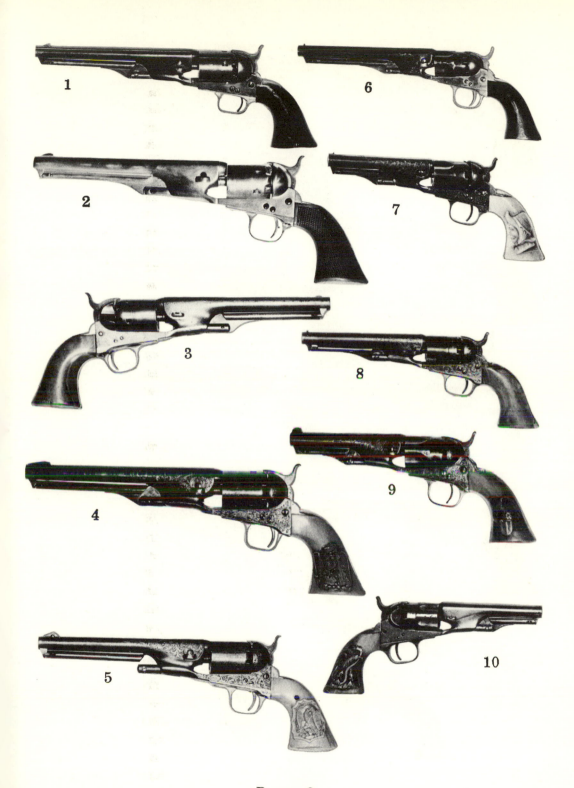

PLATE 6

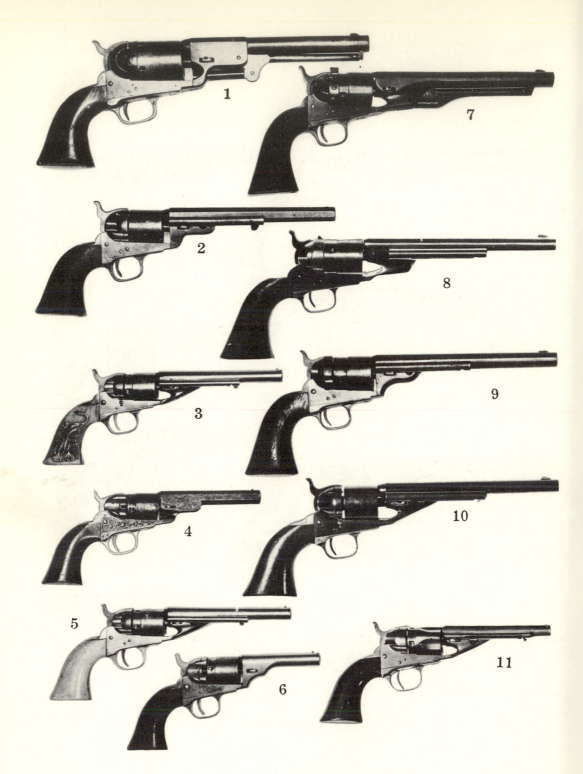

PLATE 7

inch round barrel, total length 12 inches, and weight about 1 lb. 10 oz. This revolver was carried as a personal arm by some Union and Confederate officers, so it can be regarded as a U. S. secondary martial revolver. Also, it was extensively used in the West during the Civil War, and afterward.

Percussion Colt Revolvers Converted to fire metallic cartridges. With the appearance of the self-contained metallic cartridge weapons, thousands of percussion guns still remained in Hartford, in the hands of dealers and of individuals—as well as in the U. S. armories, which also had percussion shoulder arms on hand—that needed only the work of competent gunsmiths to convert them over to the new, more efficient firing method.

Although there is little mention of these revolvers in the historical literature of the West, they did exist and served their purpose, as shown by the accompanying illustrations (Plate 7) with the descriptive captions.

These were all big-calibered revolvers, and when a man filled his holster with one of them, he knew he was packing a powerful argument.

Many other makes of pistols were used on the frontier during this time, but in song and story and in actual use, it was the Colt revolver that seemed the outstanding favorite.

PLATE 7. Colt Percussion Revolvers Converted to Fire Metallic Cartridges.

1. Army Revolver, Model 1848, caliber .44 long r.f., 6-shot, 8-inch round barrel. Loading lever retained.
2. Model 1851 Navy Revolver, caliber .38 long r.f., 6-shot, with loading gate and side-rod ejector.
3. New Model Pocket Pistol of Navy Caliber, caliber .38 c.f., 5-shot, 4.5-inch round barrel, with loading gate, side-rod ejector, and one-piece ivory grips, carved on right with Mexican eagle.
4. New Model Pocket Pistol of Navy Caliber, caliber .38 r.f., 5-shot, 4.5-inch octagon barrel, without loading gate or side-rod ejector, with all metal parts engraved, and silver-plated guard and straps.
5. New Model Pocket Pistol of Navy Caliber, caliber .38 r.f., 5-shot, 5.5-inch round barrel, with loading gate, side-rod ejector, and ivory grips.
6. New Model Pocket Pistol of Navy Caliber, caliber .38 long c.f., 5-shot, 3.5-inch round barrel, with iron back strap, and made without loading gate or side-rod ejector.
7. Army Revolver, Model 1860, Thuer's conversion, caliber .44 Thuer c.f., 6-shot, 8-inch round barrel. Iron back strap, brass guard and strap.
8. Army Revolver, Model 1860, caliber .44 Colt c.f., 6-shot, 8-inch round barrel, with loading gate and side-rod ejector. The firing pin is in the frame and not on the hammer.
9. Army Revolver, Model 1860, caliber .44 Colt O.M., 6-shot, 8-inch round barrel, made with loading gate, side-rod ejector, and iron guard and straps.
10. Model 1861 Navy Revolver, caliber .38 c.f., 6-shot, 7.5-inch round barrel, made with loading gate, side-rod ejector, and brass guard and straps.
11. New Model Police Pistol, sometimes called Belt Model 1862, caliber .38 r.f., 5-shot, 4.5-inch round barrel, half-fluted cylinder, made with loading gate and side-rod ejector.

Stampede by Sioux Indians at Fort Union, at the Mouth of the Yellowstone River, Dacotah Territory. Frank Leslie's Illustrated Newspaper, May 30, 1868.

X *Martial Percussion Hand Guns on the Frontier: U. S. Martial and Secondary Martial Pistols and American Martial Revolvers*

THE hand guns discussed and shown in this chapter are all of the percussion type. All were carried to a greater or less extent by United States troops before and during the Civil War, by civilians—and also by Confederate soldiers. The guns had a long and frequently a colorful life. Even after Samuel Colt's introduction of the percussion revolver in 1836 and its subsequent manufacture by other arms makers, the big, heavy-calibered single-shot pistols continued to be made and bought by the government as a regulation-issue arm, chiefly for certain units of the cavalry.

Inevitably many of these pistols, regular issue or not, and the revolvers as well, found their way into the hands of frontier civilians, often those attached to the frontier army posts. They were sutlers, contract surgeons, wagoners and freighters, civilian scouts, packers, mule skinners, as well as the "washerwomen." Many of these were young and pretty and their talents, in that lonely and womanless land, were not necessarily limited to the washboard; some of them made excellent wives for grizzled NCO's awaiting their discharge papers. The women and families of the "Washerwomen's Rows" carried guns of all types, from the heavy martial to tiny derringers, and these are classified as American martial arms, as opposed to the U. S. martial weapons actually made for and supplied by the government to its troops.

Outside the log stockades of many remote frontier posts straggling settlements sprang up, brought by the security of the breeze-whipped flag, the stout log walls and the reassuring sounds of military routine from within. The population was largely drifting, often wild and always resentful of the same authority it looked to for protection from Indian attack. Such a place was at once the bane of the post CO, and the delight of the enlisted man.

Here were the skin tepees of an Indian band come to trade—and to steal—a gang of freighters with their huge-wheeled, heavy-laden wagons, bearded buffalo skinners and hunters, white traders, a crew of punchers with beef-on-the-hoof for the fort, covered-wagon emigrants awaiting the spring opening of the mountain passes; and in times of peril, ranch families huddling close for safety. Also, if conditions warranted, tinhorn gamblers, saloonmen and honkytonk girls, plus assorted renegades and frontier riffraff.

These were trouble spots in more ways than one. Lack of sanitation invited widespread pestilence; carelessness or ignorance threatened flaming destruction; and if hostiles moved against the garrison in force, driving the population inside the walls, it meant at least short rations of food and water; all the confusion and danger of a small, vastly overcrowded place where discipline, at best, was not too effective.

There is no doubt that these army-post villages often formed ready outlets for stolen government arms and ammunition. The profit in supplying Indians with good firearms was high and soldiers' pay proverbially low—fifteen dollars a month or less for a recruit—when, as, and if the paymaster reached the fort. For many a resentful, homesick city-bred recruit, the temptation of being close to another source of wealth was too much:

powder-and-ball and guns smuggled out would buy just the medicine he needed—gambling, whisky and girls—and well worth the risk of guardhouse or even court-martial. And frequently deserters were involved in stealing case shipments of government arms, including the percussion single-shot pistols and revolvers.

These percussion hand guns continued to play their important part in Western history through the years. They were blooded in early Indian troubles, in conflicts between rival fur and trading outfits, in the Texas war for independence against Mexico and in the later Mexican War. They were also carried by military escort details guarding government scientific expeditions, stagecoach routes and railroad builders. With the percussion shoulder arms, these weapons cleared the way for the men who worked with ax, sledge hammer and shovel, breaking trail for the civilization to follow.

To qualify as a U. S. martial arm, the percussion single-shot pistol, shown and discussed further in this chapter, had to be made in the United States arsenals at Harpers Ferry, or at Springfield, Massachusetts, or made under government contract by these arms makers: Henry Aston; the reorganized firm of H. Aston & Co.; Ira N. Johnson—all of Middletown, Connecticut; William Glaze & Co., Columbia, South Carolina, doing business as the Palmetto Armory; N. P. Ames, Springfield, Massachusetts; and Henry Deringer, Philadelphia, Pennsylvania. These weapons bear the model years of 1842, 1843, and 1855.

American secondary martial percussion single-shot pistols were those of large caliber and size, but which were not known to have been bought by the United States and issued to government troops. They were pistols carried either officially or unofficially by state troops, semi-official military and naval organizations, by officers and crews of privateers, or manufactured—usually in limited quantity—on speculation by those seeking government contracts.

While the U. S. martial and the American secondary martial single-shot percussion pistols shown and described below do not comprise the entire story of such weapons, these specimens give a fair representation of this classification. As big, heavy-caliber hand guns, they served in the transition toward the development of American martial percussion revolvers the detailed description of which follow that of the single-shot pistols.

Plate 1 is a complete display of U. S. martial percussion pistols, but it is more than that. In this group, figure 1 is the U. S. Pistol, Model 1842, made by the Palmetto Armory, which later produced arms for the Confederate States of America. Figure 2 is the U. S. Pistol, Model 1843, made by Deringer for the army. Figure 3 is the U. S. Pistol-Carbine, Model 1855, Springfield, which is really a revolver with a shoulder stock so that it can be fired as a shoulder weapon. Figure 4 is U. S. Pistol, Model 1843, Army, made by N. P. Ames, who also made many of the swords and sabers for the armed forces of the United States. Figure 5 is the Elgin Cutlass Pistol, made by C. B. Allen, of Springfield, Massachusetts, along with the scabbard. This weapon was not only used by the U. S. Navy but also by merchantmen and by some who were no better than pirates. Thus, it is not only a U. S. martial percussion pistol, but can be classified as a sword-pistol, knife-pistol, dagger-pistol, a combination weapon, or grouped with freaks and oddities.

Figure 6 is another view of the U. S. Pistol, Model 1842, Palmetto Armory, identical to figure 1, but photographed to a larger scale. Figure 7 is the U. S. Breech-loading Percussion Martial Pistol bearing the stamp of the inspector in two places, which is not too remarkable for the period, but all its characteristics indicate that it was made by Simeon North, one of the great arms makers of American history.

Figures 8 and 9 are two views of the U. S. Army Signal Pistol, Model 1862, which, like modern signal pistols, was used to fire small rockets or flares as signals to commence artillery fire, to cease it, to order an infantry advance after a preparatory artillery barrage, or for any other purpose. Such signal pistols are sometimes classified as freaks and oddities, like the Elgin Cutlass Pistol, but weapons of this type are definitely not freaks or oddities, and are usually grouped under that heading merely for ease of classification.

Plate 1: Detailed Descriptions of U. S. Martial Percussion Pistols

U. S. Pistol, Model 1842, Palmetto Armory, caliber .54; 8.5-inch, smoothbore, round barrel marked "Wm. GLAZE & Co.," "P," "V," with a palmetto tree and the date on the breech. Lock plate marked "COLUMBIA S.C." and the date. Except for the marks, this pistol is almost exactly like the U. S. Pistol, Model 1842, Army, H. Aston, and the same model made by I. N. Johnson. Figures 1 and 6.

U. S. Pistol, Model 1843, Deringer, Army, caliber .54, smoothbore, identical with U. S. Pistol, Model 1843, N. P. Ames, except that lock plate is marked "US DERINGER PHILADELa." There may be "USR" behind the hammer, but it is usually absent. This is the abbreviation for United States Mounted Rifles. Barrel may be unmarked, it may be marked "RP," or it may be marked "DERINGER PHILADELa RP." Brass-blade front sight. No rear sight. Figure 2.

U. S. Pistol-Carbine, Model 1855, Springfield, caliber .58, Maynard tape lock, 12-inch, round, rifled barrel having a low-blade front sight, a triple-leaf rear sight, marked "P" and "V" with an eagle head and the model year, 1855, on the tang. Total length of pistol without detachable stock 17.75 inches. Weight of pistol alone 3 lbs. 13 oz. Brass mountings. Trigger guard 5.25 inches long with round ends. One band. Full-length oil-finished walnut stock, with ring in butt. Flat, beveled-edge lock plate marked "U.S.: Springfield" in front of hammer and "1855" behind the hammer. Maynard primer recess cover marked with spread eagle. Brass-mounted, detachable, oil-finished walnut stock, 26.5 inches long, with sling swivel. Butt plate of stock marked "US." Total length of pistol and detachable stock, when assembled, 28.25 inches. Total assembled weight, 5 lbs. 7 oz. Dragoons carried this weapon in two pieces on the saddle. When they dismounted to fight, they used it as a carbine. This weapon is also listed under U. S. martial percussion shoulder arms.

Same, but without the detachable stock. Figure 3.

U. S. Pistol, Model 1843, Army, N. P. Ames, caliber .54; 6-inch, smoothbore, round, browned barrel without sights, marked "USR" (United States Mounted Rifles), "RP" and "P" with the date. Three-quarter, 10.625-inch walnut stock extending to the swivel ramrod. Total length 11.625 inches. Brass mountings. Casehardened box lock, with hammer inside lock plate. Rounded, countersunk, brass butt plate. Flat lock plate 4.3 inches long and 1.25 inches wide, marked "N. P. AMES," "Springfield Mass." and "USR," with the date. Trigger guard 4.75 inches wide with square ends. One band. Brass-blade front sight. No rear sight. Figure 4.

Elgin Cutlass Pistol, C. B. Allen, Springfield, Mass., caliber .54; 5-inch, smoothbore, octagon barrel bearing iron-blade front sight, and marked "Elgin's Patent PM CBA 1837," with a serial number, such as 149, as on the specimen illustrated, on the left side. No rear sight. Total length 15.75 inches. Weight 2 lbs. 7 oz. Left side of iron frame marked "C. B. Allen Springfield Mass." with same serial number as on barrel. Side hammer. Iron back strap. Walnut grips. Iron trigger guard loops at rear to the butt to serve as a hilt when the blade is used. Knife or cutlass blade is 11.5 inches long and 2.063 inches wide, fastened in front of trigger guard under the barrel. Leather scabbard. This was formerly regarded as a U. S. martial secondary percussion pistol, but recent information shows that it belongs in the U. S. martial classification. The United States contracted to purchase 150 of these pistols on September 8, 1837. Figure 5.

PLATE 1

Unverified U. S. Breech-Loading Percussion Martial Pistol, caliber .54; 6.5-inch, smoothbore, round, iron barrel. Total length 14 inches. Center hammer similar to that of percussion carbines of the same period made by Simeon North. Spring catch on the underside allows the barrel to drop for loading. Stamped "NWP" on top of rising breechblock and also NWP in oval on left side of stock. These are the initials of Ned W. Patch who was an arms inspector at the armories of Simeon North and Asa Waters from 1831 to the 1850's. The workmanship indicates that it may be a North product. This is a unique specimen, unknown to most of the leading collectors and dealers, and owned by Mr. Sam E. Smith, Markesan, Wisconsin. Figure 7.

U. S. Army Signal Pistol, caliber .69; 1.75-inch, round, brass barrel. Center-hung hammer. Spur trigger. Nipple set on rear of barrel. Iron lever extends down from barrel along frame and is used to hold flare in barrel. Butt marked "U.S. Army Signal Pistol 1862." Brass frame. Figure 8.

U. S. Army Signal Pistol, caliber about .75; 1.625-inch, brass barrel. Center-hung hammer. Spur trigger. Walnut grips. Iron lever extends down from barrel along frame to hold flare in barrel. Brass frame. Butt marked "U.S. Army Signal Pistol 1862." Figure 9.

Plate 2 shows 12 pistols that belong in the classification of American secondary martial percussion single-shot pistols.

Figure 1 is another version of the Elgin Cutlass Pistol or Bowie Knife-Pistol, made by Morrill & Blair, Amherst, Massachusetts. Figures 2, 3, and 4 are three different versions of the Lindsay 2-Shot Single Barrel Pistol, which is sometimes classified among freaks and oddities, but was merely an attempt to develop from the single-shot pistol to the revolver. Figure 5 is the Marston Breech-loading Pistol, which was remarkable in its time as an effort to get away from muzzle-loading. Figures 6 and 7 are versions of the Perry Breech-loading Pistol, one with, and one without, the automatic capping (priming) device. Figure 8 is the Sharps Breech-loading pistol, made

PLATE 1. U. S. Martial Percussion Pistols.

1. U. S. Pistol, Model 1842, Palmetto Armory.
2. U. S. Pistol, Model 1843, Deringer, Army.
3. U. S. Pistol-Carbine, Model 1855, Springfield.
4. U. S. Pistol, Model 1843, Army, N. P. Ames.
5. Elgin Cutlass Pistol, C. B. Allen, Springfield, Mass., with scabbard.
6. Another view of the U. S. Pistol, Model 1842, Palmetto Armory, identical to figure 1 but photographed larger.
7. U. S. Breech-loading Percussion Martial Pistol bearing the stamp of the inspector in two places, possibly made by Simeon North, and probably unique.
8. U. S. Army Signal Pistol, 1862.
9. U. S. Army Signal Pistol, 1862.

by the same men who produced the Sharps buffalo rifles, and figure 9 is another version of the same. Figures 10, 11, and 12 are pistols by A. H. Waters & Co., Constable of Philadelphia, and Tryon of Philadelphia, respectively.

Plate 2: Detailed Description of American Secondary Martial Percussion Single-Shot Pistols

Elgin Cutlass Pistol or Bowie-Knife Pistol, Morrill & Blair, caliber .36, 3-inch round barrel. Iron frame. Side hammer. Knife blade 7 inches long, 1 inch wide, etched with "Horn of Plenty" on right side and "Morrill & Blair Amherst Mass." on left side. Figure 1.

Lindsay 2-Shot Single-Barrel Pistol, caliber .45; 8.25-inch, half-octagonal, smoothbore barrel bearing brass-blade front sight, marked in front of cones "Lindsay's Young America Patented Oct. 9, 1860." Rear sight is a notch in the brass frame. Total length 12 inches. Walnut grips. Spur trigger. Simple trigger operates two centrally hung hammers. Right hammer falls on right cone to discharge forward load, and then, if trigger is pressed, left hammer falls on left cone to discharge rear load, since loads are placed one in front of the other in the single barrel. No ramrod. Figure 2.

Lindsay 2-Shot Single-Barrel Pistol, caliber .41; 4-inch, part square, part octagonal barrel. Walnut grips, brass frame, spur trigger. Hammers like those on the .45-caliber model. Blade front sight. Groove rear sight. Marked "Lindsay's Young America. Man'f'd by J. P. Lindsay-Man'f'g Co. New York" on right side of barrel, and "Patent'd Feb. 8, 1859. Patent'd Oct. 9, 1860" on under side of barrel. Frame engraved with deer and dog. Left side of barrel engraved with lion, flags, etc. Figure 3.

Lindsay 2-Shot Single-Barrel Pistol, caliber .40; 4.875-inch, tapered, octagonal barrel marked "Lindsay's Young America" on top and "Patent Apd. For" on right side, at the breech. Walnut grips, engraved brass frame, and double spur triggers. Brass-blade front sight and no rear sight. This model with two separate triggers, one for each hammer, is the first type of Lindsay made, and less than 200 were produced. Figure 4.

Marston Breech-Loading Pistol, caliber .36; 5.75-inch, rifled, blued barrel, round at front and octagonal at rear, bearing brass-blade front sight and V-notch iron rear sight, and marked "W. W. Marston Patented New York" on top and "Cast Steel" on right. Total length 10.75 inches. Weight 1 lb. 12 oz. Walnut grips. Oval iron trigger guard. Engraved side hammer and engraved silver-plated bronze frame. Blued barrel, casehardened hammer, trigger, and lever for operating sliding breechblock. This pistol fired a peculiar cartridge having a cardboard case with a leather base. The earlier, bronze-frame specimens are worth more than the later ones having iron frames.

Same, with 6-inch barrel.

Same, with 7-inch barrel.

Same, with 8-inch barrel.

Same, with 8.5-inch barrel. Figure 5.

Perry Breech-Loading Pistol, caliber .52; 6.188-inch, round, rifled barrel with brass-blade front sight and V-notch rear sight grooved in barrel over breech. Total length 12.75 inches. Weight 2 lbs. 15 oz. Walnut grips. No forearm. Side hammer. Breechblock marked "A. D. Perry Patented" and "Perry Patent Fire Arms Co. Newark, N.J." Blued finish. To load, the trigger guard is lowered, thus tilting the breech up and the barrel down, and permitting the loading of the pistol with loose powder and ball or with a paper cartridge. A projecting beveled ring fits into the chamber and forms a gastight joint which is an improvement on the Sharps Breech-loading Pistol which the Perry otherwise resembles. When the breechblock is closed, a percussion cap is fed to the nipple by an automatic capping magazine extending through the butt. This is the model usually listed. Figure 6.

Same, but without the automatic capping device. Figure 7.

Sharps Breech-Loading Pistol, caliber .38; 6.5-inch, rifled, round, tapered barrel with brass-blade front sight. Total length 11 inches. Weight 2 lbs. V-notch rear sight in frame. Walnut grips. No fore end. Steel back strap and frame. Side hammer. Frame marked on left "C. Sharps & Co. Rifle Works Phila. Pa. C. Sharps Patent 1848." Lawrence pellet priming device is a tube in the frame which automatically feeds priming pellets to the cone when the hammer is cocked. Trigger guard serves as breechblock lever. Figure 8.

Same, but 5-inch round barrel marked "Sharp's Patent Arms Manufacturing Co., Fairmount, Philadelphia, Pa." Total length 12 inches. Figure 9. 9.

A. H. Waters & Co. Pistol, caliber .54; 8.5-inch round, smoothbore, bright-finished barrel bearing brass knife-blade front sight, with a large open rear

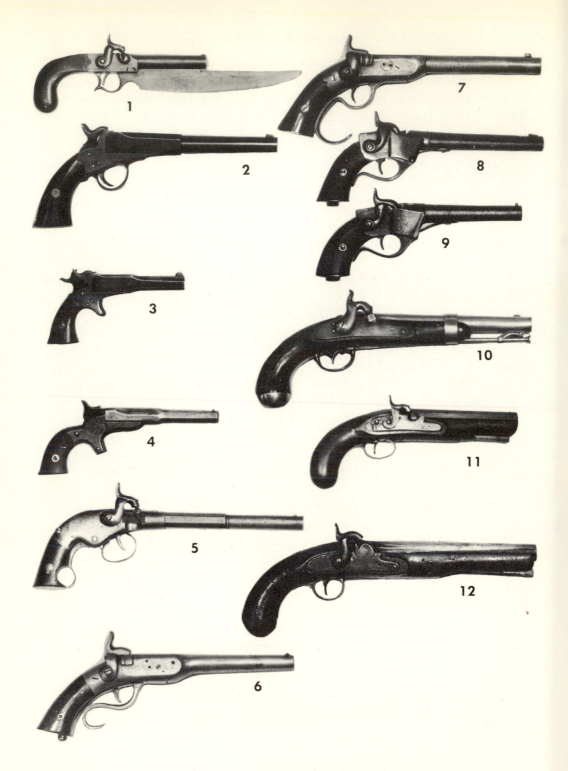

PLATE 2

sight on the tang, and marked with initials, probably of an inspector or possibly the barrel maker. Total length 14 inches. Weight 2 lbs. 6 oz. Three-quarter-length black walnut stock ends near ramrod swivel. Iron mountings. Barrel fastened to stock by a single branch-band fastened through the front side screw on the left. Back strap formed by extension of the butt cap. The cone is set on a side lug. This pistol superficially resembles the U. S. Pistol, Model 1836, A. Waters, and the U. S. Pistol, Model 1836, A. H. Waters & Co. (see U. S. Martial Flintlock Pistols), except that those had beveled lock plates whereas this percussion pistol does not have a beveled lock plate. Furthermore, this pistol was made as a percussion weapon and is not an alteration from the flintlock system. The lock plate is marked "A. H. Waters & Co. Milbury Mass," with the date. The trigger guard may be either iron or brass. Figure 10.

Constable, Philadelphia, Pistol, caliber .54; 6-inch, smoothbore, octagonal, pin-fastened barrel marked "Philadelphia." Total length 10.5 inches. Lock plate marked "Constable." Iron-pin front sight and no rear sight. Full stock. Horn-tipped ramrod. Iron-mounted. Made about 1840 by Richard Constable, famous Philadelphia gunsmith. Figure 11.

Tryon, Philadelphia, Pistol, caliber .64, 9.25-inch, smoothbore, round, iron, pin-fastened barrel marked "Tyron Philadelphia" with English proof marks. Lock plate marked "Tryon." Total length 14.5 inches. Tryon imported the barrel from England, probably because it was often cheaper to import barrels and locks than it was to make them here, but he apparently made the rest and assembled the pistol. Figure 12.

Before going into detailed descriptions of American martial percussion revolvers, it might be well to name—if only for the sake of the record—the private American manufacturers who made and sold percussion revolvers under contract to the government, for issuance to federal troops during

PLATE 2. American Secondary Martial Percussion Pistols.

1. Elgin Cutlass Pistol or Bowie-Knife Pistol, Morrill & Blair, Amherst, Mass.
2. Lindsay 2-Shot Single-Barrel Pistol, caliber .45, 8.25-inch barrel.
3. Lindsay 2-Shot Single-Barrel Pistol, caliber .41, 4-inch barrel.
4. Lindsay 2-Shot Single-Barrel Pistol, caliber .40, 4.875-inch barrel.
5. Marston Breech-loading Pistol.
6. Perry Breech-loading Pistol, with automatic capping device.
7. Perry Breech-loading Pistol, without automatic capping device.
8. Sharps Breech-loading Pistol, with 6.5-inch barrel.
9. Sharps Breech-loading Pistol, with 5-inch barrel and different marking.
10. A. H. Waters & Co. Pistol.
11. Constable, Philadelphia, Pistol.
12. Tryon, Philadelphia, Pistol.

the Civil War. These do not include revolvers imported by the government from Europe, but which also come under the same classification—that of U. S. martial percussion revolvers:

Allen & Wheelock, Colt, Joslyn, Pettingill, Remington calibers .44 and .36; Remington-Beals caliber .44; and Whitney Navy revolvers.

The American martial percussion revolvers we are specifically concerned with are those bought and carried as private arms by officers and enlisted men of the U. S. forces and civilians associated with federal military and naval units.

Colt revolvers are not discussed here, as it is customary in books on firearms to classify Colts by themselves. The revolvers described below include not only those in common use by military personnel during the two wars with Mexico, the various Indian campaigns and the Civil War, but also some revolvers of especial interest because of their unique characteristics, such as the Walch 12-shot Navy Revolver, by no means a common arm.

All these guns, at one time or another—along with the single-shot pistols previously described, and a good many more—found their way to the Western frontier, and were carried and used by various individuals of that historic time and place.

Plate 3: Detailed Descriptions of American Martial Percussion Revolvers

Allen & Wheelock Army Revolver, caliber .44, 6-shot, S.A.; 7.5-inch, rifled, round barrel, octagonal near breech, marked on left "Allen & Wheelock Worcester Mass. U.S. Allen's Pt's. Jan. 13, Dec. 15, 1857. Sept. 7, 1858." Total length 13.25 inches. Weight 2 lbs. 14 oz. Brass front sight on barrel. V-notch in lip center hammer serves as rear sight. Cylinder, 1.94 inches long, removed by pressing spring catch at front of frame and removing cylinder pin to front. Walnut grips. Blued barrel, cylinder, and frame. Hammer and trigger guard casehardened in mottled colors. Trigger guard serves as rammer when dropped by pressing spring catch. Called "Last Model." Figure 1.

Allen & Wheelock Navy Revolver, caliber .36, 6-shot, S.A.; 8-inch, octagonal, rifled barrel marked "Allen & Wheelock Worcester Mass. U.S. Allen's Pts. Jan. 13, Dec. 15, 1857, Sept. 7, 1858." Total length 13.5 inches. Weight 2 lbs. 6 oz. Cylinder, 1.845 inches long, is engraved with scene of animals in forest. German-silver-blade front sight on barrel. V-notch rear sight grooved in frame. Blued barrel, cylinder, and frame. Casehardened hammer and trigger guard. Side hammer on right. Trigger guard serves as loading lever and operates rammer. Cylinder removed by pulling cylinder pin from rear. Figure 2.

Alsop Navy Revolver, caliber .36, 5-shot, S.A.; 4.5-inch, octagon, rifled barrel marked "C. R. Alsop Middletown Conn. Patented July 17th, August 7th 1860, May 14th, 1861." Total length 9.875 inches. Weight 1 lb. 4 oz. Round cylinder marked "C. R. Alsop Patented Nov. 26th, 1861." Spur trigger. Brass cone front sight on barrel. V-notch rear sight grooved in frame. Blued cylinder and frame. Casehardened hammer and loading lever. Walnut grips. Made with loading lever. Cocking hammer revolves cylinder and forces it against barrel. This is the description of the standard Navy model. Figure 3.

Cochran Patent Monitor or Turret Pistol, caliber .40, 7-shot, S.A., 5-inch, rifled barrel, round except for 1 inch at the breech which is octagonal. The strap at the top lifts to remove the turret-like cylinder for loading and priming. Underhammer. No trigger guard. Total length 10 inches. Top strap marked "Cochran's Patent C.B. Allen Springfield, Mass." The specimen illustrated bears serial number 106 on the barrel, frame, top, strap, and cylinder. This is one of the rarest of all American revolving weapons and was patented by J. W. Cochran of New York City on April 29, 1837, with C. B. Allen as the maker. Figure 4.

Butterfield Army Revolver, caliber .41, 5-shot, S.A.; 7-inch, octagonal, blued, rifled barrel. Total length 13.75 inches. Weight 2 lbs. 10 oz. Brass knife-blade front sight set in barrel. Grooved rear sight in frame. Bronze oval trigger guard. Bronze frame marked on top "Butterfield's Patent Dec. 11, 1855 Philada." although many specimens are found unmarked except for a serial number on the barrel, cylinder, cylinder lock, loading lever, hammer block, and the inside of the frame side plates, which number is usually above 560. Disk primer magazine in front of trigger guard. Cocking the hammer feeds primers to cones from magazine tube. Blued cylinder, 1.69 inches long. Figure 5.

Freeman's Patent-Hoard's Armory Army Revolver, caliber .44, 6-shot, S.A.; 7.5-inch, round, rifled barrel. Total length 12.5 inches. Weight 2 lbs. 13 oz. Steel-blade front sight. Rear sight grooved in frame. Blued barrel, cylinder, and frame. Casehardened hammer and loading lever. Walnut grips. Frame marked "Freeman's Pat. Decr. 9, 1862, Hoard's Armory, Watertown, N.Y." Loading lever operates rammer. To remove the cylinder and cylinder pin, a slide in front of the cylinder is pushed forward. Figure 6.

Joslyn Army Revolver, caliber .44, 5-shot, S.A.; 8-inch, octagonal, rifled barrel marked on top "B. F. Joslyn Patd May 4th 1858," or it may be

PLATE 3

marked "B. F. Joslyn, Stonington, Conn." or "B. F. Joslyn Worcester Mass." Total length 14.375 inches, and weight 3 pounds, but the total length and the weight vary with the barrel length, which in some specimens is either more or less than the standard 8 inches. Steel knife-blade front sight set in barrel. Grooved-frame rear sight. Partly checkered walnut grips. Blued finish. Made with loading lever which operates rammer. Side hammer is curved to strike through the center of the frame, not to one side. Iron trigger guard and frame. Figure 7.

Mass. Arms Co.–Wesson's & Leavitt's Patent Army Revolver, caliber .40, 6-shot, S.A.; 7.125-inch, round, rifled barrel marked on top of barrel extension "Mass. Arms Co. Chicopee Falls," and on the barrel locking device "Patented Nov. 26, 1850." Frame marked "Wesson's & Leavitt's Patent." Total length 15 inches. Weight 4 lbs. 6 oz. Brass-blade front sight on barrel and V-notch rear sight on barrel extension. Walnut grips. Brass oval trigger guard. Cylinder, 2.25 inches long, is removed by first turning a catch in front of the cylinder and then raising the barrel. Blued back strap and barrel. Cylinder, frame, and hammer may be either casehardened or finished in a gray color. Cylinder is revolved by cocking hammer. Figure 8.

Same, but Navy Revolver, caliber .36, 6-shot, S.A.; 7-inch, round, rifled, tinned barrel.

Same, Navy Model, but caliber .31, with 3.5-inch barrel. Figure 9.

Pettingill's Patent Army Revolver, caliber .44, 6-shot, D.A., hammerless; 7.5-inch, rifled, octagon barrel sometimes marked "Pettingill's Patent." Frame marked on top "Pettingill's Patent 1856" and "Raymond & Robitaille Patented 1858," and sometimes with only the latter phrase when the former phrase, minus the patent date, appears on the barrel. Total length 14 inches. Weight 3 lbs. Brass-cone front sight. Rear sight grooved in frame. Walnut grips. Hammer concealed in frame. Blued barrel and either blued

PLATE 3. American Martial Percussion Revolvers.

1. Allen & Wheelock Army Revolver.
2. Allen & Wheelock Navy Revolver.
3. Alsop Navy Revolver.
4. Cochran Patent Turret Pistol, C. B. Allen.
5. Butterfield Army Revolver.
6. Freeman's Patent–Hoard's Armory Army Revolver.
7. Joslyn Army Revolver.
8. Mass. Arms Co.–Wesson's & Leavitt's Patent Army Revolver, caliber .40.
9. Mass. Arms Co.–Wesson's & Leavitt's Patent Navy Revolver, caliber .36.
10. Pettingill's Patent Army Revolver.
11. Remington Army Revolver, Model 1861 (Old Model) Revolver.
12. Remington Army Revolver, Model 1861, with ivory grips.

or browned frame. Made with loading lever. Made by Rogers & Spencer, Willowdale, New York. Squeezing trigger cocks, revolves cylinder, and fires. Figure 10.

Remington Army Revolver, Model 1861 (Old Model) Revolver, caliber .44, 6-shot, S.A.; 8-inch, octagonal rifled barrel, marked on top "Patented Dec. 17, 1861 Manufactured by Remington's Ilion N.Y." Total length 13.75 inches. Weight 2 lbs. 14 oz. German silver cone front sight. Rear sight grooved in frame. Brass oval trigger guard. Blued throughout except for casehardened hammer. Walnut stocks. Made with loading lever, cut away on top to permit removal of cylinder without dropping level. Figure 11.

Same, but with ivory grips. Figure 12.

Plate 4: Detailed Descriptions of American Martial Percussion Revolvers

Remington-Beals Army Revolver, also called Remington-Beals Old-Model Army Revolver, caliber .44, 6-shot, S.A.; 8-inch, octagonal, rifled barrel marked "Beals Patent Sept. 14, 1858. Manufactured by Remingtons Ilion New York." Total length 13.875 inches. Weight 2 lbs. 14 oz. Low-blade brass front sight set in barrel. Rear sight grooved in frame. Brass oval trigger guard. Walnut grips. Blued finish. Cylinder, 2 inches long, is removed by lowering loading lever and pulling cylinder pin to front. No hammer-rest indentations in cylinder. Figure 1.

Remington-Rider's Pt. Navy Revolver, 6-shot, D.A., caliber .36; 6.5-inch, octagonal, blued, rifled barrel marked on top "Manufactured by Remington's Ilion N. Y. Rider's Pt. Aug. 17, 1858, May 3, 1859." Brass-cone front sight. Rear sight is V notch in frame. Blued cylinder, barrel, and frame. Brass oval trigger guard. Casehardened hammer. Walnut grips. Total length 11.5 inches. Weight 2 lbs. 1 oz. Full fluted cylinder. Figure 2.

Rogers & Spencer Army Revolver, caliber .44, S.A., 6-shot; 7.5-inch, octagonal, rifled barrel. Total length 13.375 inches. Weight 3 lbs. 2 oz. Brass-cone front sight. Grooved-frame rear sight. Frame marked on top "Rogers

PLATE 4. American Martial Percussion Revolvers.

1. Remington-Beals Army Revolver.
2. Remington-Rider's Pt. Navy Revolver.
3. Rogers & Spencer Army Revolver.
4. E. Savage—H. S. North Navy Revolver, also called Savage First Model Navy Revolver.
5. E. Savage—H. S. North Navy Revolver, with iron instead of bronze frame.
6. E. Savage—H. S. North First Model Navy Revolver.
7. Starr Double-Action Navy Revolver.
8. Starr Single-Action Army Revolver.
9. Walch 12-Shot Navy Revolver.
10. Warner-Springfield Arms Co. Third Model Revolver.

PLATE 4

& Spencer Utica N.Y." Blued cylinder, barrel, and frame. Hammer and loading lever casehardened in mottled colors. Bell-shaped, square-bottom, black walnut grips. Figure 3.

E. Savage–H. S. North Navy Revolver, also called Savage First Model Navy Revolver, caliber 36, 6-shot, S.A.; 7.2-inch, octagonal, rifled barrel marked "E. Savage Middletown Ct. H. S. North Patented June 17, 1856." Total length 14 inches. Weight 3 lbs. 7 oz. Made without trigger guard. Brass-cone front sight. V-notch rear sight set in frame. Blued barrel and cylinder. Casehardened hammer and loading lever. Walnut grips. Trigger is large and shaped like figure 8, hence this revolver is sometimes called the Figure 8 Model. This trigger cocks the hammer and operates the cylinder, but the piece is fired by another trigger which is inside the upper circle of the figure 8. Made with loading lever. Bronze frame. Figure 4.

Same, but made with iron instead of bronze frame. Figure 5.

E. Savage–H. S. North First Model Navy Revolver, caliber .36; 6-shot, S.A., 6.75-inch, octagonal, rifled barrel marked "E. Savage Middletown, Ct. H. S. North Patented June 17, 1856." Total length 13.5 inches. Made without trigger guard. This type is the rarest of all the rare so-called figure-eight models and is distinguished by its flat iron frame and the very slight spur on the back strap as compared with the round iron frame and more pronounced back strap spur on the other models. Figure 6.

Starr Double-Action Navy Revolver, caliber .36, 6-shot, D.A.; 6-inch, round, rifled barrel. Total length 12 inches. Weight 3 lbs. 3 oz. Barrel tips down to permit cylinder removal for loading, as distinguished from Army Double-Action model, in which barrel tips up. Marks on both D.A. models are the same. The cylinder on this Navy model is 0.375 inch longer than the cylinder on the Army model. Also, the curve of the frame at the grip is different, thus making this Navy model 0.375 inch longer in total length. Figure 7.

Starr Single-Action Army Revolver, caliber .44, 6-shot, S.A.; 8-inch round, rifled barrel. Total length 13.75 inches. Weight 3 lbs. 1 oz. Otherwise the same as the Starr Double-Action Army Revolver. Figure 8.

Walch 12-Shot Navy Revolver, caliber .36, 12-shot, S.A.; 6-inch, octagonal, rifled barrel marked "Walch Firearms Co. New York Pat. Feb. 8, 1859." Total length 12.25 inches. Weight 2 lbs. 4 oz. Brass front sight. No rear sight. Blued barrel, cylinder, and frame. Casehardened hammers and triggers. Walnut grips, partly checkered. Made with a loading lever which operated a rammer. Two hammers, two triggers, and twelve cones, since it was loaded with two loads, one on top of the other, in each of the six chambers, and each load was fired from its own cone.

Same, but not marked. Figure 9.

Warner–Springfield Arms Co. First Model Navy Revolver, caliber .36, 6-shot, S.A.; 6-inch, round, rifled barrel marked "Springfield Arms Co." Total length 12.5 inches. Weight 2 lbs. 2 oz. Iron frame and trigger guard. Side hammer. Walnut grip. Blued. Cylinder shaft forms lower part of frame. Made with loading lever which operates rammer. Brass-cone front sight set in barrel. V-notch rear sight on barrel extension. Two triggers. The front trigger turns the cylinder; the rear trigger releases the hammer. Frame marked "Warner's Patent Jan. 7, 1851."

Same, but Second Model. There is a latch instead of the rear trigger. This latch is tripped by a slight pressure on the single trigger, which was formerly the front trigger.

Same, but Third Model. There is only one trigger, as described for the Second Model. Instead of the side hammer found on the first two models there is a center hammer. Figure 10.

Painting the Town Red. R. F. Zogbaum, Harper's Weekly, 1886.

XI *Johnny Kept His Gun: Confederate Firearms in the West*

ONE warm spring day in mid-Virginia two former comrades-in-arms met, saluted each other, shook hands and proceeded to write a document, dated April 9, 1865, that would strongly affect the lives of all Americans for generations yet unborn.

Grant handed Lee the rough draft after refusing the Confederate general's proffered sword. Lee glanced at the paper, suggested a minor correction in the wording, for which Grant thanked him. The fours years of bitter, bloody strife had ended. Although sporadic resistance continued until May 26, when Kirby Smith surrendered to General E. R. S. Canby at New Orleans, the Confederate States of America had ceased to exist.

The surrender itself would also have its impact on the development and settlement of the Western frontier. Thirty-five thousand gaunt, battle-weary veterans of a lost cause were to be paroled to return to their homes. Officers were permitted to keep their side arms; the men, their private horses and mules, and all official matériel would be turned over to the United States. But at that particular hour it is probable that the men in gray and butternut were more interested in the twenty-five thousand rations coming from the Union camp kitchens than in almost anything else.

By the following day the preliminary conditions of the surrender had been completed; after a brief farewell to his troops, Lee left on Traveler for his Virginia home. The men—only two weeks past there had been almost twice that number engaged in the futile attack on Ft. Steadman—started toward their homes. Or whatever might be left of them.

For many of these men, the journey was an Odyssey of hardship, danger and heartbreak. The physical destruction of the South, from Mason and Dixon's Line down through the Carolinas, and from the Mississippi eastward to the Atlantic, had been as completely ruinous as cannon and torch could make it. Cities had been leveled—Vicksburg, Atlanta, Richmond, and others. Great plantation houses and modest farmsteads had been burned, the fields of cotton and corn given over to weeds and vines.

And the families of these footsore, war-scarred men—what of them?

Many, of course, had managed to remain in or near their homes. Many others had died of hardships inflicted by the war, from disease or gunfire as they tried to protect their property. Still others had fled before the swift advance of ravaging armies that had to live off the country rather than be burdened by supply trains. Along the big rivers, civilians existed in caves or starved or sought safety in flight, as the naval guns and mortars of Farragut's and Foote's flotillas battered the cities and towns. Almost all communication lines had been wiped out; civilians seldom heard whether their men were living or dead, and soldiers had scant word of how their families fared.

Throughout the war-torn South, for weeks and months, emaciated gray-clad men returned to find the homes they had left now reduced to rubble and charred timbers, to see once fruitful fields now barren, fire-scorched earth—who was there now to work the land, anyway?—and to the recent graves of those who had gallantly waved as they marched away beneath their brave banners.

To thousands of these returning soldiers, here was a blank wall of hopelessness and despair. Some of them doggedly started building again, but there were many others who knew themselves dispossessed. Horses, mules, and oxen could still be bought, traded for, or won at cards or dice. Wagons could be built. And if "officers were permitted to retain their sidearms," what seasoned soldier ever needed specific permission to obtain and carry anything he really wanted—provided it wasn't too noticeable to the eyes of the damyankees?

Something to ride, to carry a man where he could find a future, was not too hard to come by. And a weapon to protect a man's property, his person and his honor was usually already in his pocket or tucked under his arm. So the needle swung—and pointed West.

To the average young Southerner who had a traditional appetite for high adventure, deeds of daring that called for a good dash of physical courage, gambling in almost any form, social drinking and sociable damsels, good horseflesh, personal combat, and a dislike of tedium and drudgery, the frontier acted as a powerful magnet. For here was an almost endless scope of country that had hardly known the War had existed. Towns and cities offered excitement and employment to young men who had a way with a deck of cards. It was a growing country, a building country, with work enough for everyone—and better still, often work spiced with danger. So some transplanted Southerners helped to build railroads, some joined the Plains army as saddle mates of their former enemies in the almost hopeless job of policing thousands of miles of rugged, hostile country. Some sought their fortunes in the mines, or found adventure as express guards or lawmen, or as professional gun hands or outlaws. A legion of them became cowpunchers, trail hands or ranchers. Usually the guns they had owned during the War they continued to carry and use in their new occupations. And a strange and wonderful assortment they were, too.

Despite the sympathy of President Franklin Pierce with the Southern cause and slavery, and the gradual strengthening of Southern defenses during his term and later by certain high officials of Buchanan's administration, the War's outbreak found the South in urgent need of firearms. The situation was not unlike that which, nearly a century before, faced the Colonies. In 1776, anything that could fire a projectile was welcome; and there were actions in which spears, pikes and pitchforks were brought into the fray by the Colonists. In 1861, although there were a few Southern armories and arms factories, they could not produce a fraction of the firearms needed. And it was probably small comfort for Southern young men, as they marched and countermarched in the village squares with shouldered brooms, to know that even the booming factories of the North were a lamentable way from meeting the Union need for weapons.

Anything the Union army had, the Confederate army got, by the seizure of federal arsenals and forts at the outbreak of hostilities, and later by capture and salvage on the battlefields. But it was never nearly enough, at any time. During the first engagements the Confederates went into battle with every kind of arm imaginable ("If it can shoot a Yank, we need it!"), including single-shot, muzzle-loading flintlock muskets and rifles, muzzle-loading and breech-loading shotguns of various bore sizes, and all kinds, sizes and shapes of flintlock, percussion and cartridge pistols and revolvers.

Confederate pistols, revolvers and shoulder arms, broadly speaking, are those guns, whether flintlock, percussion, or cartridge, made within the borders of the Confederate States of America; imported from foreign countries for Confederate use; bought from organizations or persons in the United States outside the Confederacy; captured from the United States forces; or in the possession of Southern persons and organizations prior to the outbreak of the Civil War. Furthermore, for any weapon to be truly Confederate, it must meet one or more of the above conditions of origin, and also have been carried and used by Confederates during the Civil War.

The problem for a historian or an arms collector is not so much what to include as what to exclude. Since the Confederates did not mark all their firearms with "C.S.A.," or with any other identifying stamp, the antique firearms market today is plagued by hundreds of weapons fraudulently marked "C.S.A." either on metal or wooden parts, because this raises the value above that of the same weapon without the Confederate mark. In addition to the unethical stamping of "C.S.A." on any firearm made before 1865, there are several gunsmiths who openly advertise that they make excellent reproductions of desirable antique arms, including Confederate weapons, complete with marks which look to the beginner like the real thing.

Virginia Manufactory Flintlock Rifle

The arm known as the Virginia Manufactory Flintlock Rifle is an example of a well-known Confederate shoulder arm, and is of interest to students of the Civil War, particularly to those who specialize in the history of the Confederacy.

Resembling to some degree the Kentucky rifle of its period, especially because of the full octagon barrel, this piece, in its original flintlock form and marked with the dates of 1808 and of 1809 to the rear of the cock, was issued to troops of the state of Virginia in 1861. The same rifle, but dated 1806, altered to percussion fire and bearing the motto on the patch box "Don't Tread On Me," was also issued to Virginia troops in the same year. Again, the same rifle, dated 1812, altered to percussion, with the barrel cut from 39 to 30 inches, was issued to the Confederate army from 1861 on; it is

Virginia Manufactory Flintlock Rifle.   FULLER

supposed that this issue was not confined to the troops of Virginia.

The Virginia Manufactory Flintlock Rifle, caliber .54, has a 39-inch, full octagon barrel; a total length of 54.5 inches, and weighs 9 pounds, 14 ounces. The walnut stock extends to the muzzle of the barrel, and it has the heavy brass tip characteristic of many Kentucky rifles of the time. The lock plate is marked "Virginia" between the cock and the pan. The word "Richmond" appears to the rear of the cock in a curve with the date, which may be 1817 on some specimens and other years on others.

Confederate Hand Guns

Shown and described here are typical specimens of Confederate hand guns made in the South during the Civil War, or otherwise correctly identified as Confederate arms. These, of course, do not attempt to include the multitude of European and United States arms that were also used by the Confederacy.

Dance Brothers & Park Percussion Revolver, caliber .44; 8-inch, part octagon, rifled barrel. Brass trigger guard, back strap, and blade front sight. Flat frame. No recoil shield. No rear sight. Serial number 89 on various parts of specimen illustrated. Not marked. Made at Columbia, Texas, 1863–64. Exceedingly rare. Plate 1, figure 1.

Dimick-Colt Percussion Revolver, caliber .36, 6-shot; 7.5-inch rifled barrel marked "H. E. Dimick, St. Louis." Total length 14 inches. Brass front sight, trigger guard, and strap. Historians believe that this was made for Dimick by the Manhattan Fire Arms Co. Plate 1, figure 2.

Griswold & Grier Percussion Revolver, caliber .36, 6-shot; 7.5-inch barrel, rifled with 6 grooves, right. Brass frame. Unmarked except for serial numbers. Known as Brass-Frame Confederate Colt to some collectors and dealers. Made near Macon, at Griswoldville, Georgia. Confederate newspapers called this a "Colt's Navy Repeater." Plate 1, figure 3.

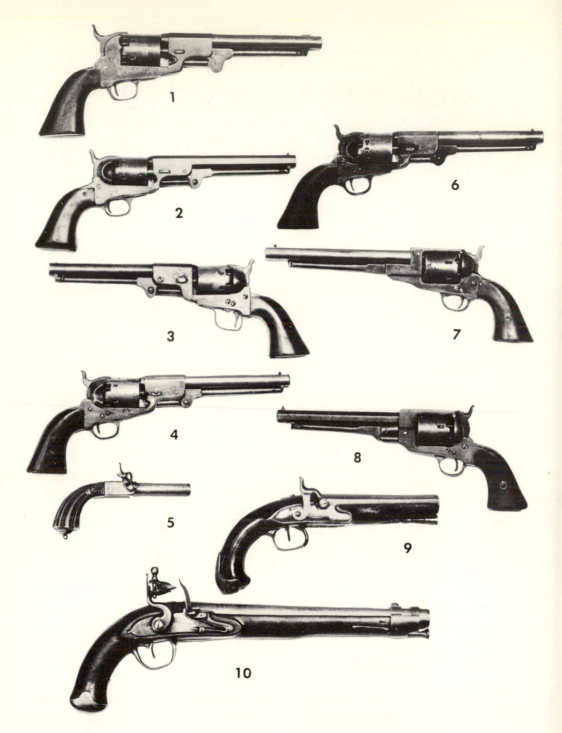

PLATE 1. Confederate Pistols and Revolvers.

1. Dance Brothers & Park Percussion Revolver.
2. Dimick-Colt Percussion Revolver.
3. Griswold & Grier Percussion Revolver.
4. Leech & Rigdon Percussion Revolver.
5. Radcliffe & Guignard Percussion Pocket Pistol.
6. Rigdon & Ansley Percussion Revolver.
7. Shawk & McLanahan Percussion Revolver.
8. Spiller & Burr Percussion Revolver.
9. Samuel Sutherland Percussion Pistol.
10. Virginia Manufactory Flintlock Pistol.

Leech & Rigdon Percussion Revolver, caliber .36, 6-shot; 7.5-inch rifled barrel marked "Leech & Rigdon, C.S.A." Brass front sight, trigger guard, and handle strap. Some specimens marked "Leech & Rigdon" without the C.S.A. The manufacturer made imitation Colt Navy revolvers. The factory was moved from Memphis, Tenn., to Columbus, Miss., and from there to Greensboro, Ga., and finally to Augusta, Ga., because of the approach of the United States Army in each case. Also see Rigdon & Ansley Revolver, below. Plate 1, figure 4.

Radcliffe & Guignard Percussion Pocket Pistol, caliber .44, single-shot, 3-inch, round, rifled barrel. Total length 7 inches. Engraved iron mountings. Folding trigger. An example of the type of pocket pistol sold in the Confederacy during the Civil War. Plate 1, figure 5.

Rigdon & Ansley Percussion Revolver, caliber .36, 6-shot; 7.5-inch rifled barrel marked on top "Augusta, Ga. C.S.A." There are 12 cylinder stops. Brass trigger guard, front sight, and handle strap. Serial numbers are on the cylinder, trigger guard frame, barrel lug, handle strap, and loading lever. Plate 1, figure 6.

Shawk & McLanahan Percussion Revolver, caliber .36, 6-shot; 8-inch round barrel. Brass frame. Back strap marked "Shawk & McLanahan, St. Louis, Carondelet, Mo." Manufactured about 1858–59 at Carondelet, St. Louis, Missouri. Most specimens have a serial number inside the trigger guard frame. The specimen illustrated is unmarked. Plate 1, figure 7.

Spiller & Burr Percussion Revolver, caliber .36, 6-shot; 7-inch octagon barrel marked "Spiller & Burr." Resembles a Whitney. The letters "C.S." followed by the serial number are usually found on various parts, such as the cylinder, the underside of the barrel, underside of the frame, the loading lever, and the grip strap. Plate 1, figure 8.

Samuel Sutherland Percussion Pistol, caliber .60, single-shot, 6.25-inch, octagon, brass barrel. Lock plate marked "Sutherland, Richmond." This was a French flintlock pistol converted to percussion by Sutherland during the Civil War. Plate 1, figure 9.

Virginia Manufactory Flintlock Pistol, caliber .69, 12.5-barrel. Total length 18.5 inches. Iron mountings. Lock plate of specimen illustrated is marked "Richmond 1807" in rear of hammer. See discussion of U. S. Secondary Martial Flintlock Pistols for a more complete description of this pistol. Plate 1, figure 10.

Pilgrims of the Plains. A drawing by A. R. Waud which is generally recognized by authorities on pictures of the Old West as one of the most accurate of all illustrations showing the animals, equipment and people of an early wagon train. LIBRARY OF CONGRESS

XII *Revolving Shoulder Arms and Related Weapons*

LIKE other arms makers whose popular fame rests largely on the hand guns bearing their names, Colt also manufactured shoulder arms. It was inevitable that he should apply his patented idea of the revolving cylinder to the rifle and carbine to make them multishot weapons, as well as making the more conventional single-shot long arms. It was also natural that other arms makers should follow his lead, apparently without infringing on his patent. But it's doubtful if Samuel Colt was aware, when he opened the Paterson factory, of the long bloodline behind the revolving shoulder weapons he was busily turning out for the army of the new Texas Republic and for the United States forces.

Almost two centuries before the wheels started to turn in the plant at the falls of the Passaic, a revolving matchlock with a manually operated cylinder had been made, probably in India, sometime between 1650 and 1700. The outstanding arms authority and historian Charles Winthrop Sawyer was one of the first to point out some of the venerable ancestors of this type of gun. Another weapon, made about the same time and probably in the American Colonies, is a revolving snaphance, quite similar to the flintlock. And a specimen well known to collectors is the revolving flintlock made under an English patent obtained in 1818 by the Boston gunsmith, Elisha Haydon Collier.

Specific information on the use of the Colt revolving shoulder arm as well as on its production is somewhat sketchy. We know that the Paterson models, especially one called the Model 1836, was bought in carbine and rifle form by the United States for martial use in 1837. Later, production of these continued in the Hartford factory, and during the Civil War about seven thousand Colt revolving long arms of all types were used by the troops. One of the famous units, the First and Second Regiments of U. S. Army Sharpshooters, often called Berdan's Brigade, or Berdan's Sharpshooters, was armed with the Colt Model 1855, caliber .56 rifles with the 31.312-inch barrels, and other outfits also carried these or similar weapons, which would bring them under the classification of U. S. martial shoulder arms in some cases, and almost all of them could qualify as U. S. secondary martial shoulder arms. In its short-barreled carbine form, the caliber .56 was sometimes carried by officers as personal side arms.

These guns were not popular with the troops for one reason or another, and were displaced by the issuance of the Sharps. In the official records and periodicals from 1836 onward, only scattered and vague references to the Colt revolving long arms appear, but it is extremely difficult to pinpoint these comments. Over twenty years of production of this type of weapon, there seems no doubt that it was in use in the West during frontier times, even though it is not usually associated with the dramatic highlights of that period.

PLATE 1

1. Collier Flintlock Revolving Shoulder Arm Mechanism.
2. Colt Revolving Shoulder Arm.
3. Colt Percussion Revolver.
4. Colt Percussion Revolver fitted to shoulder stock.
5. Revolving Matchlock Gun.
6. Revolving Snaphance, American, about 1650.
7. Flintlock Revolving Shoulder Arm, 1700-1725.
8. Flintlock Revolving Gun, American, made by Elisha Haydon Collier.

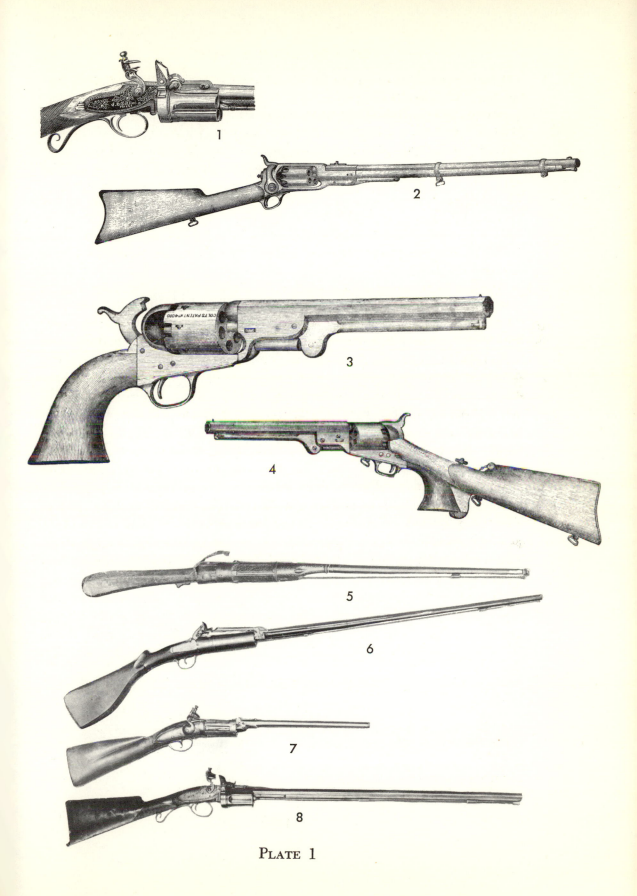

PLATE 1

Whether or not these guns were popular with the Civil War soldiers, the fact that they were in production over two decades shows that there was a reasonable demand for them. If they were bought by the government of Texas in 1836, it's a certainty that they were used after Texas joined the Union, and gravitated to the personal armament of early cattlemen and frontiersmen generally, at one time or another and in various places where guns were badly needed. The chances were that these revolving long arms were satisfactory enough during the percussion period, but other rifles were simply better adapted to the needs of the men who had to battle a hostile wilderness.

In the accompanying illustrations, Plate 1, figures 1 to 4 inclusive are from the author's collection, and are drawings appearing originally in an English publication of the early nineteenth century. Plate 1, figures 5 to 8, and Plate 2, figures 1 to 6 inclusive are from the collection of Charles Winthrop Sawyer.

Figure 1. The essential mechanism of a Collier flintlock revolving shoulder arm, based on the English 1818 patent of Elisha Haydon Collier. 2. Early drawing of a Colt revolving shoulder arm. 3. Drawing of the same period of a Colt percussion revolver. Figure 4. Same, fitted to a shoulder stock to be used as a shoulder weapon. These are shown for comparison with the revolving mechanism of the shoulder arms.

Figure 5. Revolving matchlock gun, manually operated cylinder, made 1650–1700, probably in India. 6. Revolving snaphance, similar to the flintlock, about 1650, probably made in the American colonies. 7. English flintlock shoulder arm, marked "John Daste, London"; 1700–1725. 8. Flintlock revolving gun made by John Haydon Collier.

Plate 2, figure 1. American flintlock shoulder arm, altered to percussion fire, about 1825. 2. Colt percussion shoulder arm, Model 1836, Paterson, bought for martial use by U.S.A. in 1837. Plate 2, figures 4 to 6 inclusive are Colt Paterson percussion revolving shoulder arms, with stocks shaped

PLATE 2

1. Flintlock Shoulder Arm altered to concussion.
2. Colt Percussion Shoulder Arm, Model 1836.
3. Colt Paterson Revolving Shoulder Arm.
4, 5, 6. Colt Paterson Revolving Shoulder Arms ornamented like Kentucky rifles.
7. C. B. Allen's, Cochran Patent Percussion Turret Rifle.
8. North & Skinner Revolving Percussion Rifle.

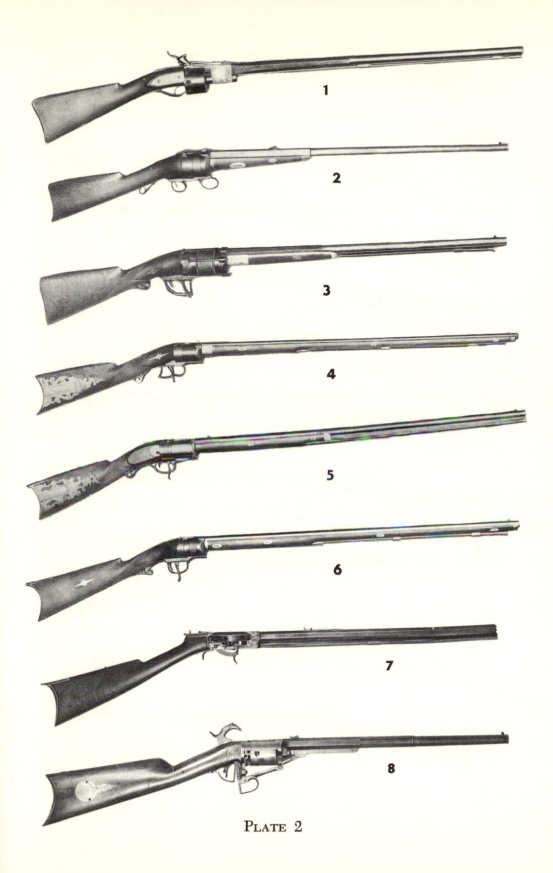

1

2

3

4

5

6

7

8

PLATE 2

PLATE 3

and decorated something on the order of the Kentucky rifle and bearing the superficial characteristics of that famous arm.

Figure 7 is the C. B. Allen, Cochran's Patent, Percussion Turret Rifle, caliber .44, 7-shot, with a 30.5-inch octagon barrel and a frame marked on the top strap "Cochran's Patent. C. B. Allen Springfield Mass." A similar rifle was made like the above but 8-shot, with a 31-inch octagon barrel and the barrel marked only "Cochran's Patent." The turret, which corresponds to the cylinder in the Colt revolving rifles, revolves horizontally.

Figure 8 is the North & Skinner revolving percussion rifle, marked "H. S. North Pat 1852," referring to the North & Skinner U. S. Patent No. 8982, dated June 1, 1852. A revolving percussion shotgun of similar design, based upon the same patent, is known as the "H. S. North Revolving Percussion Shotgun," caliber .60, with 27-inch barrel, marked "H. S. North, Middletown, Conn."

Plate 3 is a group of eleven Colt shoulder arms, the first nine of which are revolving shoulder arms. Figure 1. Carbine, caliber .44. 2. Shotgun, 30-gauge. 3. Rifle. 4 and 5: Carbines made with loading levers. 6. Model 1855 revolving-cylinder percussion rifle, caliber .36. 7. Model 1855 revolving-cylinder percussion shotgun, caliber .75. 8. Model 1855 revolving-cylinder percussion musket (smoothbore), U. S. Army Model, equipped with bayonet (not fixed in the illustration). 9. Model 1855 revolving-cylinder percussion rifle, caliber .56. 10. Colt Berdan Russian-type single-shot, breech-loading cartridge rifle. 11. Colt Berdan Russian-type, single-shot, breech-loading cartridge carbine. The phrase "Russian type" relates to the fact that Colt had a contract with Russia to supply that country with arms, which he did.

Although these revolving shoulder arms are not too familiar to the layman, they form an interesting and important step in the development of the multishot shoulder arm that was to culminate in the breech-loading repeating cartridge guns we know today. Because really accurate and definite information on this type of weapon is so meager, it is customarily treated separately in any discussion of American firearms. Collectors of revolving

PLATE 3. Colt Rifles and Carbines.

1. Paterson-Colt Revolving-Cylinder Percussion Carbine, caliber .44.
2. Paterson-Colt Revolving-Cylinder Percussion Shotgun, 30-gauge.
3. Paterson-Colt Revolving-Cylinder Percussion Rifle.
4. Paterson-Colt Revolving-Cylinder Percussion Carbine with Loading Lever.
5. Paterson-Colt Revolving-Cylinder Percussion Carbine with Loading Lever.
6. Colt Model 1855 Revolving-Cylinder Percussion Rifle, caliber .36.
7. Colt Model 1855 Revolving-Cylinder Percussion Shotgun, caliber .75.
8. Colt Model 1855 Revolving-Cylinder Percussion Musket, U. S. Army Model, with bayonet.
9. Colt Model 1855 Revolving-Cylinder Percussion Rifle, caliber .56.
10. Colt Berdan Russian Single-Shot, Breech-loading Cartridge Rifle.
11. Colt Berdan Russian Single-Shot, Breech-loading Cartridge Carbine.

shoulder arms, even those specializing in the Colt, usually include other makes; therefore it does not quite fit exclusively into the Colt story in a book of this rather general nature. And although many of these weapons could qualify as U. S. martial or secondary martial shoulder arms, we have no precise or accurate knowledge what models and types were actually used in military action.

The year 1865 is a milestone in United States history, and no less so in the history of firearms. That year marked the end of the percussion era, with its awkward and often dangerous process of muzzle loading. Specifically, the salvage of shoulder arms by the U. S. ordnance department from the field at Gettysburg did the trick. After the inspection of the unfired guns of both sides, the discovery that many of the men, in the excitement and stress of combat, had rammed home suicidal charges that would have inflicted as severe casualties on the riflemen as enemy bullets, must have been startling, to say the least. Perhaps the ordnance officers recalled the remarks of the British general, after inspecting a unit of green troops already committed to battle: "I don't know if they'll frighten the enemy or not, but, by God, they scare hell out of me!"

Of course, percussion arms continued to be used well into the cartridge period, just as breech-loading, metallic-cartridge weapons were in use by both sides during the Civil War, and had been introduced even before that. At first, many prospective purchasers of the new type of weapon were afraid that the metallic, self-contained cartridges would be liable to accidental discharge.

In demonstrating the safety of metallic cartridges, Mr. Wesson, of Smith & Wesson, once hurled one with all his might into a fireplace; unfortunately for the success of the experiment, the edge of the shell struck the sharp corner of an andiron, causing it to fire. "There," remarked Wesson, in a tone of complete satisfaction, "did you note the terrific blow it required?"

After the Civil War, the preponderant demand was for breech-loading, metallic-cartridge arms, and the gunmakers made every effort to supply the demand, sometimes by converting percussion guns, but more often by manufacturing the complete new type of firing system.

With the passing of the flintlock and later the percussion era, the first wilderness exploration phase of the Western frontier had also passed. Now we will see the West during the days of the thundering longhorn trails, the establishment of the vast, unfenced open range and the boom of the cattle industry, with its dramatic and violent end at the close of the 1880's.

The tide that swept the High Plains and some of the mountain states was from south to north and also west, from a cattle-glutted Texas to the lush untouched grazing land of Arizona and New Mexico, of Oklahoma, Colorado, Wyoming, the Dakotas, and Montana. There settled the big cattlemen and their cowpunchers, ready to protect their land with .44 and .45 caliber Colts, the .30–30 lever-action Winchester repeater and other makes of relatively modern arms.

At the same time through the northern ranges, another strong wave was pushing from the East, heralded by the black smoke spouting from diamond-stacked locomotives, and followed by legions of emigrant farmers, to take up homestead claims often on range used but not legally owned by cattlemen. The meeting of these two currents was frequently explosive and marked by bloodshed and the fire of the guns that we will describe and see in the following chapters.

Another important and dramatic part of Western settlement was the last desperate stand of the Plains Indians against the encroachments of white settlers and gold stampeders on their traditional hunting grounds and reserves, and against the broken promises of venal politicos, from Washington all the way down to the local Indian agents. We will find out about the arms and equipment used by the U. S. troops in their Indian campaigns, as well as the firearms used against them, in many cases ironically supplied to the hostiles by the government.

According to some Western historians, another weapon was even more important in winning the West than the carbines and revolvers of the troopers or the guns of the cattlemen and law officers. This was the heavy-calibered buffalo rifle that in a few short years exterminated millions of bison from the plains—and in so doing wiped out the larder of the Indians.

Were it not for these guns and other firearms, the stirring saga of the Western frontier might still be untold.

A Recent Robbery near Leadville, Colorado.—Searching a Commercial Traveler for Valuables. DENVER PUBLIC LIBRARY WESTERN COLLECTION

XIII *When the Colt Was King: The Immortal '72 Model Peacemaker, and Others*

Sam Bass was born in Indiana, which was his native home.
Before the age of seventeen, the boy began to roam.
He first came out to Texas, a cowboy for to be—
A better hearted fellow you scarce could hope to see.
                              —Ballad of Sam Bass

· · · · · ·

Samuel Bass
Born July 21st, 1851
Died July 21st, 1878
A brave man reposes in death here. Why was he not true?
                    —Epitaph in Round Rock Cemetery.

BETWEEN the first line of the song quoted above and the last, forever unanswered question lies a saga of gunplay and violence so typical of the cattle country of the 1870's and 1880's that it could have been the history of a thousand other reckless youngsters.

Sam Bass, although a good deal more than just another "poor cowboy who knew he done wrong," wasn't greatly different from the average cowpuncher on the north Texas ranges, except for his inborn streak of wildness. Unlike Billy the Kid and Jesse James—contemporaries with whom he was to share the apocryphal reputation of a Western Robin Hood—young Bass was no hate-driven, dedicated killer. Nor was he any great shakes as a fancy pistol artist. There were probably dozens of men who used Colt six-shooters on both sides of the law more dangerous and far more deadly in performance. Among them might be named Wild Bill Hickok, Wyatt Earp, Clay Allison, and—perhaps the most lethal gentleman of them all—Ben Thompson.

Like the above-mentioned men, Bass was to depend on a Colt six-shooter for both his livelihood and his life. The reason why Sam Bass's exploits are relevant here is that he was not a "special" type; he was a pretty good working cowhand, but one who would rather race good horses than nurse longhorns. That he could do it and still stay within the law is probably a tribute to his virtuosity. But there came the time, when he awoke in Deadwood with a splitting head and a natural desire to help a friend, that sent him on the trail where a man lives by the gun and usually dies by it. Sam Bass did both.

Oddly enough, in each instance, the gun was probably a Colt revolver, Frontier model, caliber .45, center fire.

The "cowboy for to be" landed in Denton County, Texas, sometime in the late '60's, a likable lad not yet twenty, with a go-to-hell gleam in his eye; a youngster who favored a good horse, plenty of excitement, and not too much else. According to the story, he got his first job as cowboy for Sheriff Everhart (Dad, Egan, sheriff of Denton County, according to some versions); he acquired—honestly—a fast little sorrel, famous in the ballad as "the Denton mare," which successfully backed Sam's judgment in one cowtown race after another. Given the choice of continuing as a twenty-dollar-a-month cowhand or racing, naturally Sam Bass did what almost anyone else would do. He quit. He liked horses, and they liked him enough to bring him fast and easy money. From northeast Texas he drifted down to San Antonio, then to Uvalde County and other places, wherever there was a county-fair track. . . .

> He fairly coined money and spent it frank and free
> He drank the best of whiskey wherever he might be. . . .

[**210**]

Possibly it was a time when feathers instead of chicken headed Sam's menu; possibly his winnings were too consistent for his popularity. At any rate, one day in San Antonio, he signed on as point rider with a cattleman named Joel Collins, who was heading a herd that he'd bought on credit up to Deadwood, South Dakota. In the new gold diggin's, beef helped a man swing a pick and hoist a shovel. They'd pay in dust and nuggets for Texas beef.

From San Antonio, Texas, to the Black Hills of South Dakota was a long and rugged thousand miles of cattle trail, and by the time Collins and his crew reached Deadwood, they had built up a real thirst to settle the trail dust they'd been eating and breathing for the past months.

Deadwood, a wide-open gold camp in 1877, was just the town to take care of weary trail hands. Here, only a year before, Wild Bill Hickok had succumbed to the marksmanship of one Jack McCall, who cautiously had shot the marshal in the back. Here, Collins and Sam Bass might have stared at a swaggering female arrayed in boots, pants, flannel shirt and gun belt, who barged into bars stating in her sea-lion roar that Calamity Jane was by God settin' 'em up for the house! Honkytonks, gambling halls, saloons and brothels abounded; there was money to throw at the birds, and six-shooters were worn openly on the hip.

Collins sold the herd, paid off the boys; then, laden with the cattle money, he joined his crew in painting the town—a procedure that had proved perilous, if not fatal, to many a trail boss before him. . . .

The sun was shining when the drover awoke, but it wasn't shining for Joel Collins. He was engulfed in the dismal realization that last night it had taken almost all the herd money to try to fill inside straights. Now his reputation back in Texas as a fine rancher and an honest man was as empty as his pockets. Panicked and desperate, without credit, he knew he'd be disgraced and likely jailed if he faced his creditors empty-handed. He'd betrayed his friends, and in a country where hundreds of thousands of dollars changed hands on no more than a man's given word, Collins' misstep was about the blackest crime in the book. What to do?

This was gold country, and a little "road mining"—the current euphemism for stage-robbing—he thought, might restore his fortunes and his face. Sam Bass, never one to run out on a friend or to be bothered by moral scruple, would back his old boss to the last damned cap. So would another cowboy. But though they stopped several stages, they only succeeded in accidentally killing the driver of one. Badly planned and amateurishly executed, the operation not only had proved unprofitable, but now they'd soon be sought as murderers. Better make themselves hard to find around Deadwood.

Ogallala, on the South Platte, was a wild, end-of-trail town and in that seething throng of Texas cowboys their arrival was unnoticed. Collins and

Bass took stock—and it is more than probable, in the light of his later career, that Sam Bass's voice now became more predominant in making plans. They determined to profit by their past blunders. This time, they'd pick a good target, line it in their sights, and make a killing. If they planned it right, and luck was on their side, they could ride back to Texas with heads high and gold chinking in their pockets.

The target was found. In a couple of nights, on April 18, the UP Express, said to be carrying a heavy gold shipment, was due to stop for water and dispatches at Big Springs, about twenty miles southwest on the South Platte, and close to the Colorado line. That was a good strategic position. To do the job right, they recruited three more from among . . .

His chums they was all cowboys, rough and hard as they could be. . . .

who probably, as the saying went, "had seen the elephant," and were trustworthy, seasoned hands at extralegal activities. They rode out at dark studying the ground and perfecting their plans.

The afternoon of the big night, they stopped at Sam Leach's Mercantile, purchased supplies, a pair of boots and other things. Collins bought a couple of yards of calico from a bolt Leach had on display. Then they casually rode through the dusk down toward Big Springs.

In a hollow near the water tank they dismounted, picketed their horses and checked their armament. As they adjusted the calico masks, someone swore: "Damn threads tickle my chin." Collins moved, his knife out, and trimmed the cloth. As the distant rumble grew louder and the long, lonesome-sounding whistle hooted, they crawled up the grade toward the rails. They crouched there, waiting, their palms clammy on their pistol grips.

The train left the station and chugged slowly toward the tank, its headlight beam stabbing the blackness and silvering the rails. Collins had already cut the telegraph wires, and as the locomotive and tender ground to a stop beneath the tank's nozzle, two of the bandits clambered up into the cab. Under the gun, the engine crew drew the fires. Collins and another swung up to the patform and made their way into the express car, getting the messenger busy with the safe. The third pair, having secured the train crew, started working their way through the passengers, shaking them down for arms and cash.

In the express car Collins and his pardner were having a bad time. The safe was equipped with a time lock, which the messenger was unable to open. It seemed that the ex-trail driver and his bunch were still pursued by the hoodoo luck that had fastened onto them in Deadwood. Apparently, all these fine plans would net only what the passengers contributed. About to jump down from the car, Collins spied four small boxes in a shadowed corner. One of the tops was loose, and Collins' foot shoved it aside. The glint of newly minted twenty-dollar gold pieces struck his eyes. He lost no time. . . .

By dawn, well satisfied with their night's labors, the six were snoring peacefully in their beds, back in Ogallala.

That morning, Collins, Bass & Company, according to plan, played it cagey, hiding their elation behind stolid poker faces. Their confidence increased as they heard the story of the robbery recounted in their accustomed saloons. This was startling news, indeed. Men could be murdered or killed in gunfights, but it was seldom that a bunch of nervy gents calmly looted the UP Express of $100,000 in gold, without a shot being fired. Not a trace of the bunch who did it, either. A smart, fast job; Jesse James himself couldn't have done it no slicker. . . . So ran the comments, laudatory rather than otherwise.

Collins and his bunch had reason to strut. Of course, the gold, now cleverly stashed away, was $60,000 rather than $100,000. Passengers had kicked in with another five thousand. Collins, and Bass as well, though tough enough, were not killers—the thought of the Deadwood stage driver who had been killed by an accidental discharge of one of their guns still might have galled them—and the fact that they had pulled this without having to shoot anyone somehow made it seem better.

Collins wondered: Now, at last, he could go back and face his Texas friends, pay them off, and resume his former life as a solid, respected cowman, with the additional satisfaction of a nice little stake in the bank. Or, he could ride his luck for a while. If it held like this, he'd be a rich man before he knew it. Collins the Cattle King . . . that had a real sound to it!

It's doubtful if Sam Bass did much wondering. Here was a fine way to get big money—they had agreed on an even split; $10,000 plus was a good stake for any man, and without any sweat. There were plenty of thrills in this occupation, too. He could live high, wide and handsome, as he used to when he was racing, back in Texas. If he did anything, he'd raise blooded horses. He had a lifelong passion for fine horseflesh, just as other men had for gambling, whisky, or women. Not that there was anything wrong with those. But with Sam Bass, horses came first. . . .

By noon, most of the town was out at the hollow near the water tank. It would have been strange if the six robbers had not joined the crowd. Sam Leach, the storekeeper, was certainly there, leaning down to squint at the hoof tracks. While some of the boys acted out their version of the holdup, others were gesticulating, arguing, and making wide guesses, all warmed by the reflected excitement of this astounding crime.

Unlike many others, Sam Leach didn't wave his arms and try to outshout the amateur detectives. He was still studying the ground, and at one point he leaned down for a closer look. When he strtaightened up, he had a tiny slip of calico in his pocket. He recognized it at once, just as he remembered who had bought it. Perhaps he passed a few words with Collins and some of his pardners, then said something about having to get back to tend store. He climbed into his rig and headed up the road; a quiet, methodical man, burdened now with a fateful secret.

Back in Ogallala, he paused to read a poster, the ink still damp, which offered $10,000 reward for the capture of the robbers and return of the loot. He reopened his store, fingering the bit of cloth that was to bring violent death to three men and make hunted fugitives of three more.

According to plan, Collins and the others hung around town for a couple of days. The robbery and the reward were still big news, and the men joined in the barroom discussion, watched their drinking, and finally bought necessary supplies—at Leach's store, of course—for their return trip to Texas. Presently they headed back, six trail-seasoned cowboys with three led pack horses, appearing no tougher than the average, riding easy toward their home range. The dust of their going hid a swarm of sheriffs, special UP and Wells Fargo agents and some U. S. marshals, all bird-dogging for a scent they couldn't find.

Behind them, too, they left Sam Leach—but not far enough behind. . . .

Some hours after his former customers had started south, Leach pulled down his shutters, locked his store, and saddled his horse. Possibly he left a laconic note: "Gone fishin. Back next week, maybe." At any rate, he took the trail of the six men and stuck to it, always keeping out of sight during the day, but crawling through brush and rock at night to listen and watch the bandits about their campfire. After three or four days of cautious riding, and nights of Injuning around their camp, Leach's risky vigil paid off. He held his breath as he watched Collins, within a few yards of where Leach hid, give $10,000 in twenty-dollar gold pieces to each man. He heard them make their plans to split up: Collins and another would head for San Antonio; two more would start for Mexico, Missouri; and Bass and another would aim for Denton.

That was all Sam Leach wanted to know. He lost no time making tracks for the nearest town that had a telegraph and an alert lawman. Before long, the wires stretching south and east were humming with important news.

A day or so later, in Kansas, Collins and his partner led their pack horse into Buffalo Station and were at once confronted by a Wanted poster describing themselves, as well as Bass and his saddle mate.

If Joel Collins had ever pondered whether to return to the fold of respectability or to continue to take his chances along the owlhoot trail, that decision was abruptly yanked from his hands. He knew it now, and together the two bandits wheeled their horses, dug in their spurs, and with the led horse following, lit out down the road. They were too late, however, for a townsman had recognized them and warned a detachment of U. S. cavalry camped on the edge of town. Overtaken and questioned by the troopers, Collins tried to laugh it off. It was useless, and at Collins' signal both men went for their guns. For once, the horse soldiers didn't wait to do it by the book. They got in their shots first and when the smoke cleared, two men who had robbed their last train lay dead in the dust, while the pack horse stood up the road a piece, sides heaving from its run under the weight of more than $20,000 in gold.

Of the two bandits who had started for Missouri, one reached his home near Mexico where he was killed by a posse; the other escaped and faded from history.

Meanwhile, Sam Bass's trail was hot and growing hotter. At the Texas state line, the two fugitives managed to evade a delegation of Rangers who had prepared a suitable welcome for them. Sam's companion decided that the climate of South America would suit his complexion better than that of Texas and made tracks for Galveston. Sam, however, elected to stay on . . .

> And in the town of Denton he did his money share.
> The lad he was so reckless, three robberies did he do,
> The passenger and express car and U.S. mail car, too.

But not single-handed. As leader of the now famous Big Springs train robbery—smart, dead-game, and lucky—he had no trouble in recruiting a few kindred wild spirits; tough hands who'd ride out their string to the bitter end. Possibly visions of gold pieces danced in their heads as they hit the Texas Pacific Railroad, according to legend, at Eagle Ford. They faded fast, then later held up another train at Mesquite Junction. But no such jackpot as the UP ever came their way.

According to James Gillett, of the Frontier Battalion, Texas Rangers, probably a hundred officers were constantly on the lookout for Bass, yet he rode boldly into Dallas and Fort Worth night after night for guarded relaxation. At length, however, the campaign of attrition began to tell. Sam's gang was partly broken up and he had to move his operations south, in the vicinity of Austin. Already he had become a figure of legend, a sort of minor giant in the popular mind, whom it was impossible to picture without a Colt .45 handy at his hip or smoking in his fist.

Because it's an important part of the Colt story, let's see how such an image—the man, the horse, and inevitably the gun—takes root and grows in people's imagination.

Sam Bass, years before he trailed up to Deadwood, had been well known throughout Texas. The chances were, too, that he was pretty well liked; in a horse country, the owner of an animal like the Denton mare was likely to be looked upon with admiration and a little envy. He was probably a good gambler, and cowmen were by nature gamblers; they had to be in the days before stock-raising became almost a technological science. He was one with thousands of other cowpunchers; perhaps a little wilder, but when his luck was rolling high, a soft touch for any man faced with the grim necessity of having to sell his gun or saddle, or in need of medicine money for an ailing family. He was probably "just as common as you or me"; as comfortable as an old boot, and without a mean bone in his body.

The Big Springs holdup marked a new high in the train-robbing business. To date, no other looted train had yielded such a large sum of money. Moreover, it was all in gold—not in prosaic paper currency. There's something about boxes overflowing with fresh-minted double eagles that keeps haunting a man's mind like the memories of good times that can never come again. . . .

So the picture of Sam Bass abruptly changed. Only yesterday, or a couple of years ago, he was playing the county-fair circuit like a lot of other fellows, or occasionally punching cattle. Aside from owning some pretty fast horses, there wasn't anything outstanding about him. But now he was shooting up to near ten foot tall, and maybe he got into his pants both legs at a time instead of the way you and I do it. Even so, Sam Bass was still remembered as the good-hearted stranger who'd buy you drinks if you were dry and busted, and likely bail you out of the hoosegow next morning.

In cowtown saloons, around the supper fires on roundup or in bunkhouses, men shook their heads and grinned. Who'd have guessed that behind that easy grin were the brains and the rawhide toughness to make his desperate gun gamble, then to ride away, winner on all counts! If he was lucky, he was also smart and plenty brave; and those big, far-off companies could well afford to lost a little cash. It wasn't like he'd taken the money from *people!*

During the '70's, in certain parts of the cattle country, ranchers and cowboys had no love for the railroads that cut across their ranges, expropriating —at a price—whole sections of the land they'd been using, often without legal title. Railroads—like the express companies—in the minds of many frontier people were "soulless corporations" running rough-shod over the average rancher, and fair game for anyone who could get a claim against them. They were owned by smart Wall Street dudes with countless millions behind them, and if any bunch of nervy men could stick up a train and get away with a good haul, more power to them! The inconsistency that a large part of the cattle industry was dependent on the railroads for its prosperity was, in many instances, conveniently overlooked. Of course a really serious matter, such as rustling horses and cattle, or even sticking up a cowtown bank, called for harsh, summary settlement, via Colts, Winchesters, or a lariat and a cottonwood limb.

[216]

To many of those who remembered him "back when," Sam Bass had done a daring thing successfully; a piece of business to excite at least tacit admiration. Now, loaded with gold pieces, he was further engaged in a life-or-death game against not only local law officers but the formidable Texas Rangers—and outsmarting them all at every turn! The underdog, the lone running target before a manhunting pack, the fugitive who is tough and dangerous but not snake-mean, by his own dramatic and precarious situation exerts a strong bid for popular sympathy.

The man on the dodge is in a poor bargaining position to obtain the things he most needs: a fresh horse, ammunition, food, and a safe place to hole up when the chase gets too hot or when he's wounded. He also needs trustworthy, close-mouthed friends, and a lot of luck.

Like many a fugitive from the law, both before and since, Sam Bass spread his gold as needed: twenty dollars tossed down for a tin of biscuits or a dozen eggs; three double eagles to buy a night's lodging from a worried ranch widow, with Bass riding herd on his men to keep them quiet and to allay the woman's fears. Perhaps he took time out to chop needed firewood for some invalid, or dropped a gold piece into the cradle of a hard-luck rancher's ailing baby. . . .

He was famous—or infamous—and feared, just as anyone would be who led such a desperate, kill-or-get-killed existence. A hunted man whose life span was measured from moment to moment, he had, knowingly or not, committed himself irrevocably to a way of violence, bloodshed and deadly gunfire. That such a fearsome figure would pause to do some little act of human kindness fired popular imagination, as it has for centuries. Outlaw, gunman and bandit he might be, still he exemplified the important Pioneer virtues—at least in legend—of physical courage and daring, open-handed generosity, and unswerving loyalty to his friends. And his end did nothing to detract from the growing hero image.

One of his gang betrayed to the Rangers his plan to rob the bank at Round Rock. Into the town, filled with waiting deputies and Rangers, rode the gang, although earlier than expected. Two officers were killed as they tried to arrest the bandits in a store. That opened the ball.

Four Rangers joined in the shoot-out. One of the gang was killed as they made for their horses. Ranger Dick Ware sent a .45 slug into Bass's kidney. Frank Jackson, youngest member of the crew, helped Bass upon his horse with his left hand while firing his revolver with his right. In a hail of lead, Jackson covered his chief's back as they galloped out of town.

Deep in a thicket, they drew up. Jackson dismounted and helped Bass to the ground. Bass told the boy that he was done for; to get out while he could. It took some argument before the kid reluctantly left him. Sam Bass was picked up by the pursuing posse and brought back to Round Rock. He died there three days later.

According to the story, young Jackson hid in the swamps for a while, then vanished. For the next fifty years, rumors located Jackson in various parts of the world, but none was ever verified. Jim Murphy, Judas of the gang, committed suicide while in prison.

For several reasons, Sam Bass lingered in the popular mind. Tales of his buried treasure—those yellow, chinking twenty-dollar gold pieces—became current. Every cave and thicket from the Llano River north to the Red were supposed to have been his hiding places. Around the turn of the century, faded maps began to appear, pinpointing for the gullible various caches, supposedly holding as much as two hundred thousand. And in gold, of course. As late as 1928, within the city limits of Dallas, nocturnal excavations failed to uncover any of the bandit's fabled loot. Such romantic myths die hard.

Not long after his death, personal souvenirs and relics said to have belonged to Sam Bass began to sprout like willow shoots in the spring throughout northern and central Texas. Wayne Gard, in his biography of Sam Bass, says, "If all the 'authentic' Bass guns could be gathered in one place, they would stock an arsenal."

And then there's the song. Who first sang it or made it up, no one knows. Like most genuine folk ballads, it just grew, with variations and new verses added according to the ability and preference of the singer. It was a song that used to be sung on the cattle trails, around chuck-wagon fires, or hummed by the night guards as they jogged their circle around the drowsing longhorn herd. It's a romantic song about a Texas cowpuncher whose streak of recklessness would always remind one of the outfit of some half-forgotten cowboy acquaintance; and it's a song in which that all-but-indispensable tool of frontier survival—the .45 revolver—played an active and dramatic part.

The gallery of frontier gun-fighters who blasted their lasting place in Western history is a large one. Just to begin to list those who became famous through their professional use of the six-shooter, both for and against the law—and sometimes playing it on both sides!—is beyond the scope of this book. To try to compare their lethal skills, attributes and motivations would not only fill several volumes with discussion of a largely academic nature, but would also take us far off our present range. The reader of frontier history of this period probably has his own favorite among the great gun-toters, and it would idle to dispute it.

The challenge of the rugged, shifting frontier border was answered by those with iron in their souls as well as in their holsters. It took a man strong in determination and sinew to work for years, from before dawn well into deep dark, in order to build up a small cattle outfit so that he could make a living. There was always risk and he carried the threat of disaster on one shoulder to balance his hopeful plans on the other. That is, if he was honest. Many a substantial cowman, however, was supposed to have got his start with a careless loop and a running iron, especially during the years just following the Civil War, when a cowman's poverty, instead of his wealth, was in direct proportion to the number of cattle bearing his brand. A man could be cow-poor, with perhaps five thousand head of cattle.

These men, and the early homesteaders, and those who built the settlements to furnish them with supplies, were for the most part fighting pioneers. They had to be, for they left organized law behind them as they pushed into new and untamed land. That land, of course, offered a different kind of challenge to others fleeing from the law; all varieties of riffraff, scoundrels, thieves and murderers sifted in. At one time, the letters "GTT" chalked on the door of a vacated cabin or farmhouse meant "Gone to Texas," a mighty wide scope of country, where a man in trouble with the law could conveniently lose himself, or change his identity. One popular music hall song of the early days contained the line, "Oh, what was your name in the States?"—a too-personal inquiry which, if asked seriously, provoked a surly answer backed by a six-shooter. During the post-Civil War years, the Wanted book of the Texas Rangers contained a list of more than three thousand names of fugitives from the law.

The settlers, the townsmen and the ranchers wanted and needed established law and order. Running a herd of longhorns, or proving up on 160 acres of homestead land is tough enough, without having to keep constantly on the alert for marauding bands of Comanche, Kiowa, Apache, Blackfeet or Sioux. In certain localities where the hostiles were not active, organized bands of rustlers continued to harass the ranchers; in frontier towns and cities, badmen swaggered along the boardwalks, invoking the law of Judge Colt to settle their grudges or to force merchants and businessmen to pay them tribute. In the gold-mining country, especially, stage stick-ups furnished some gun-hung ruffians with a temporary source of income, as later they would prey upon the railroads, and small-town banks contributed their gold to heavily armed, masked horsemen.

In order to make this new country habitable for men with families, to establish schools and churches and to realize the economic possibilities of its agricultural wealth and other resources, wholesale lawlessness had to be curbed. It took strong men; men characterized by instant decision, fearlessness, swift action and integrity to do the job. Most of the territorial and state rangers were such men; less often were the county sheriffs and town or city marshals.

Not infrequently the latter were pretty tough characters themselves, whose back trail might have been shadowed but whose gun-fighting prowess was judged formidable enough to stand as a bastion between a town's peaceful citizens and newly arrived troublemakers. Of such were the deadly Ben Thompson, Wild Bill Hickok, King Fisher, possibly Doc Holliday through his close association in Tombstone with the Earps, and—at the end of his life—Tom Horn, as a Wyoming cattle detective.

This idea, one version of the "if you can't lick 'em, j'ine 'em" tactic, was better in theory than in practice, for eventually a man with a killer's innate disposition and an unbridled temper would forget his responsibility to the public weal and start to blaze away with his Colts for purely personal reasons—and sometimes for personal gain.

There were other gun-wise men, however, who were good and solid citizens; willing and able to risk their lives in the fight against frontier crime. Men of high purpose, courageous and responsible, the ranks of those who upheld the badges of local law included men like John Slaughter and Billy Breakenridge, of Cochise County, whose small statures belied their determination and daring; "Bear River" Tom Smith of Abilene, whose right fist proved better than the guns of lesser men; Bucky O'Neill, of Arizona; U. S. Marshal Bill Tilghman, of Oklahoma, and a host of others who used the '72 Colt to help tame their parts of the frontier.

Here, chosen more or less at random, are sketches of a few of the men who, one way or another, wrote their names in the flame of Colt six-shooters across the pages of frontier history.

James B. Gillett, sergeant in the Frontier Battalion, Texas Rangers, and subsequently marshal of El Paso during its wild days. Gentle of speech, mild of manner, he was dynamite when action was called for. As a Ranger on the trail of a killer, he was apt to throw the rule book into the river, as he did after a Mexican had murdered in cold blood the editor of the Socorro, New Mexico, *Sun*. The killer fled to Texas, thence to Zaragoza, Mexico. Gillett knew there was no use entangling himself in the red tape of extradition, and he also realized that a request to his CO to make a little pasear across the Rio would probably be denied, and he'd be in the uncomfortable spot of having to disobey an official order. With another Ranger, he rode into the small town and spotted the murderer clerking in a store. Gillett backed him out at gunpoint, mounted him behind his companion, and in broad daylight made it back across the Rio, while behind them pounded every able-bodied man in town, armed with rifles and pistols, and shooting for keeps.

Gillett got a dressing-down from his captain, and as disciplinary action was sent to Socorro as the prisoner's escort, where the man was delivered and later taken from jail and hanged by a mob.

After six years of battling Indians and outlaws with the Rangers, and a brief but effective tour as head law-enforcement officer in the gunsmoke climate of El Paso, Gillett retired his caliber .44-40 Frontier Colt, and became a cattleman.

Ben Thompson, raised in Austin, was a reckless, undisciplined youngster who seemed to need the sauce of mortal danger to make life palatable. He fought Comanches before the Civil War, and enlisted in a Texas outfit after having fatally shot an acquaintance over a young woman. He was in camp barely a week before he quarreled with his sergeant and killed him in a pistol duel. He escaped the guardhouse and joined another regiment, but the monotony of military life was not for Ben. He wandered down to Laredo, where he got into a fight with a roomful of local men, and got out leaving three corpses behind him.

After the downfall of the Confederacy, he went to Mexico, fought with the forces of Maximilian, but made his escape after the capture of the emperor with his remnants of troops in 1867. Thereafter he became a professional gambler along the cattle-trail towns; running the famous Bull's Head saloon in Abilene, then moving on to Ellsworth as that town became the focal center of the cattle-trail trade. Its stable population took a dim view of the wild Texas cowboys who drove up the great herds for shipment, and Ben Thompson never forgot that he was a Texan. With his brother Bill, he answered some drunken insults about Texas and Texans with hot lead, during which altercation the sheriff was accidentally killed. While Bill galloped out of town, Ben and other Texans lined themselves across the road, guns out, to prevent pursuit.

In search of pastures new, Ben hit the gold-camp circuit where the pickin's were rich for a high-rolling gambling man, and after a few successful years returned to his family in Austin and to the home-town saloons. Lately, when in liquor, he was apt to become unmanageable and explosively playful with his Colt .45. Barred from the Senate Saloon after a display of destructive target practice, he served notice on the owner that he intended to drop in and drink what and as he wished, naming day and hour for his return engagement. A shotgun and rifle reception was arranged, and Ben, with foolhardy recklessness, made a bull's-eye of himself for No. 1 buck and .30-30 slugs. He then went to work with his hand gun, killing both the owner and the bartender, and walked, unharmed, to the police station where he gave himself up. His arrest, speedy trial and fast acquittal followed.

As a straight-shooter both with cards and Colts—he always paid for the property damage he inflicted and contributed generously toward the funeral expenses of his victims—he was fast becoming an outstanding citizen. Since no law-enforcement officer in his right mind would ever remonstrate with Ben when he was in a shootin' mood, he seemed a natural to run for city marshal. Elected, he proved a remarkably good and efficient head peace officer, he ran the town "like it was his own," and there was remarkably little crime during his administration. Nobody wanted to tangle with Ben Thompson.

On a holiday visit to San Antonio, he dropped into the Vaudeville, a saloon, gambling house and entertainment resort run by local politicians, and a tough place. After a few drinks Ben bucked the tiger, lost heavily and claimed the deal had been crooked. He refused to pay his losses, and backed out with his gun covering the enraged but helpless gamblers.

After his election, he made a return visit to the dive. "Where's the shotgun brigade?" Ben wanted to know, looking around for his enemies. At last he sighted the manager on a balcony, scattergun in hand. "What do you think you're doing with that gun?" Ben roared.

"I'm here to kill you," announced the saloonman, foolishly. Ben fired and the Vaudeville Saloon was out one manager.

Ben gave himself up and was tried for murder in San Antonio. While in jail, he resigned from his Austin job. Acquitted, he returned to Austin to find himself regarded as a public hero. Again he started around the gambling circuit in the Texas towns and the places along the Mississippi. Wherever the stakes were high and cards were hot, there would be Ben Thompson, duded out in silk hat, frock coat, with an expensive cheroot beneath his opulent mustache, dealing 'em out.

Patching up a quarrel with another gunman and outlaw—famous as the man who put up the sign on a public highway—"This is King Fisher's road. Take the other."—the two gunslingers journeyed to San Antonio to cement their friendship in good whisky. Of course, the Vaudeville drew them; Ben expansively claimed he wanted to bury the hatchet with the owners, good friends of the late manager, and who carried figurative notches on their own guns, as well. It was a happy little gathering until, it is claimed, Ben recalled the perfidy of the defunct manager and became abusive. The two owners moved back from Fisher and the well-lubricated Thompson. A volley of shots crashed from a curtained box toward the bar below, and Ben Thompson died without a chance to draw his gun.

Tombstone, Arizona, during its wild days of the early '80's, offered a colorful example of almost every phase of frontier life—and sudden, smoky death. For here was a big silver-strike town; the shudder and thump of the stamping mills furnished obbligato to the day-and-night crash of cowboys' six-shooters, the pound of honkytonk pianos, the shuffle of dancing feet, and the thud of hoofbeats pounding in and out of town.

It was fine country for cattle-raising, and for lawlessness. Nearby were the Dragoons, the Huachucas, the Mule Mountains; deep canyons, and twisting arroyos, peaks and rugged terrain stretched toward the border, making fine spots for rustlers and other outlaws. Here, too, the famous Skeleton Canyon Massacre took place, when some tough hands from the Tombstone country hijacked a Mexican mule train of silver, killed off all the drivers, and disappeared with the loot, said to be still buried in that up-and-down country. And it was ideal for tough outfits to make swift nocturnal raids into Mexico and return with wet cattle to be rebranded and sold—until a bloody reprisal occurred and a bunch of cowboys were wiped out by pursuing Mexicans and the stolen longhorns driven back by their former owners.

There was money and wealth in Tombstone, in Galeyville and Charleston. Silver and gold ingots and bars rolled out on guarded stages and wagons for shipment to the refineries. From running wet cattle, the wild element found profit in sticking up stages. Quarrels, personal jealousies, local power politics, brought on feuds. Men were waylaid, murdered.

Historians estimate that there were some three hundred part-time small ranchers and cowhands scattered in the rough country between Tombstone and the border. From this rugged and remote natural stronghold, they ran wet cattle in from Mexico, "stood up" gold-laden stagecoaches, knocked off mine payrolls, quarreled, murdered, shot up town saloons, and terrorized those whom they could, which meant almost all peaceably inclined citizens. This leather-chapped, loose-knit army operated under the leadership of two renegade families who had proved tougher than any of their cohorts. Old Man Clanton of the San Pedro Valley had been run out of California by the Vigilantes in his younger days and, with his three wild, hard-shooting sons, continued his lawless ways, no longer troubled by the threat of any miners' hang-rope committee. With the Clantons, the two McLowerie brothers, equally deadly, held forth from their headquarters in Sulphur Springs Valley. Between them, this killers' empire grew and prospered.

It is doubtful that it would have lasted as long as it did, had it not been for the county and territorial political situation, not so surprisingly similar to the basic pattern of modern municipal corruption which periodically makes the headlines. County offices, and especially that of sheriff, were ripe political plums, and although there has been no record of an official retiring to enjoy his loot in the fleshpots of European capitals, the job could be made easy and productive of a comfortable living. The Clanton-McLowerie country was good for about three hundred votes—enough to wield heavy influence in any election. All they asked was to be let alone, a not unreasonable demand so long as they confined their horse and cattle raids to Mexico, and were not too open and bold in their stagecoach holdups, and didn't use prominent and well-liked citizens as targets for their guns. It was a pleasant regime of live and let live for all concerned. And certainly Johnny Behan, the stout, well-liked sheriff of Cochise County, wasn't one to mess up the status quo. A man could easily get himself shot full of holes by such a damfool procedure.

If the vote-conscious sheriff lacked the drive and desire to ramrod his bailiwick, he had a deputy who was later to show that he had what it took. This was William Breakenridge, a nervy, pint-sized youngster with a cool head and a fast gun; a relative newcomer to Tombstone. Thinking, perhaps, to have some fun with his new assistant, Behan allowed that if Billy expected to get paid, he'd better get out and rustle up some taxes. Galeyville—favorite hangout of some of the toughest Clanton-McLowerie crew, including such formidable gunsmoke gladiators as Curly Bill Brocius, the cryptic and deadly John Ringo, Pony Deal, Zwing Hunt and a dozen others —the sheriff suggested as a good starting point.

The deputy was fully aware that no tax collector had ever won a popularity contest, and had heard that it was always open season on any stranger who interfered with this hard-bitten bunch. Coolly, Breakenridge said he guessed he'd give it a whirl, and rode to Galeyville, where he entered the saloon favored by the gang. Curly Bill and some of his pals were drinking at the bar.

Curly Bill Brocius was built like a grizzly and was proud of his muscles as well as of his gun-slinging ability. Alone and bare-handed he had made a shambles of several barrooms, smashing furniture and fixtures, and finally upending the bar amid the blood and broken bottles covering the floor. He was proud of his ferocity in a free-for-all fight when he supplemented his bludgeoning fists by kicking, butting, gouging and biting. His forte, however, was in the enormous strength of his arms and torso, and he had boasted of the men he had crushed to death by slowly tightening that relentless embrace. He was a bully, but one who could back up his brags, and was noted for his unpredictable disposition, especially with a load of whisky under his belt. A good man to ride a wide circle around, was this renegade chief.

Billy Breakenridge, like most frontier lawmen, was a mighty hard man to scare, He had courage, plus—a quality noted by Captain Bill McDonald of the Texas Rangers, who said, "No man in the wrong can stand up against a fellow who's in the right and keeps a-comin'." Quietly Breakenridge told Curly Bill his errand, bought him a drink and invited him to ride with him into the Clanton-McLowerie territory—as his deputy.

Brocius squinted down at the slender lawman, tossed off his drink and burst into bellowing roars of laughter. The joke, he swore, was on him. Besides, this youngster had the kind of nerve he liked. "Be damn', I'll go along!" he roared.

[224]

For the next few days, the two tax collectors made the rounds among some of the toughest, most ornery renegades of the Southwest. Curly Bill laid it on the line to his rough neighbors: "Dig it up, or I'll rassle it outa you!" They paid. And Bill Breakenridge rode back to Tombstone toting over a thousand dollars in tax money—and the friendship of Curly Bill and his bunch.

That sort of friendship, however, could be stretched to the breaking point. So it was when Billy Grounds and Zwing Hunt, a wild pair who had recently anted up tax money to Breakenridge, rode into Charleston one night, and there held up the offices of the Tombstone Mining Company. They murdered in cold blood an employee who had offered the robbers no resistance. Word of this soon reached Tombstone, ten miles distant, and Breakenridge quickly raised a posse of citizens and took the trail of the killers.

The two outlaws had at last outraged public feeling, for the victim of their guns had been well-liked in the community; a quiet, hard-working, affable young man. They probably knew well that if they were captured they would hang, either legally or at the hands of angry townsmen, and it was soon apparent that they had no chance of outrunning the pursuit. They would have to make a last-stand fight of it. Using Indian tactics, they drew off, one to each side of the road, and, concealed by undergrowth, waited silently with their guns ready. Breakenridge and his handful of men rode on, straight into sudden, deadly gun flame. Horses and men went down together in a screaming tangle under the deadly fire of the killers. Only Breakenridge himself escaped; all the others of his party were hit; some were killed. Billy Breakenridge coolly fought on, at last lining his Colt on Grounds, who fell dead from the deputy's .45 slug. Another bullet caught Hunt in the lungs. The battle was over. The deputy then loaded the dead in one wagon and the wounded into another, and drove his grim cargo back into Tombstone.

Breakenridge was Behan's deputy during the Earp-Clanton feud, with its brief and bloody climax in the OK Corral—the culmination of bitter quarrel inflamed by personal animosity perhaps as much as by the conflict of lawman against outlaw. In his book, *Helldorado*, Breakenridge makes noncommittal reference to the Clanton faction, but claims that Wyatt Earp and his brothers and Doc Holliday goaded them into that history-making battle. Along with other famous frontier characters and incidents, Wyatt Earp remains a figure of controversy, especially concerning his time in Tombstone as U. S. marshal. Many people invest him with a smoky halo.

In his book, *Wyatt Earp, Frontier Marshal*, Stuart Lake portrays him as a forceful and righteous bringer of the law into a land seething with trouble and violence. Others believe that he and his brothers—and their compadre, the consumptive homicidal Doc Holliday—were too quick to unlimber their artillery; that they wanted to dominate the Tombstone country, and were legal murderers, impelled by their own interests.

After the laissez-faire regime of Johnny Behan, Breakenridge was elected sheriff and found frequent use for the '72 Colt that helped him to enforce the law in that still-troubled county. During his later career as a railroad special officer, he favored the more compact Bisley model Colt. As one of the relatively few who took active part in the gunsmoke frontier, Colonel Breakenridge lived on into another, perhaps less colorful, era. He died at the age of eighty-five, of a coronory condition in a Tucson hospital, in 1931.

Tom Horn, Indian-tracker, scout, expert roper, packer, cowboy, stage-driver, private law-enforcement man, expansive boaster and warmhearted two-fisted drinking man, was also handy with his Colt .45. He was tried, convicted, and hanged for murder in 1903 in Wyoming. Among aficionados of local frontier history you can still stir up a hot argument as to whether or not he was framed. In one sense, Tom Horn, and many of his acquaintances were casualties of the passing of the frontier. The law, brought first by the Colt '72, and now administered through subpoenas and windy lawyers in dusty courtrooms—backed, to be sure, at times by six-shooter or .30-30 Winchester—was changing the way of life for the pioneer. Where now was the old-time, ringtailed rancher and trail-driver? Busy with their accountants, celebrating the good old days at organized conventions in fancy hotel dining rooms, playing high-stake poker at the Cheyenne Club or warming memories of more virile days in Dallas and Fort Worth.

To understand the type of man Tom Horn was—and many of his contemporaries—we have to look briefly at the changing picture of the cow country. Its tradition was deeply bred in the great men who made it—most of them Texans whose roots went back to the cavalier and feudal days of the pre-Civil War South. Their hair-trigger sense of personal honor sprouted from their shoulders in a forest of lethal chips. An insult spoken or a physical trespass could be answered only by the gun. Yet they had a wonderful and generous sense of responsibility toward those less lucky or energetic. A man whose family needed beef to eat was welcome to slaughter a steer or two. Others, who ran off a jag of longhorns, were apt to pay with their lives. No stranger was ever turned away from the sprawling main houses of the old-time cattle kings, contentious and quick-triggered though they were apt to be with overambitious neighbors.

Those were the men, that was the tradition, that came up the trail, in the 70's and 80's chasing 'em north, to settle in Oklahoma, Wyoming, Colorado, Montana and the Dakotas—and other places that offered graze for big herds. They were gamblers and fighters—against blizzard and drouth which were as unpredictable as their own tempers and more economically destructive than the raids of Cheyenne, Apache and Sioux used to be. A freezing white winter would dot the range with costly skeletons of cattle in the spring; a parching summer might be even more disastrous, making feed scarce at the time and preventing the storing of hay for the winter.

And there were other imponderables to battle. Disease, such as Texas fever; a poor calf drop for no apparent reason; losses in trail-driving due to stampedes and drownings in flooded river crossings; rustling. And there was always the fluctuating price of cattle, figured per head on the range or —the determining factor—at per hundredweight in the Chicago and Kansas City markets. In 1883 one Texas rancher wasn't anxious to part with his herd at $25 a head; a few years later he begged a buyer to take his cattle at six dollars, calves thrown in, and all f.o.b. the nearest loading point.

Prices started climbing in the early eighties and the cattleman was—so he thought—knee-deep in clover. Thirty dollars a head was paid for range stock; feeders went quickly at the unheard-of price of $40 and $50. Money, spectacular and fast money, started to roll in. It was a real boom, a miraculous sparkling, golden bubble that attracted speculators, promoters and private investors and jugglers of high finance. Stock companies and foreign syndicates bought huge tracts of land and cattle. The Prairie Land & Cattle Company, owned chiefly in England, ran three big ranches totaling more than 8,000 square miles in various grazing states and territories, ran almost 140,000 head of cattle and a capital investment of almost $5 million. Swan Land & Cattle, the Matador, and the famous XIT were some other huge outfits.

There were many other syndicates, some of them existing chiefly on paper; others managed by men who had no knowledge of the cattle business, run with prodigious waste. Projected dividends of 40 and 50 per cent were promises that produced more money from starry-eyed investors. It was a simple formula: The more cattle, the more profit. Pack 'em in on the range—they'll make out somehow. But beef cattle need good graze and lots of it. They couldn't build up tallow from land where the grass had already been eaten. Gaunt and weak from undernourishment, the herds suffered and all it needed was the severe winter of 1884–1885 to spread the cow country with carcasses. William MacLeod Raine and Will C. Barnes, in *Cattle*, tell of one Brazos rancher ruinously overstocking his range by running some 25,000 head on 100,000 acres, who found himself with a herd of only 10,000 gaunted skeletons at the end of spring roundup. He was not alone.

Only yesterday, it seemed, a steer was almost literally worth its weight in gold. But now, try to find a buyer! They'd taken to cover as if they'd been hunted with guns. Some of the outfits went bust. Others—and especially the big syndicates and companies—hung grimly on. But the old careless methods of cattle-raising were gone and would never return. Now it was a bitter struggle for bare survival. Their mistakes of the past would not be repeated, and the idea of endless, free range—meaning endless fodder—had proved only an empty mirage.

Wyoming at the time was a one-industry state. It raised, sold and lived cattle, as opposed to Montana and Colorado, for example. To ensure plenty of graze, to safeguard the springs and creeks, fences were necessary. And fence they did—especially the big syndicates. That their range fences might run on public land didn't bother them, naturally. They'd been using it for years, anyhow. Nor did they look with a welcome eye on the small ranchers and nesters that were coming in increasing numbers, to settle on government land where some of their cattle grazed. Now, if a man slaughtered a beef or two for his family, he was in bad trouble. He was destroying capital assets belonging to stockholders.

Cattlemen got together to form associations to protect and promote their interests. They hired inspectors to watch shipments, to keep an eye on calves branded at roundup, to see that cattle in shipping pens had clean brands. The big companies also often made their weight felt in politics at all levels. There is no doubt that frequently they were overbearing and bullying to the small, independent ranchers, some of whom, but by no means all, were known rustlers. Laws were passed in the state legislature favoring the big companies. An unbranded calf was no longer the property of the first man who could slap his brand on the critter. All mavericks, according to law, belonged to the Stock Growers' Association. That law, many small ranchers felt, was stepping right on their toes. How could a man get an honest start in this business, anyhow, unless he had the money or credit to buy a herd of cattle? Almost no one had.

Association detectives were viewed by the settlers, nesters and small ranchers as dimly as the Colonists more than a century before looked upon King George's redcoats. They were often strangers and as such had no business sticking their noses into a man's private affairs, much less hauling him before a judge to be fined if he happened to have a cowhide that carried one of the Association brands.

The local small ranchers looked upon the big companies as fair game for rustling. Most of the time, it was done on a small scale. Range detectives arrested many of the rustlers. But repeatedly a judge and jury made up of neighbors refused to convict. "How," one Association man wanted to know, "can you hope to convict a cow thief, when he's brought before a jury of cow thieves and tried by a cow-thief judge?" The man gladly paid twenty-five dollars for contempt.

So the breech widened, and—as we will see in the next chapter—resulted in one of the most spectacular cow-country shootin' wars that ever made a man grab his Winchester, buckle on his Colt, and with a fistful of bullets in his chaps pocket, hit the saddle to fight off an invading army.

Meanwhile, who cared about the big companies that were driving formerly honest settlers into becoming criminals, if they wanted to live at all? So one argument ran. The usual cowman's interests and loyalties were characteristically intensely local and personal. If he was going to be branded a rustler by dabbing his loop on a range maverick—a time-hallowed custom all over the cattle country—then he'd by God have the game as well as the name! Who cared what the board of directors in the Netherlands, in London or Berlin felt or did or said?

One kind of man did care—the cowmen who owned or managed the big outfits for their absentee employers. As rustling persisted, they took steps to stop it. The remedy was classic: guns and ropes had always done the job when the courts would not or could not.

Tom Horn, along with other frontier-raised men, hungered for excitement. He got a job as cattle detective, probably keeping his badge and credentials out of sight, for it was an occupation both unpopular and dangerous. Horn was an imposing figure and he knew it. Like some others—Wild Bill Hickok, Buffalo Bill Cody, and the lesser Russian Bill, of Tombstone—he had a good streak of ham actor in him. Perhaps he saw too clearly the passing of the old days, the days of his glory. He loved nothing better than to recall them over a convivial jug. Drunk, he did not have the truth in him; he was, it was said, one of the most expansive .45-caliber liars in the West. Incredible tales of derring-do; the men he'd known, the badmen he'd killed, held the saloon customers enthralled. Tom Horn, with his fire-red shirt, banging his hamlike palm on the bar, bellowing his brags in classic frontier style.

Rumors sifted around; ugly rumors, too. Some dead men—small ranchers —were found in remote parts of the range. Some had been killed when they hadn't been packing a gun, or with their pistols still in their holsters, their rifles unfired. They were all men suspected of rustling, and some of them had been tried and, as usual, found not guilty. Some of the corpses had three pebbles resting on their chests or at their heads. Must be the killer's signature, men whispered. The killer who collected in gold for every corpse marked with those stones.

A settler named Nickell was suspected of stealing cattle. Early one morning, his fifteen-year-old son went out of the cabin to start the morning chores. It was cold, and he put on his father's hat and jacket. From some rocks and undergrowth a shot shattered the early stillness. Willy Nickell fell dead. Horn was arrested for the murder. It is claimed that a U. S. marshal who had known him for years purposely got him drunk and led him into a confession of the Nickell killing and several others. He was tried in Cheyenne, was convicted on circumstantial evidence and hanged, November 20, 1903.

Despite all efforts to make him talk, he refused to give the names of the men who had employed him. For months and years his trial was argued back and forth in the cow country. To take a stand one way or another was to invite a fight right there. But the day of the big rancher who enforced his own law with the gun was passing. The sound of Tom Horn's .45 Colt Frontier was its sunset gun.

In the Montana cattle country around the 1890's, at the ranches situated near the Little Rockies between the Missouri and the Milk River, a medium-sized good-natured cowboy named George Parker was welcome at any time, either to sign on as a working cowhand or to drop in for a bait of grub and to josh with the boys. There was something appealing about him; he could laugh at himself as well as at others, and he was a mighty good man to have riding beside you in any kind of tight spot. George Parker was as game as they come and would share his last dollar with any cowhand. He drifted down to Wyoming and ran afoul of the law—a matter involving some cows that weren't his—and was sent to the pen at Laramie. It was his first misstep, and his friends got a governor's pardon for him. Not very long after that, however, began a series of spectacular train and bank robberies that were to become part of the legend of the West—the work of the last of the old-time frontier outlaws.

Butch Cassidy—Parker's *nom de guerre*—and Harvey Logan (alias Kid Curry) headed up the crew sometimes called The Wild Butch and The Hole-in-the-Wall Gang, that numbered around a dozen or fifteen members and had loose affiliations with other groups, including Black Jack Ketcham's gang that operated in New Mexico.

The Wild Bunch operated over a wide spread of territory, from northern Idaho and Nevada, through Montana, Wyoming, Colorado, Utah, the Dakotas, Texas, New Mexico and Arizona. Seldom if ever did they all appear in one raid. Their headquarters were in Lost Canyon, near Thermopolis, Wyoming; but Robber's Roost knew them, as did Brown's Hole. It was wild, rough, rugged country and admirably fitted the characters of the men who rode there.

With his companions, Cassidy was said to have robbed a bank at Belle Fourche, South Dakota, another at Montpelier, Idaho. Soon after that, Wilcox, Idaho, was the scene of a UP Express stick-up by the gang. Pursued into Wyoming by a posse, they decided to give battle and killed the sheriff, then they holed up in the mountains until things quieted down.

Cassidy and Longabaugh drifted down south, probably at least part of the way riding the old Outlaw Trail, which was, properly speaking, not a trail at all but a series of relay stations, isolated ranches in the wild, mountainous country where gulches and deep pockets offered natural refuge from the law. Along this twisting, sparsely settled route, a man in a hurry could swap his mount for a fresh horse and no questions asked. He could get food, bullets, a six-shooter or rifle if one was needed; or he could hole up while his wounds healed under the rough surgery of the ranchers, whose short memories and tight lips could be depended upon.

In August, 1900, another Union Pacific train was held up at Tipton, Wyoming; the following month, the bank at Winnemucca, Nevada, suffered an involuntary withdrawal of funds under the guns of the gang. Part of the crowd were chased all the way to Texas, where some of them were killed. Not many weeks passed before Harvey Logan, Ben Kilpatrick and another—some say Butch Cassidy was also present—swung aboard the Great Northern westbound train at Malta, Montana; forced the engine crew to stop the train near Wagner, and rode off, leaving behind them an empty express safe.

Authorities, bankers, railroad and express companies were tired of making their contributions to this ubiquitous crew of pistoleers. The Pinkertons offered $6,500 for the capture of the Wagner train robbers.

This seemed a propitious time to lie low. They knew Fort Worth; Cassidy was popular and perhaps had some connections. There Cassidy and Harvey Logan, Ben Kilpatrick, Harry Longabaugh and Will Carver lived well for a while, but not too well. Duded up in iron hats and store clothes and sporting heavy gold watch chains across their vests, they dined quietly at the best restaurant, then sauntered the streets, content to take in the sights. One of the sights was a photographer's shop, and whether it was bravado or carelessness no one will know, but the quintet of bandits decided to pose for their famous photograph that hastened the end of their activities.

It wasn't long after they had left town that the Pinkerton operatives nosed along their cold trail. The photographer recalled the bunch by their description; showed the negative to the officers. This was a jackpot! How many copies of the group picture were circulated to all law-enforcement agencies is not known, but they were enough to identify the hunted men. And the chase grew hotter.

Ben Kilpatrick was arrested in St. Louis. After a desperate gun fight, Harvey Logan was captured in Knoxville, Tennessee, and given a hundred-and-thirty-five-year sentence. He never served a day of it, escaping en route to the penitentiary.

Man trackers, including the famous Charlie Siringo, Doc Shores, Joe LaFors, Pat Lawson, and others kept on their trail. Butch Cassidy and his bunch steered clear of Wyoming. After an unsuccessful train holdup in Colorado, Shores tracked the robbers, fatally wounded Harvey Logan. Ben Kilpatrick was in prison in Columbus; his brother George had been killed in New Mexico. Other members of the gang had suffered the same fate. Only Butch Cassidy and Longabaugh remained at large. But there was now no place for them in the West. They managed to make it to South America, and were killed after robbing a mine payroll in southern Bolivia.

There are men still alive today who remember George Parker, the happy-go-lucky likable cowboy, who had on more than one occasion proved himself a friend in need to his saddle mates. They will tell you that whatever else he was, Butch Cassidy was no liar, and vociferously back up Cassidy's statement that, although he used his Colt .45, he never killed a man with it. And there are whispered stories that Butch Cassidy never did go to his death in Bolivia, but is still alive, a very old man now.

Where? *Quien sabe?*

Famous Colt Cartridge Revolvers of the Old West

Although the hand gun that is popularly associated with the winning of the West is usually called the Colt .45 Peacemaker or Frontier six-shooter, and seems to have been preferred in its single-action forms by the cow-country men who carried them, this Colt, in all its variations, is generally accepted by firearms authorities as a U. S. martial hand gun. Famous Colt cartridge revolvers of the Old West are:

1. Single-Action Army Revolver, also called New Army Metallic Cartridge Revolving Pistol, Single-Action Army, Single-Action Frontier, Peacemaker, and Colt Army Revolver, Model 1872.

2. Double-Action Army, also called the Double-Action Frontier, and sometimes the Colt Double-Action Army Revolver, Model 1878.

3. New Navy Double-Action, Self-Cocking Revolver, Model 1889.

4. New Navy Double-Action, Self-Cocking Revolver, Model 1892, which was actually nothing but a modification of the Model 1889.

5. New Army Models, 1892, 1894, and 1896.

Other, later models and modifications run from 1901 through 1911 and still later, but we are concerned here with the guns used during the days of the West that closed with the turn of the century; the days of the cattle and mining frontiers.

One of the first of the cartridge revolvers brought out by Colt after the Civil War was the Colt Old Line, Single-Action, .22 caliber revolver, pocket type; also known as the First Model .22 caliber Colt Revolver. It is a seven-shot revolver made from about 1870 to about 1871, which was not popular and did little to win the West, but we mention it to indicate the progress in Colt design.

Colt Model 1872, also called the Peacemaker, and the Frontier Model. In the regular model, this revolver was caliber .45, c.f., 6-shot, S.A., with a

7.5-inch round barrel, total length 12.5 inches, weight 2 lbs., 5 oz. Its manufacture started in 1871; it was presented for test by the U. S. Army Ordnance Department in November, 1872, and the first order was placed for 8,000 revolvers, to be issued to the U. S. Cavalry in 1873. The standard barrel lengths were 7.5 inches for most revolvers, including the Cavalry Model and Peacemaker; 5.5 inches for the Artillery Model; 4.75 inches for the so-called civilian model; and either 3 inches or 4 inches for the pocket model bought on special order, but specimens have been found with a barrel length of 3.5 inches without an ejector, hence there is no arbitrary barrel length that determines the type.

Plate 1, figure 1 is the Army Model, with the 7.5-inch barrel. Figure 2 is the Frontier Model, chambered for caliber .44-40 c.f. cartridge and with a 7.5-inch barrel. Figure 3 is a Frontier Model but with a 5.5-inch barrel, owned by George Parker, who was known as "Butch Cassidy" and was the leader of "The Hole in the Wall Gang," also known as "The Wild Bunch of Robber's Roost." Notice the short barrel and the ivory grips.

Collectors' Items

Figure 4 is the Colt Model 1872 Revolver, caliber .44-40, with a 4.75-inch barrel. Figure 5 is the same model, but caliber .45, with a 5.5-inch barrel, silver-plated except the cylinder and hammer are gold-plated, and the head of a bull is carved on ivory grips. Figure 6 is Model 1872, caliber .32-20, with a 7.5-inch barrel and fancy grips. Figure 7 is the Model 1872, caliber .32-20, with what the Colt factory called "Type B" engraving, 6-inch barrel, gold-plated hammer, and gold-plated trigger. The trigger is known as the "Bisley type." Figure 8 is the Model 1872, caliber .22, with 5.5-inch barrel and stag grips.

Figure 9 is the Buntline Special, a Colt Single-Action Army Revolver, Model 1872, with the true "Peacemaker" characteristics, made at the Colt factory with a 16-inch barrel and an attachable skeleton shoulder stock, supplied with a holster. This model was made for Ned Buntline, whose true name was Edward Judson, author, showman, and soldier of fortune. According to tradition and some records, Buntline gave several similar outfits to people in public life, but with 12-inch barrels and attachable walnut shoulder stocks. Wyatt Earp, Bat Masterson, Bill Hickok and other prominent figures of the frontier were on his gift list. Buntline was also a promoter and early, self-appointed publicity man for Buffalo Bill Cody and for Annie Oakley.

One of the most interesting facts about guns of the Old West is the fact that the Frontier Model, Colt Single-Action Revolver, Model 1872, was chambered for the .44-40 cartridge used in the Winchester Model 1873

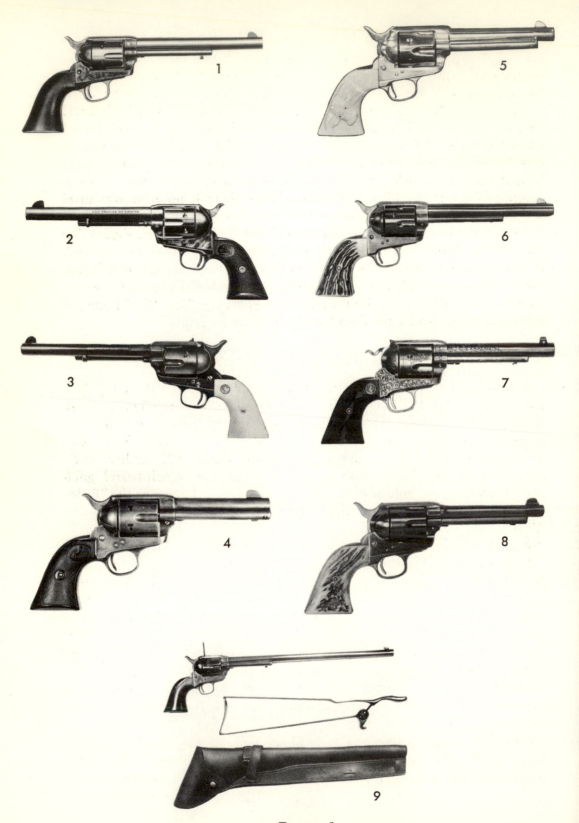

PLATE 1

Repeating Rifle, especially when this Colt revolver was made with a 7.5-inch barrel. The theory behind this was that it was desirable for a man to have only one make, type, model and caliber of cartridges, which he could use in both a hand gun and a shoulder arm.

Variations of the Model 1872 Colt Revolver

The Cavalry, Peacemaker and Artillery Models of the Colt 1872 Revolver are without doubt U. S. martial cartridge revolvers, but the Frontier version is a secondary U. S. martial cartridge revolver, depending upon the size, caliber, barrel length and use. All of these versions have been chambered at the Colt factory and by many gunsmiths for an infinite number of cartridges, hence it is impossible to be arbitrary about them.

Colt House Pistol

The Colt House Pistol, also called the Cloverleaf Colt, the Jim Fisk Pistol, and the Old Model Cloverleaf House Pistol, is caliber .41, r.f., 4-shot, with a 3-inch round barrel marked "Colt's House Pistol, Hartford, Ct., U.S.A." It is called the "Cloverleaf" because of the shape of the cylinder. It was made from 1871 to about 1875 with few variations. From the mechanical viewpoint, this was the first revolver to use the recessed chambers that the Colt people now call the embedded-head cylinder. This arm, as its name indicates, was probably intended for inside work, as opposed to the martial type of hand gun carried by cowboys, frontier lawmen, express messengers, and others. It was primarily a gun to be used in town or cities by gamblers, bankers, merchants, and members of what used to be called "the sporting element."

Plate 2, figure 1 is the Colt House Pistol with a round cylinder, caliber .41 r.f., and figure 2 is the Colt House Pistol with a cloverleaf-shaped cylinder, in the same caliber, r.f.

The Colt House Pistol was made with barrels from 1.5 to 3.5 inches long, and some were made with a round cylinder, which was a decided departure from the cloverleaf-shaped cylinder, hence the latter characteristic is not a determining factor in classifying this revolver.

PLATE 1

1. Colt Army Model 1872.
2. Colt Frontier Model, 7.5-inch barrel.
3. Colt Frontier Model, 5.5-inch barrel.
4. Colt Model 1872, .44-40, 4.75-inch barrel.
5. Colt Model 1872, caliber .45, 5.5-inch barrel.
6. Colt Model 1872, .32-20, 7.5-inch barrel.
7. Colt Model 1872, .32-20, 6-inch barrel.
8. Colt Model 1872, caliber .22, 5.5-inch barrel.
9. Colt Buntline Special, 16-inch barrel, with attachable skeleton shoulder stock.

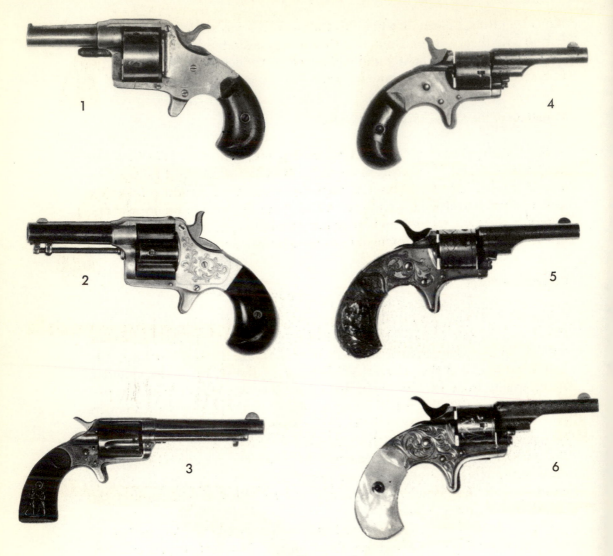

Plate 2

1. Colt House Pistol, caliber .41.
2. Colt House Pistol with cloverleaf-shaped cylinder.
3. Colt "New Line Single-Action Pocket Revolver."
4, 5, 6. Colt, caliber .22—the "Open-Top Revolver."

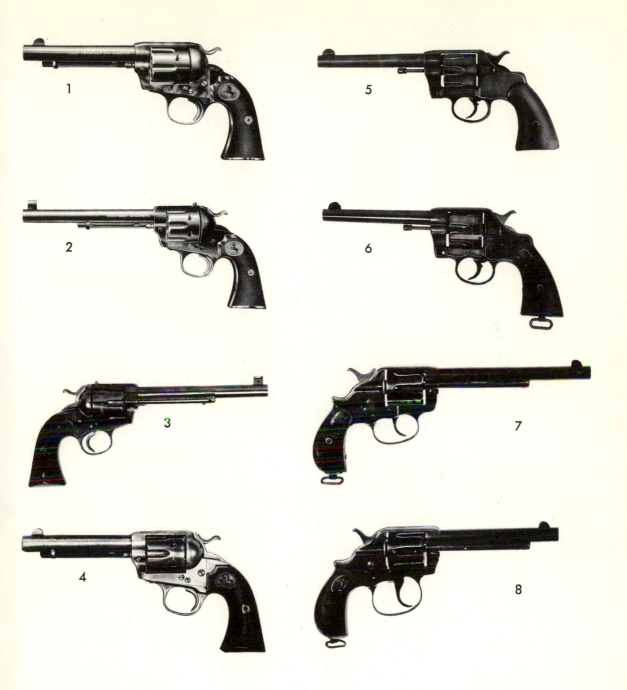

PLATE 3

1. Colt Bisley, standard model.
2. Colt Bisley Model 44.
3. Colt Bisley "Flat-Top" Target Model.
4. Colt Frontier Model converted to a Bisley.
5. Colt New Navy, Double-Action, Self-Cocking Revolver, Model 1899.
6. Same, Model 1892.
7. Colt Double-Action Army or Frontier Revolver, Model 1878.
8. Same, Model 1878, variation with large trigger guard.

Colt New Line Pocket Revolvers

The Colt company, from about 1873 to about 1890, manufactured "New Line Single-Action Pocket Revolvers" in a variety of sizes, barrel lengths, and calibers, many of which have been given unofficial names by collectors and dealers through the years, such as "Big Colt," "Ladies' Colt," "Little Colt," "New York Police Pistol," "Police and Thug Model," etc. All these were used in the Old West. Figure 3 illustrates a typical specimen.

Colt So-Called Open-Top .22-Caliber Revolvers

While the above-mentioned Colt New Line Pocket Revolvers were being developed, manufactured, and sold, the Colt company continued to market a .22-caliber revolver without a top strap generally called by collectors and historians the "Colt Open-Top Revolver," sold both with and without the ejector which was a holdover from percussion days. This model and type is illustrated by figures 4, 5, and 6, Plate 2.

First Colt Double-Action Revolver

The first double-action revolver made by Colt, manufactured from 1877 to 1912, was called the Colt New Double-Action, Self-Cocking, Central-Fire, 6-Shot Revolver; and also known as the Lightning Model; and the New Model, Double-Action Revolver. As far as we know, this revolver was generally made in caliber .38 c.f., 6-shot, with 2.5-, 3.5-, 4.5-, and 6-inch barrel lengths, although we have found specimens made for caliber .41, c.f., with various barrel lengths.

Colt Bisley Models

The Colt Bisley Model revolvers were developed gradually from the Colt Single-Action Army Revolver, also known as the Peacemaker and the Frontier Model, and by many other names, into a target revolver by changing the trigger, hammer and grips. It was manufactured from 1896 or possibly from 1897 to 1912, hence the period of its sale does not cover the true frontier era. In addition, it may be gently mentioned that a revolver made for target practice was not popular with men who wanted to kill at close range, although target shooters have always liked this model since its inception.

Plate 3, figure 1 is generally called the standard or regular model of Bisley because the barrel is marked in two lines "Bisley Model" and "Colt Frontier Six Shooter." Figure 2 is marked in one line: "(Bisley Model) 44 Russian Ctg." Figure 3 is the Bisley "Flat-Top" Target Model. Figure 4 is definitely a revolver made originally as a Frontier model and then converted to a Bisley by changing the trigger, hammer and grips, but it is still marked as a Frontier on the barrel.

First Colt "Swing-Out" Model

The Colt New Navy, Double-Action, Self-Cocking Revolver, Model 1889, was the first of the swing-out-cylinder, simultaneously ejecting Colt revolvers. It was manufactured from 1889 to 1892, hence it covers the period when cowboys were beginning to act civilized. The usual caliber was .38 short and long Colt, but caliber .41 short and long Colt was common in the Old West. This is illustrated in figure 5.

Colt New Navy, Double-Action, Self-Cocking Revolver, Model 1892

The Colt New Navy, Double-Action, Self-Cocking Revolver, Model 1892, illustrated in figure 6, was made by Colt from 1892 to 1908, in caliber .41 short and long Colt, and caliber .38 short and long Colt; six-shot, 6-inch barrel.

Colt D.A. Army or Frontier Revolver, Model 1878

The Colt Double-Action Army or Frontier Revolver, Model 1878, illustrated in figure 7, was first put on the market by the Colt company in January, 1877, and was then called the New Double-Action, Self-Cocking, Central-Fire, Six-Shot Revolver, but it was later advertised as the Lightning Model. The Army received this revolver with walnut grips, but civilians were persuaded to buy hard-rubber grip plates, for no reason we can understand. It was made in various barrel lengths and calibers, and was the first large, heavy, double-action cartridge revolver made by Colt. Figure 8 is the Double-Action Army or Frontier Model 1878, caliber .45 c.f., 6-shot, with a 7.5-inch round barrel, made with hard-rubber grips, a variation with the larger trigger guard, intended originally for Alaska but sent to the Philippines.

Winchester Catalogue Cover, 1867.

XIV *Gunsmoke Over Powder River: The Winchester Rifle*

The mysterious train which left the city yesterday over the Union Pacific had a very important mission to fill, namely to get about 35 or 40 detectives to the northern part of Wyoming as rapidly as possible. The cattlemen in Buffalo, Sheridan, Bonanza, and Riverton, Wyoming, and in Red Lodge, Billings, and Fort Smith, Montana, have formed an organization with the intention of exterminating the rustlers and have called on a detective agency for assistance.

The U.P. officials here when asked about the train denied any knowledge of its having left the city.

—The Denver *Sun*, April 7, 1892.

[241]

THE conflict between the big cattle companies in Wyoming and the nesters, settlers and small ranchers that had been growing since the boom years of the early '80's, finally exploded in the spring of 1892 in bitterness and bloodshed, in the crack of Winchester rifles and the roar of Sharps .45 and .50 caliber buffalo guns. This action, without parallel in Western history, was amazing in more ways than one; in its open and well-publicized defiance of legal procedure on the part of half a hundred imported gunmen and their leaders (among whom were many honest if hot-headed men), and in one of the most courageous last-stand gun fights against overpowering odds in a country and time characterized by a high order of individual fighting nerve.

This smoldering situation later resulted in the killing of a number of settlers and the controversial execution of Tom Horn, for the results of the Powder River invasion, or Johnson County War, were not conclusive. The war between cattlemen and grangers (or small ranchers) dragged on for more than a decade, and ended only with the ultimate victory of the grangers. The day of the rustler was ending too; rustlers had thrived on the open range, and when it was gone, rustling became difficult and unprofitable. It was the persistence of the grangers, once the rustlers' allies against the big cattlemen, that finally established law and order in the cattle country.

In Wyoming in 1891 the lines were sharply drawn between the big cattlemen and their powerful Association on one hand, and the grangers and "rustlers" on the other. To the big cattle companies, small settlers and rustlers were synonymous; their accusations against the grangers were widely publicized in the press and created the impression that organized rustling was widespread. The Association maintained that Johnson County authorities worked hand in glove with the rustlers, that it was impossible to have them prosecuted.

The big companies were up against it; the severe winter of 1886–1887 had nearly wiped them out; cattle prices were dropping simply because they had glutted the markets of the East. The obvious scapegoat was the granger, or rustler. The Denver press collaborated with the Association in building up the impression that Wyoming was in their hands. News leaked out of the lynching of rustlers. A father and his son who accidentally roped some marked calves were noisily arrested and charged. Killings that had no connection with cattle were attributed to rustlers.

The grangers had their complaints too, perhaps more justified. They were intimidated by the big cattle companies, they charged; their small herds disappeared mysteriously into the large herds of the big cattle operators. Roundup outfits slapped the big ranchers' brands on small herds on the open range. Big outfits would not employ cowboys who owned cattle of their own; the motive and the opportunity for increasing their herds made them suspect.

It is hard now to know how many grangers actually were rustlers; grangers and rustlers by this time had a common name and a common cause. A cowhand who acquired a small herd of his own would be called a rustler. An independent man, handy with a gun, got the name of an outlaw. One of the "rustlers" the Association wanted most to exterminate was Nate Champion, a top cowhand, a cool man with a gun, in fact the most dangerous gun fighter in Wyoming. He had become the acknowledged leader of the "grangers and rustlers." In the fall of 1891 four men entered a cabin where he was staying and fired on him; the shots went wild, and Champion returned the fire and drove the men away. It was virtually a declaration of war.

A month later two settlers named Jones and Tisdale were ambushed and killed near Buffalo in Johnson County. The settlers cried for the blood of the cattlemen and the sheriff too, and one of the Association's loudest spokesman, F. M. Canton, was charged with the murders, released, and later rearrested and placed under bond.

H. C. Davis, a Cheyenne cattleman, claimed that a gang of two hundred rustlers, chiefly Texans (perhaps the fact that Nate Champion was a Texan lent color to the charge), were openly defying the Cattle Association. The Denver papers obligingly published the statement without crediting the source.

The small ranchers repudiated the Association and planned an early roundup in the spring of 1892 to circumvent the Association rules and the official supervision of branding. One of the things that rankled among the small settlers was a law requiring that cattle suspected of having been stolen be seized, sold, and the money held until the alleged owner could prove his innocence. The implication that a man was guilty until proved innocent was an outrage to the frontiersman's deeply ingrained individualism and the traditions of Anglo-Saxon law. Now the grangers prepared to defend their own property.

Early in April the Association held a brief meeting. Shortly afterward, three stock cars were loaded with horses in the freight yard at Cheyenne along with a flatcar with wagons and camp gear. The next day an unscheduled train arrived on the Union Pacific from Denver; it consisted of a passenger car with curtains drawn, a baggage car, and a caboose. It coupled onto the loaded freight cars and the train was closely guarded even from railway employees. Some people may have noticed that there had been a run on Winchester rifles in a Cheyenne store the past two days, but nobody really knew what was going on.

The train pulled out of Cheyenne that night en route to Casper. On the way it made one stop, at Fort Fetterman, where the foreman of a ranch belonging to Senator Carey, a big cattleman, was delegated to cut the telegraph wires from Casper.

The train carried a party of men called the Regulators—about twenty-five "detectives" recruited in Denver, and that many more cattlemen and their employees. Each was armed with pistols and a new Winchester rifle. They were accompanied by a surgeon and—to tell the world their side of the story—a Chicago newspaper correspondent. The Denver *Sun* had already announced the train's departure, adding that rustlers had herds of stolen cattle numbering thousands in the Big Horn mountain.

It was not the first time in the history of the West that private citizens had taken the law into their own hands. The Vigilance Committees in San Francisco had a sanction almost above the law; public officials abandoned their offices to join them, with general approval. And vigilantes had ridden against rustlers all over the West with popular approval. In Johnson County, however, the cattlemen were defying both law and public opinion. They had always *been* the law, they believed, and they still were. They hardly expected the reception they got.

Detraining at Casper, they mounted their horses and rode northwest toward a ranch that was to serve as headquarters. Before they got there a foreman from the Western Union Beef Company rode out to meet them and told them that Nate Champion and some other rustlers were holed up at the KC Ranch on the North Fork of the Powder River.

Champion was the man they wanted, and they headed toward the KC. Surrounding the house before daylight, they shot two men who emerged after sunrise—two trappers who happened to have spent the night there— and sent fusillades of bullets into the house where two other men remained —Nick Ray, also a wanted man, and Champion. When Ray went out to see what had happened to the trappers, he was shot. Champion hauled him back inside still alive. The cattlemen kept up their fire all day, with Champion firing back when he could. In the afternoon a neighboring farmer and his son came past the farm. The cattlemen fired on them but they escaped and went to the town of Buffalo to give the alarm.

Inside the cabin, Nate Champion looked after his dying comrade, took occasional shots at the cattlemen whenever he could sight a target, and started writing a note. He had an idea that this time the chips were down.

> April 9. Me and Nick was getting breakfast when the attack took place. Two men here with us Bill Jones and another man. The old man went after water and did not come back. His friend went out to see what was the matter and he did not come back. Nick started out and I told him to look out, that I thought there was someone at the stable and would not let him come back. Nick is shot but not dead yet. He is awful sick. I must go and

wait on him. It is now about two hours since the first shot. Nick is still alive; they are still shooting and are all around the house. Boys, there is bullets coming in like hail. Them fellows is in such shape I can't get at them. They are shooting from the stable and river and back of the house. Nick is dead, he died about 9 o'clock. I see smoke down at the stable. I think they have fired it. I don't think they intend to let me get away this time.

It is now about noon. There is someone at the stable yet; they are throwing a rope out the door and drawing it back. I guess it is to draw me out. I wish that duck would get out further so I could get a shot at him. Boys, I don't know what they have done with them two fellows that staid here last night. Boys, I feel pretty lonesome just now. I wish there was someone here with me so we could watch all sides at once. They may fool around until I get a good shot before they leave. Its about three o'clock now. There was a man in a buckboard and one on horseback just passed. They fired on them as they went by. I don't know if they killed them or not. I seen lots of men come out on horses on the other side of the river and take after them. I shot at the men in the stable just now; don't know if I got any or not. I must go and look out again. It don't look as if there is much show of my getting away. I see twelve or fifteen men. One looks like [name scratched out]. I don't know whether it is or not. I hope they did not catch them fellows that ran over the bridge toward Smiths. They are shooting at the house now. If I had a pair of glasses I believe I would know some of those men. They are coming back I've got to look out.

Well, they have just got through shelling the house like hail. I heard them splitting wood. I guess they are going to fire the house tonight. I think I will make a break when night comes, if alive. Shooting again. I think they will fire the house tonight. It's not night yet. The house is all fired. Goodbye, boys, if I never see you again.

Nathan D. Champion.

Late in the afternoon the cattlemen loaded a buggy with hay and pitch pine, fired it, and ran it into the ranch house, setting it ablaze. Nate Champion was forced out and he made a break to get past the cattlemen's fire, but fell under a fusillade from a score of Winchesters. The note he had written while under siege in the house was found on his bullet-torn body and published in the Cheyenne *Daily Leader* of April 14, 1892. It was probably the last time in the history of the West that a single gun fighter made such a dramatic last stand against such odds.

The cattlemen mounted and rode to the headquarters of the Western Union Beef Company to get fresh horses, and thence toward the town of Buffalo, hoping to take it by storm. They were met by the hastily organized Home Defenders' Corps, two hundred strong. A local merchant had armed every able-bodied man with rifles and ammunition. Churches and schools had been turned into barracks. The entire community—townsmen, grangers, rustlers, and "men about town"—was up in arms. The Regulators beat a quick retreat to the TA Ranch and barricaded themselves in the house.

There the grangers besieged them for nearly two days. When they failed to bring out the cattlemen, they constructed a "go devil," a wagon which would protect several men from gunfire while they moved a load of dynamite toward the house.

Conflicting reports of the war in Johnson County reached Cheyenne, since the telegraph wires were cut and the news was only hearsay. The acting governor made no move so long as there was no adverse word from the cattlemen. But when news came that they were besieged, he quickly sent a wire to President Harrison in Washington, saying that a state of insurrection existed in Johnson County and asking that federal troops be sent from nearby Fort McKinney. The troops arrived just as the grangers' movable fort was advancing on the beleaguered cattlemen, who surrendered without ceremony to the federal commanding officer. The prisoners included high officials of the Cattle Association, including F. M. Canton, its eloquent inspector, and twenty-five or thirty Texans who had apparently been recruited from the saloons of Denver.

When the time came to prosecute the prisoners, Johnson County was bankrupt, and the men were released on personal bond to appear in January. By that time the Texans had vanished and the prosecution's chief witnesses had been kidnaped and taken to Nebraska. The case was dismissed and the cattlemen went free.

After the smoke had cleared from the Johnson County war, Wyoming was no longer a frontier. The rule of law had prevailed; the homesteaders and townspeople had rejected the rule of force and domination by the big cattle companies.

But isolated incidents occurred for a decade after; the cattlemen did not give up, and range detectives still sought out cattle thieves, even though county officials now assured the cattlemen of legal protection. Winchesters still sang out on lonely trails where cowboys and rustlers were ambushed. While the trial of the insurrectionists was fizzling out, two young cowboys who had worked for large outfits but now had small holdings and herds of their own were arrested on rustling charges. Dab Burch and Jack Bedford were blamed for all the rustling activity still alleged to be going on in the county, given a hearing, and sent to Buffalo for trial. They were disarmed and placed in the keeping of guards, John Wickham and Joe Rogers, who promised safe conduct, and set out across the mountains. Some time later Wickham and Rogers returned alone, and reported they had been ambushed and the prisoners kidnaped. The bullet-riddled bodies of Burch and Bedford were later found near the trail. Wickham and Rogers, suspected of collusion with two prominent cattlemen, were arrested, but as there were no witnesses, they were not held. Such sporadic shooting continued; few rustlers were legally executed.

The case of Tom Horn marked the end of the struggle in Wyoming, although strong feeling lingered on for years after his execution. Nickell, father of the boy Horn had slain, asked the sheriff to see Horn's body after the hanging. Fearing mob violence, the sheriff refused. Thereupon the legend grew that Horn had never really been hanged, and he "reappeared" from time to time in various places for years, becoming a minor folk hero. It was the last notable episode in the waning conflict between the big ranchers and the grangers.

In the history of firearms in the Old West two names stand out: Colt and Winchester. Although Colt made shoulder arms of various kinds, the word "Colt" came to mean revolver, first percussion, then cartridge types. In the same way "Winchester" means rifle, from the beginning of the cartridge period into our own time. The hunters, trappers, miners, cowboys, outlaws, and sheriffs of the West were not always specific in designating the make, model, or caliber of their weapons. After the Civil War, when the use of cartridge arms had become widespread, Winchester got the credit for almost all shoulder arms, carbine or rifle. It became a generic term. The reason for this was that the Winchester was the most widely used shoulder arm of the postwar era. It became popular almost as soon as it was available.

In such flare-ups as the Johnson County war, it is likely that the Winchester far outfired any other kind of arm used. The cattlemen specifically bought their gunmen new Winchesters; the armed populace that besieged them carried a variety of shoulder arms, among which Winchesters probably predominated.

The history of the rifle begins with the founding in 1855 of the Volcanic Repeating Arms Company, manufacturers of a line of repeating pistols and later carbines. After financial difficulties the company failed in 1857 and was reorganized by Oliver F. Winchester and others as the New Haven Arms Company. Smith and Wesson, earlier members of the Volcanic firm, had already withdrawn to develop their own line of pistols.

In 1860 the New Haven Arms Company began to manufacture the Henry rifle, which used a new rimfire cartridge as well as the repeating mechanism of the Volcanic pistol. This gun became famous in the Old West and revolutionized the fighting tactics of Indians as well as white settlers. Its use became widespread very shortly after it was introduced because Winchester, failing to obtain government contracts for it, concentrated on developing its sales to nonmilitary users, largely in Western territory. It was an early favorite with Indian fighters. The Indians themselves called it the "spirit gun" because it would fire repeatedly.

The usual Indian maneuver in attacking a single white man or a small band was to come within charging distance, with one or several of their number advancing to draw the fire of the white man's single-shot rifle. Then they would rush him before he had time to reload. A story is told of two white prospectors who were carrying Henry rifles when they were attacked by a band of Blackfeet Indians. Familiar with Indian tactics, both discharged a single shot when the Indians showed themselves as targets. Then when the red men rushed them they resumed fire with all fifteen remaining shots of both rifles. In the ensuing rout, they had time to reload and charge the Indians, killing all forty of them.

It was the Model 73 that made the name of Winchester. It is said to have "killed more game and more Indians, and more United States soldiers when the Indians awoke to its virtues, than any other type rifle." It was fast, reliable, and strongly constructed, and adapted for short-range shooting and mobile warfare. No less an authority than Buffalo Bill Cody endorsed it enthusiastically as the best gun he had ever used, saying that an Indian would give more for one of them than for any other gun he could get.

Model 94, firing the .30-.30 cartridge, was much used by cattlemen. It was compact, rugged, easy to carry in a saddle, long in range and ideal for game hunting. It became the most popular of American sporting rifles.

The term "Winchester" refers both to rifles and carbines. The long-barreled models are rifles, those with short barrels carbines. There is no definite barrel length that determines whether a gun is a rifle or a carbine. This text designates them by the terms most commonly applied by the manufacturers and users.

Volcanic Pistols

These were made by the Volcanic Repeating Arms Company of New Haven from 1855 to 1857. They are actually the first of the Smith & Wesson line.

Plate 1 includes five illustrations. Figure 1 is caliber .41 with a 4-inch barrel and round butt and a spur on the lever. Figure 2 is a caliber .36, with 8-inch barrel, square butt and unfinished steel frame. Figure 3 is caliber .41, 6-inch barrel, square butt, and unfinished steel frame. Figure 4 is caliber .41, with 8-inch blued barrel, square butt and brass frame. Figure 5 is caliber .31, with 3.75-inch blued barrel, square butt, nickeled brass frame and engraved parts.

Winchester Shoulder Arms

Plate 2, figure 1 is the Model 1894 Rifle, caliber .30-30, lever action, with 26-inch barrel, still being made by Winchester in the carbine type as Model 94.

Figure 2 is the Model 1892 Carbine, caliber .44-40, with a 20-inch barrel, having the same action as the Model 1886, but built for smaller calibers than that model. According to the Winchester records, it "was made in the same calibers as the Model 1873, but it was much stronger in order that cartridges of higher velocity could be used."

Figure 3 is the Winchester, Single-Shot, Lever-Action, Baby Carbine, caliber .44-40, with a 15-inch barrel. Contrary to the legends and folklore of the Old West, this was not used as a "saddle gun" for galloping alongside a buffalo and shooting it behind the ear.

Figure 4 is the Winchester-made Spencer Carbine, technically known as the Second Type, with a barrel marked "NM" for New Model, caliber .56-52, with a 20-inch barrel. This is a 7-shot repeating carbine with a tubular magazine in the butt stock. It was extremely popular as a cavalry carbine with both the Union army and the Confederates during the Civil War, and was used extensively on the Great Plains by Indians, although they did not like it as much as the First Type Spencer Carbine.

Figure 5, figure 6, and figure 7 are Winchester Model 1866 Rifles. Figure 5 has a 24-inch barrel. Figures 6 and 7 have 20-inch barrels. These Winchesters were decorated with brass tacks, a favorite method of decorating shoulder arms among the Indians of what were then known as "the Western Plains."

The Henry Rifle

Figure 8 is the famous Henry Rifle, made by the New Havens Arms Co. from 1860 to 1866, according to the Winchester records; classified in *The Gun Collector's Handbook of Values* as one of the "U.S. Secondary Martial Shoulder Arms," and correctly described as the Henry Lever-Action, Cartridge Magazine Rifle. It was made caliber .44 Henry r.f. (bored caliber .42, with grooves about 0.005-inch deep, making actual caliber .43 for a .44 bullet), with a 24-inch barrel. Total length 43.5 inches. Weight 9.25 lbs. The War Department bought 1,731 Henry rifles, and several of the states bought them for state troops. It is reported that about 10,000 were made. It is known that they were carried by United States soldiers on Sherman's march through Georgia and were described by the Confederates as "that damned Yankee rifle that is loaded on Sunday and fired all week." This was manufactured by the New Haven Arms Co., New Haven, Connecticut, and

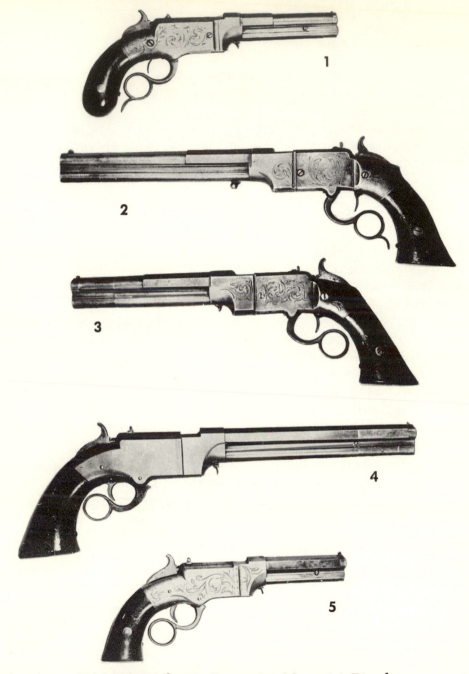

PLATE 1. Volcanic Repeating Magazine Pistols.

1. Caliber .31, 4-inch barrel with round butt and a spur on the lever.
2. Caliber .36, 8-inch barrel, square butt, and unfinished steel frame.
3. Caliber .41, 6-inch barrel, square butt, and unfinished steel frame.
4. Caliber .41, 8-inch blued barrel, square butt, and brass frame.
5. Caliber .31, 3.75-inch blued barrel, square butt, nickeled brass frame, and engraving.

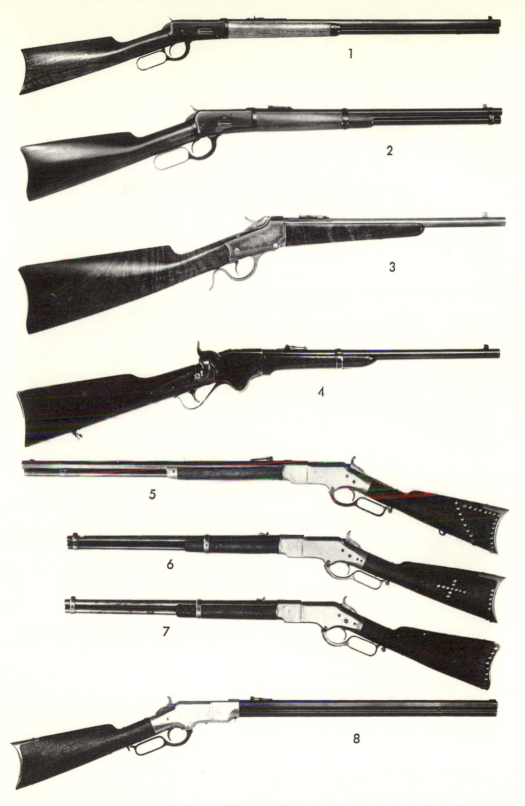

PLATE 2

1. Winchester Model 1894 Rifle.
2. Model 1892 Carbine.
3. Winchester Single-Shot Lever-Action Baby Carbine.
4. Winchester-made Spencer Carbine.
5, 6, 7. Winchester Model 1866 Rifles.
8. The Henry Rifle.

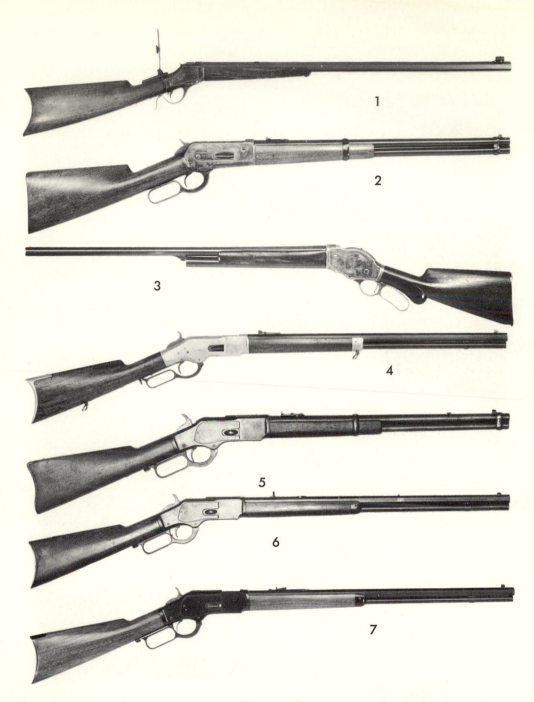

PLATE 3

1. Winchester High Wall, Model 1885.
2. Winchester Carbine Model 1886.
3. Winchester Model 1887 Shotgun.

4. Winchester Model 1886 Repeating Rifle.
5, 6, 7. Winchester Model 1873 in various versions.

marked "Henry's Patent Oct. 16, 1860," together with the name and address of the factory. Some have a brass frame and others were made with an iron frame.

More Winchesters

Plate 3, figure 1 is the Winchester High Wall, Model 1885, with a 30-inch barrel, chambered for a semi-experimental cartridge, caliber .51-25, and used extensively in the Old West for hunting and target shooting.

Figure 2 is the Model 1886 Winchester Carbine, caliber .45-90, with a 22-inch barrel, and the first Winchester lever-action repeater made with what is now regarded as a modern-type action.

Figure 3 is the Winchester Model 1887, lever-action shotgun, made in 10-gauge and also 12-gauge, with either a 30-inch or a 32-inch barrel. The 12-gauge used a 2⅝-inch shell, and the 10-gauge used a 2⅞-inch shell. This was the first really repeating shotgun made by Winchester.

Other Winchester Weapons

Plate 3, figure 4 is the Winchester Model 1866 Repeating Rifle, which indicates that the United States had it in its power to properly arm our soldiers fighting Indians after the Civil War, even though most of them were issued obsolete, single-shot muskets and rifles while the U. S. government was giving repeating rifles to Indians.

Figures 5, 6, and 7 illustrate various versions of the famous Model 1873 Rifle, also made as a carbine.

The Seventh Cavalry Charging into Black Kettle's Village at Daylight, November 27, 1868 (The Battle of Washita).
Harper's Weekly, *Dec. 19, 1868.* DENVER PUBLIC LIBRARY WESTERN COLLECTION

XV *The Indian Campaigns: U. S. Martial Arms of the Post-Civil War Era*

FROM 1847 on, a string of forts beginning with Fort Kearney in Nebraska and extending into the Pacific Northwest was flung across the continent in response to the need for protecting wagon trains, settlers, and railroad construction workers from hostile Indian tribes. By 1874 it had grown to a vast system of posts manned by U. S. Army infantry and cavalry which waged an unceasing war against Indians almost to the close of the century.

Some of the major engagements, such as Custer's stand at the Little Big Horn, were historic battles; others were minor skirmishes, lightning raids, isolated assaults on lonely settlements, sudden attacks on emigrants' wagon

[255]

trains. Altogether there was hardly a moment from 1865 to 1890 when the West was not aflame with Indian warfare. Because of a total lack of understanding and coordination between government Indian agencies and the Army, it was nearly impossible to know at any given moment what territory was hostile, what tribes were technically at peace with the United States, or where Indian warfare might break out.

Companies of soldiers were sent out from the westernmost forts to establish new posts farther west. They had to pitch camp; then, sometimes with the aid of civilian contractors whose men they had to protect, erect a fort with local timber, defending themselves as best they could from Indian raids until the fort was completed.

The life of the frontier soldier was a dangerous and unrewarding one. He was underpaid, badly armed, poorly supplied with food, clothing, and medical care, and the wilderness offered him little chance for social life, diversion, or repose. Sometimes the wives and children of officers and enlisted men accompanied them, living in private quarters within the fort. It was a perilous and sometimes appallingly horrible life for them too. In the post-Civil War years many hundreds of soldiers deserted; at best they could have a mere existence of boredom and penury; at worst they could be captured and subjected to torture by Indians. Somehow the Army did at last manage to establish the security of transcontinental routes, but at the cost of a terrible waste of its own personnel, of brutal and unnecessary massacres of peaceful Indians, of frequent defeats by well-armed Indian war parties.

After the Civil War the strength of the regular Army was reduced, and much of what remained was stationed in the Southern states. The Army was maintained at a theoretical peacetime level when actually in the West a state of war prevailed. The fact that much of the Army had been withdrawn from Indian engagements in the West during the war led the Indians to attempt bolder forays on white settlements and travelers, and to impose sterner conditions in the treaties they were constantly making with the United States. In Washington the Indian Commissioner complacently believed that the tribes were at peace; he failed to realize that a treaty made with one chief would not be honored by another, and that the internal politics of Indian tribes, which no one seems to have understood, could wipe out a treaty overnight and send thousands of hostile Indians on the warpath.

It is understandable that the Army organization was in a state of flux after the war; that bureaucratic blunders made in Washington could endanger army and civilian lives on the frontier; that Indians, having virtually no conception of treaty law as the white men understood it, would violate agreements without notice. What is less comprehensible is that army units sent to the frontier posts to keep down hostile tribes should not have been given the necessary arms and equipment to carry out their mission, and that in many cases the Indians were better armed, with newer and more efficient weapons, than the army regulars.

Indians had many ways of getting guns. Nothing could prevent traders from giving them new rifles in return for furs or food; any gun dealer could sell his guns where he pleased; and the U. S. government, on concluding a treaty with an Indian tribe, frequently issued it new rifles for hunting game. Soldiers returning from the war brought with them weapons which began to circulate throughout the West. The Army repeatedly found itself hopelessly outclassed by Indian warriors bearing superior rifles and revolvers.

The short history of Fort Philip Kearny in Wyoming is a dramatic illustration of the dangers the U. S. soldier faced in combat on the frontier; of the tactics of Indian diplomacy and warfare; and of the situation that isolated army posts bucked all through the West for a quarter of a century.

Fort Philip Kearny was part of the system of posts that stretched from Fort Leavenworth westward to open a trail to the Northwest. The route it was intended to maintain was the Bozeman Trail, the most direct way to the newly discovered gold fields of Montana. Treaties had been negotiated with the Sioux, the Army was assured that the trail was open, and detachments were sent into the Powder River country in 1866 to establish a new fort.

The Indians fought every attempt to open new trails through their territory; it meant the destruction of their hunting grounds and the game they depended on. The Sioux chiefs who had treated with the U. S. negotiators were repudiated by insurgent leaders; a new chief, Red Cloud, assumed leadership of an association of far-flung tribes. Apparently this escaped the notice of the Indian Commissioner.

The army units sent to Powder River had everything they needed except arms, ammunition, and horses. Most of the troops carried old muzzle-loading Springfield muskets, although for some reason the regimental band was equipped with Spencer breech-loading rifles, and a few of the officers had Henry rifles. Very little ammunition was taken from Fort Kearney in Nebraska; it was assumed that all that would be needed could be provided at Fort Laramie; but the ammunition there turned out to be of the wrong caliber. Of the few horses available to mount the infantry (there were no cavalry units yet) a good many were stolen by Indians.

The Indians informed the commander of the fort that no further installations would be tolerated west of Fort Reno; but since the Army assumed that peace prevailed, no attention was paid to this, and Fort Philip Kearny was begun. Wood trains brought timber to the site over a seven-mile trail, and a large elaborate fort was built. During the construction, the wood trains were attacked by Indians, emigrant trains were raided, a dozen men were killed, horses and herds were run off, and still the fort fought only such defensive actions as were necessary to protect the work. Finally the commander asked for reinforcements and got sixty men, armed with old Springfield muskets and Starr carbines.

One December morning a wood train was attacked by Indians two miles from the fort, and Brevet Lieutenant Colonel William J. Fetterman was ordered to its relief. With twenty-five men he drove the Indians off and pursued them four miles, when they turned and attacked again. Fetterman stood off more than a hundred warriors until relief arrived and routed them, but two officers were killed.

Fetterman, a born soldier, courageous and often reckless, was eager to have another chance at the Indians, devoutly believing that even a poorly armed detachment of army men could hold off a superior number of red warriors. He got his chance two weeks later.

The morning was bright and calm when a force of ninety men went to the woods to haul timber. But at eleven o'clock they sent back the message that the wood train was corralled and fighting a large Indian party. Fetterman asked permission to go to its relief, and set out with a company of about eighty, including some enthusiastic volunteers who wanted Chief Red Cloud's scalp. Fetterman cut off the Indians from the wood train, which got safely back to the fort, then deployed his men to attack the main Indian force. From the fort, some musket fire was observed around noon; then it dwindled, and no more shots were heard. Knowing that Fetterman's force was short of ammunition, the anxious commander sent out all available men to the rescue.

The relief party saw no signs of soldiers, only Indians in great numbers withdrawing from the valley that Fetterman had entered. Proceeding along a ridge the relief party came upon the bodies of Fetterman, Captain Brown, and sixty-five men, all in a space of forty square feet, dead and mutilated beyond description. Only five or six empty cartridges were found near them— indicating that they had never had a chance to reload their rifles. They had been suddenly rushed by such great numbers of Indians that they died almost without a shot. No one survived to tell exactly what had happened; but it appeared that Brown and Fetterman, after their men were lost, had shot themselves, or each other, rather than fall into the hands of the Indians.

Beyond this spot, the bodies of the rest of the company were found, with a good many empty cartridges around them and blood spots that indicated that a number of Indians had been wounded. This marked the last stand of the most experienced riflemen; they had put up as brave a fight as their inferior weapons permitted. Of the whole company only six had died of bullet wounds. Their ammunition had soon been exhausted and the Indians had rushed them with clubs and knives.

The massacre evoked indignant horror from the press, the public, and in

Washington; but the Indian Commissioner insisted that the Indians had been on a peaceful mission. An army investigation resulted in some shifts in the high command; Colonel Carrington, in charge of the fort, was exonerated.

He had repeatedly asked Fort Laramie for arms and reinforcements; two days before the massacre, he had wired: "I hear nothing of my arms that left Leavenworth September 15. . . . I need prompt reinforcements and repeating arms . . . only the new Spencer's arms should be sent . . . the Indians are desperate. . . ."

Only the autumn before, General Sherman had issued orders for traders to stop selling arms to Indians. It had aroused the Indian traders, since the sale of arms was their biggest source of profit. Apparently it had continued.

For several months the Indians were quiet around the fort, although they operated with great energy elsewhere. Then in August 1867 they attacked again. Major James Powell, a brevetted officer with a brilliant record in major battles of the Civil War and a shrewd tactician, was guarding a wood train. He had divided his force of fifty-odd men, keeping thirty of them inside a corral formed of wagons whose beds had been lined with heavy iron and were bulletproof. When a band of eight hundred Indians attacked suddenly, everyone except these men withdrew to the fort, and the Indians charged the wagons. The volley of fire that met them drove them back at once.

Twelve hundred more warriors waited in the hills. They massed and attacked in force; once more the concentrated fire from the wagons mowed them down. Regrouping again, they repeated the assault, always meeting the same relentless fire. It kept up for three hours, until the Indians withdrew entirely, with losses that were never exactly known. Of the men in the corral three were dead and two wounded. The losses of the Indians were close to a thousand—one chief placed them at 1,137, and called the battle a "medicine fight"—meaning that the soldiers had had supernatural help.

What the soldiers had were new Springfield breech-loading rifles and plenty of ammunition, while the Indians were using the old muzzle-loaders they had captured from Fetterman's company.

The following year a treaty was made with the Sioux Indians by which the United States surrendered the right to the road through the Powder River country, in return for a promise that the new Pacific Railroad right-of-way would not be molested. Fort Philip Kearny was abandoned, and the Indians burned it to the ground as soon as the troops had left.

The Union Pacific Railroad began breaking ground for track in 1863, but not much construction was done until after the end of the Civil War. By 1866 full-scale operations were in progress, and the Army was called on to protect the working crews from Indians. Most in need of protection were the preliminary surveyors, who had to move in small parties into virtually uncharted territory. They were accompanied by detachments of U. S. cavalry, which preceded the railroad construction gangs into the wilderness, first establishing a camp, then building a small fort; the railroad track would then be laid up to the fort, and the process would be repeated. Around these forts gathered traders, friendly Indians, and settlers, and towns grew up along the railway lines. These station towns also had to be garrisoned against Indian raids. The farther west the railroads moved, the greater the demands that were made on the Army.

After the war, General Grenville Dodge of the regular Army resigned to become chief engineer of the Union Pacific, and he organized his track-laying gangs in military fashion. Most of his foremen were former army officers. All the workmen were armed with shoulder arms and hand guns and could fall into fighting line as readily as they formed for their daily work. In addition the working parties were escorted by army units that provided security by day, scouting for Indians for three or four miles around the working gangs, and standing guard over the camps at night.

The Indians that attacked the rail gangs were chiefly Sioux and Cheyennes and allied tribes, and were superior in number, in mounts, and in arms to the small army units, which were always short of horses, and armed, after 1867, with single-shot breech-loading rifles, usually Springfields. The Indians attacked in small groups on horseback, using every weapon from bows and arrows to repeating rifles, relying on surprise raids and quick retreats with prisoners or booty.

The engineering difficulties of building track over rugged Western terrain were formidable enough without Indian raids; without the military organization of track crews and army protection the railroads could not have been put through. Dodge said that his crews were the best organized, best equipped, and best disciplined track force he had ever seen; even after their work was completed and they were discharged they could be instantly mobilized into fighting formation. When Indians captured a freight train at Plum Creek, Nebraska, two hundred miles west of the Missouri, in 1867, they cut the telegraph lines and tied blocks of wood to the rails. When the train ran into the trap, the Indians set fire to the cars and plundered them of the merchandise they carried.

General Dodge wrote, "It so happened that I was coming down from the front with my car, which was a traveling arsenal. At Plum Creek Station word came of this capture, and stopped us. On my train were perhaps twenty men, some a portion of the crew, some who had been discharged and sought passage to the rear. The excitement of the capture and the reports coming by telegraph of the burning of the train brought all men to the platform, and when I called on them to fall in, to go forward and retake the train, every man on the train went into line, and by his position showed that he was a soldier. We ran down slowly until we came in sight of the train. I gave the order to deploy as skirmishers, and at the command they went forward as steadily and in as good order as we had seen the old soldiers climb the face of Kenesaw under fire."

The rescue party found some of the Indians riding around the wreckage with bolts of bright cloth tied to their horses' tails, and carousing with barrels of whisky they had found on the train. When they retreated they left behind stacks of dry goods, tea, coffee, and shoes they had stolen.

The history of the Indian campaign begins with the building of the railroads; it was the railroads that threatened the Indians' hunting grounds and sent them on the warpath. Once the railroads were built and towns and cities established along them, the hunting grounds were lost, and by the 1880's the Indians were largely confined to reservations. In the twenty-five years following the Civil War there were eleven major battles, thousands of raids, innumerable minor skirmishes. In the light of the famous engagements, such as Custer's stand at the Little Big Horn, it would seem that vast hordes of savages roamed the plains and mountains.

Actually, the Indians were never so numerous as the band of some five thousand that wiped out Custer's company. Precisely because they were few in number and scattered widely over vast areas, it cost the Army a few daunting defeats to learn that they were a formidable adversary. One reason was obviously their swiftness and mobility; another was the ingenuity with which they adapted white men's weapons to their fighting tactics. Indians using clumsy muzzle-loaders could reload them on horseback very quickly; with their mouths full of lead pellets which they spat into muzzles on top of an indeterminate quantity of powder, swiftly riding Indians could outrace well-aimed shots and return fire fast. They were not good marksmen, but they could deliver a lot of lead, and a sufficient number of them, using these tactics, could demoralize small bands of settlers in short order.

A third and important reason for the Indians' military prowess was that they were generally as well armed as frontiersmen and settlers, and, more often than not, better armed than U. S. Army soldiers. Firearms were a decisive factor in the winning of the West because they were just as formidable in the hands of an enemy as in one's own.

The last major Indian uprising took place in 1890, when word spread among the tribes of a new Messiah who would bring back with him the vast herds of game which the Indians had lost when the white men came. It caused a ferment of unrest, which Sitting Bull took advantage of to urge the tribes to gather in the Dakotas; whereupon the Army acted to thwart him. In a skirmish with troops sent to arrest him, Sitting Bull was killed.

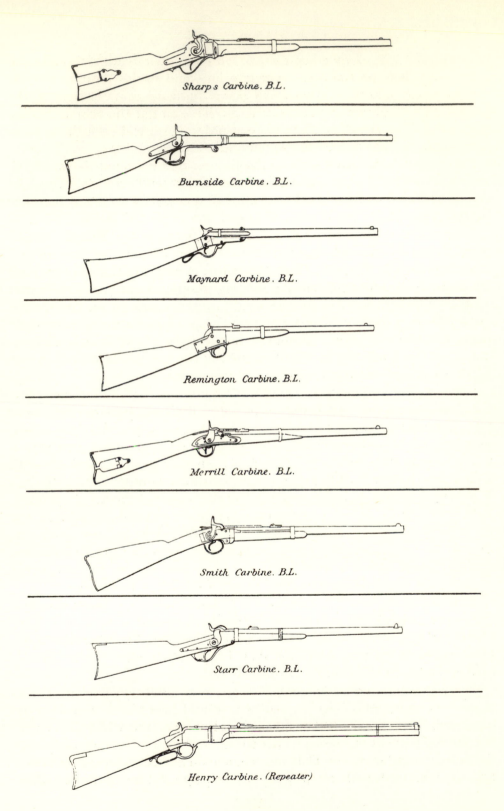

Sharps Carbine. B.L.

Burnside Carbine. B.L.

Maynard Carbine. B.L.

Remington Carbine. B.L.

Merrill Carbine. B.L.

Smith Carbine. B.L.

Starr Carbine. B.L.

Henry Carbine. (Repeater)

PLATE 1

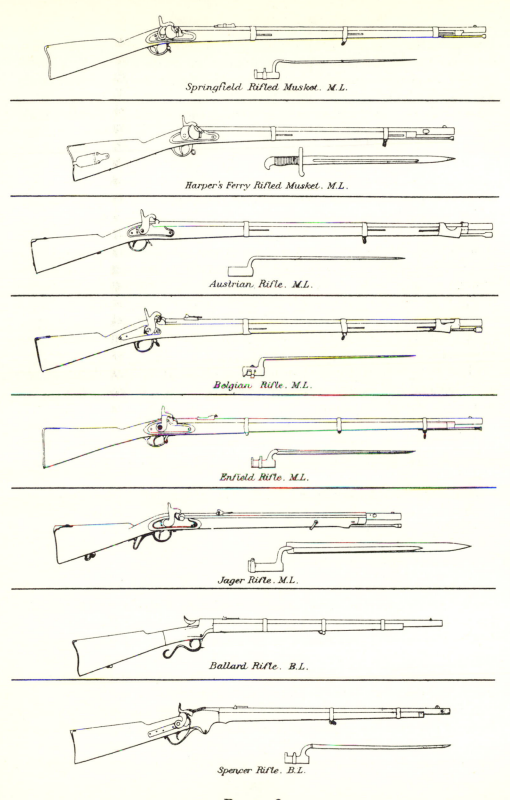

Springfield Rifled Musket. M.L.

Harper's Ferry Rifled Musket. M.L.

Austrian Rifle. M.L.

Belgian Rifle. M.L.

Enfield Rifle. M.L.

Jager Rifle. M.L.

Ballard Rifle. B.L.

Spencer Rifle. B.L.

PLATE 2

The Army then mobilized to surround the gathering of Indians in the Dakota Bad Lands, and peaceful negotiations were under way when a battle, apparently generated merely by the extreme tension between the soldiers and Indians, broke out and numbers on both sides were killed. The Indians were finally disarmed and went back to their reservations. Thereafter nothing but minor skirmishes disturbed the peace, and these too dwindled away.

Arms, Uniforms, and Equipment of the Indian Campaigns

In 1895 the U. S. Government Printing Office published an *Atlas to Accompany the Official Records of the Union and Confederate Armies*. This is an important document in the history of the West because the arms and military paraphernalia of the Civil War were used in the Indian campaigns of the West for twenty-five years with little change, except for the addition of certain rifles and revolvers to the standard equipment.

The following are selected from this *Atlas*. Most of the illustrations came from the U. S. Ordnance Manual of 1861.

Plate 1 shows Sharps and Burnside rifles, Remington, Merrill, Smith, and Starr carbines, all breechloaders. It also shows the Henry carbine, a repeater (described in Chapter XIV).

Plate 2 shows a Springfield rifled musket, a Harpers Ferry rifled musket, an imported Austrian rifle, an imported Belgian rifle, and an imported Enfield rifle, all muzzle-loading; a Ballard rifle, and a Spencer rifle, both breech-loading.

(For other shoulder arms see Chapter IV; for martial revolvers see Chapter X. The arms described in these chapters also figure in the post-Civil War history of the West.)

U. S. Martial Cartridge Revolvers

U. S. martial cartridge revolvers are those revolvers adopted by the United States government for the armed services of the United States, and for issue to the organized militia, later called the National Guard.

Revolvers owned and carried as personal weapons, but not adopted or issued by the United States, are not U. S. martial firearms. Neither are revolvers bought by the states for the use of state troops not federally recognized, and not called into the federal service with such arms.

A revolver may be called an Army, Navy, or Military model by the manufacturer but such designation does not make it a martial revolver. This was true in the flintlock and percussion periods, and is true throughout the cartridge era. In general, a revolver of large caliber and large size may be a martial revolver if it fits the above limitations, but some genuine U. S. martial cartridge revolvers were not what we regard today as having either a large caliber or a large size.

In general, cartridge revolvers bought for any of the armed forces were issued to other arms of the services. Thus the Navy has used Army models and the Army has used Navy models. The Marine Corps has used both Army and Navy models, and in addition has had two of its own, which were essentially modifications of other models.

Tabulation of U. S. Martial Cartridge Revolvers Through World War I

Although the West was tamed before 1900, there were ranches and cowboys up until World War I, and some thereafter. For this reason, we list here all genuine U. S. martial cartridge revolvers issued through World War I:

1. Colt Single-Action Army Revolver, originally called the New Model Army Metallic Cartridge Revolving Pistol
2. Colt Double-Action Army or Frontier Revolver, Model 1878
3. Colt New Navy, Double-Action, Self-Cocking Revolver, Model 1889
4. Colt New Navy, Double-Action, Self-Cocking Revolver, Model 1892
5. Colt New Army, Models 1892, 1894, and 1896
6. Colt Army, Model 1901
7. Colt Army, Model 1903
8. Colt Marine Corps, Model 1905, sometimes called Marine Corps Model 1907
9. Colt New Service, Model 1909
10. U. S. Marine Corps Modification of Colt New Service Model, 1909
11. Colt Army Revolver, Model 1917
12. Remington New Model 1874 Army Revolver
13. Smith & Wesson Army Revolver, Model 1869
14. Smith & Wesson Army Revolver, Model 1875, Schofield Patent
15. Smith & Wesson Army Revolver, Model 1899
16. Smith & Wesson Navy Revolver, Model 1899
17. Smith & Wesson Army Revolver, Model 1917

This list does not include single-shot cartridge pistols nor include semi-automatic pistols, since the latter have never been regarded as distinctly "Western."

Remington New Model 1874 Army Revolver

The Remington New Model 1874 Army Revolver is illustrated in Plate 3, figure 1. This is caliber .44, 6-shot, S.A.; with a 7.25-inch rifled, round barrel

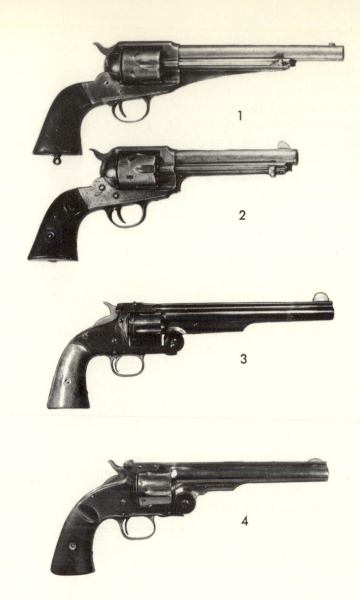

PLATE 3

marked "E. Remington & Sons, Ilion, N.Y., U.S.A." The total length is 12.875 inches. The weight is 2 lbs. 11 oz. It has walnut stocks and a lanyard ring on the butt. There is a loading gate and a side-rod ejector on the right. The Army received 3,000 in 1875, and 3,000 more, slightly modified, later.

Plate 3, figure 2 is a variation of the Remington New Model 1874 Army Revolver with a 5.5-inch barrel, hard-rubber grips, and a different rammer housing.

The Remington New Model 1874 Army Revolver also is found in caliber .45, but this was probably made and sold to civilians.

The authentic Army Model 1874 somewhat resembles the Colt Peace-maker. The Remington was originally made for a cartridge having 28 grains of powder and a 227-grain ball cartridge, but to compete with the Colt Single-Action Army Revolver, Model 1872, in its "Frontier" character-istics, the Remington Revolver was later chambered for the .44-40 center-fire cartridge used in the Winchester Model 1873 Repeating Rifle. In other words, both the Colt Frontier Model and the Remington New Model 1874 Army Revolver, when the latter was chambered for the .44-40 c.f. cartridge, could fire the same cartridge used in the Winchester Model 1873 Repeating Rifle. To what extent the Army received the benefit of chambering the Rem-ington Revolver to fire Winchester rifle cartridges is not apparent from the records. The author of this text believes that the Remington chambered for the .44-40 c.f. cartridge was sold principally to civilians in the Old West.

Smith & Wesson Army Revolver, Model 1869

Plate 3, figure 3 is the Smith & Wesson Army Revolver, Model 1869; also known as Model No. 3, Smith & Wesson; Smith & Wesson .44-caliber Single-Action American, First Issue; and further known as the American Army Model, caliber .44 S. & W. American center-fire. We give you all these names because in the literature of the Old West, in technical books written for gun collectors, and in the catalogues of antique-gun dealers, you may find any of these designations, but they all refer to the same cartridge revolver.

As the names indicate, it is caliber .44 c.f. It is a six-shot revolver with an 8-inch, round, blued, ribbed barrel marked "Smith & Wesson, Springfield, Mass, U.S.A., Pat. July 10, 1860, Jan. 17, Feb. 17, July 11, '65, Aug. 24 1869." The total length is 13.5 inches and the weight is 42.5 oz. A latch in front of the hammer operates the top-break system. The butt is of walnut. The records are not complete, but we know the Army ordered 1,000 De-cember 29, 1870, and they were delivered in 1871.

The Smith & Wesson Army Revolver, Model 1869, represents one of the first steps toward real precision manufacture of hand-gun parts. It intro-duced a genuine system of interchangeability of parts and was among the famous revolvers of the Old West, although Colt got the credit for "six-shooters" in the literature of that era and even now. This revolver was awarded a gold medal at the International Exhibition, Vienna, Austria, in 1873.

Smith & Wesson Army Revolver, Model 1875, Schofield Patent

The Smith & Wesson Army Revolver, Model 1875, Schofield Patent, also was called Smith & Wesson Model .45-caliber Single-Action, Schofield Patent; and often simply "the Schofield Model." It is illustrated in Plate 3, figure 4. It is caliber .45 S. & W., 6-shot, S.A., with a 7-inch, tapered, round, ribbed barrel, marked on left "Smith & Wesson, Springfield, Mass., U.S.A., Pat. Jan. 17th & 24th, '65, July 11th, '65, Aug. 24th, '69, July 25th, '71"; and marked on right "Schofield's Pat. Apr. 22nd, '73." The butt is stamped "U.S." The total length is 12.5 inches and the weight is 40 oz. The butt is of walnut. The Ordnance Department, U. S. Army, accepted this revolver for tests in 1872. Following acceptance, 6,000 were delivered under a contract of 1876, and 3,000 more were delivered in 1877. Those delivered in 1877 had a milled top latch with a hollow rear, providing a place for the thumb in cocking.

Wells Fargo Variation of Smith & Wesson, Model 1875

Among the many revolvers bought and used by Wells Fargo & Co. was a modification of the Smith & Wesson Army Revolver, Model 1875, Schofield Patent, which had the barrel cut to 5 inches and marked on the right side of the heavy lug, under the barrel, "Wells Fargo & Co., Express," with a Wells Fargo serial number either before or after the name of the company, and the same number at the bottom of the handle. Those specimens examined by the author also have the usual "U.S." marks which may mean that Wells Fargo bought them as government surplus, or Smith & Wesson simply turned out the same revolver for Wells Fargo that it did for the United States, with the changes mentioned.

Smith & Wesson Army Revolver, Model 1899, and Navy Model 1899

The Smith & Wesson Army Revolver, Model 1899, when marked on the butt "S.&W. Navy 1899 U.S.N.," with an anchor, "38 D.A.," an arrow, and the serial number, plus the initials of the inspector, was known as the Smith & Wesson Navy Model 1899. Both the Army and the Navy models are also known as Model .38 Hand Ejector, Military and Police, First Issue. Two thousand were made for the U. S. Navy and 1,000 for the U. S. Army. The Army model has a 6.5-inch, tapered, round, blued barrel marked on top "Smith & Wesson, Springfield, Mass., U.S.A., Pat'd. July 1, '84, April 9, '89, May 21, '95, Jul. 16, '95, Aug. 4, '96, Dec. 22, '96, Oct. 4, '98," and on the side "S. & W. .38 Mil." The grip frame of the Army model is marked "U.S. Army Model 1899."

Both versions use the caliber .38 long Colt U. S. service cartridge. The total length is 11.5 inches, and the weight is 1 lb. 15 oz. in some specimens found with a 6-inch barrel, with corresponding changes in total length and weight for one with the regular 6.5-inch barrel. Although intended for the

Spanish-American War, it was not used then, but it was used during the Filipino Insurrection and possibly during the American campaigns at the time of the Boxer Rebellion in China.

This same Smith & Wesson Model 1899 in various barrel lengths was bought by Western ranchers, sheriffs, and policemen, and was widely used by these Westerners, but for some perverse reason it is almost always referred to as a "six-shooter," or a "Colt."

A Day's Still Hunting After Buffalo. Harper's Weekly, *March 10, 1877.*
DENVER PUBLIC LIBRARY WESTERN COLLECTION

XVI *Buffalo Guns and Hunters*

IN primitive times, it has been estimated, some fifty-five million buffalo roamed the open lands of the United States; by 1883 the buffalo was virtually extinct; today only a few protected herds on national preserves still exist. The fate of the buffalo that fell before the white men's guns was linked inevitably with the decline of the Indian tribes that depended on it for their entire livelihood—for food, clothing, shelter and fuel. The fighting power of the Indian survived the extermination of the buffalo by only a few years. Indians who lived only by hunting needed vast spaces in which to find the game they lived by, and it required thousands of square miles of grass range to support the herds to supply them; no other game existed in sufficient abundance.

The white man never needed the buffalo; but he made a good thing out of it for about a decade, during which millions of buffalo hides supplied fur robes and heavy leather goods to the East. Yet despite the magnitude of the slaughter, the buffalo hunters probably earned only about two and a half million dollars from it—a paltry return for the rugged lives they led and the destruction of the twenty million bison that remained west of the Mississippi. Most of these brought no benefit to anyone except the poorest settlers who collected their calcined bones a few years later and sold them for fertilizer.

Much of the slaughter was wanton and frivolous; it attracted some of the most trigger-happy adventurers who ever lived. But the professional buffalo hunter was a shrewd tracker and an expert marksman. Uncouth, bearded, dirty—in fact, literally lousy—he could be spotted in frontier towns by the way he scratched his back with one hand and his leg with the other; but he was a vigorous, canny, generous, and good-tempered man, with the courage and the open heart that were the hallmarks of the old Westerner. An adventurer and a rover, he was not restricted by ranch or farm, but lived crudely out of doors and took his rough pleasures—such as whisky and ribald talk—beside the campfire, amid the stench of freshly killed flesh and drying hides. His career was a brief one—about a decade and a half was the span of the great buffalo drive, and the men whose careers prospered beyond that, such as Buffalo Bill Cody, were few. His active years as a hunter were divided between the open range and the railroad boom towns from which buffalo hides were shipped.

His indispensable aid and companion was his gun, and he often developed such an affection for it that he gave it pet names—"Old Leadslinger" or "Pizen-thrower." It had to be a powerful, long-range rifle capable of great shock power and penetration; it was usually a single-shot breech-loader, which was more accurate, easier to maintain, and less subject to mechanical failure than a repeater. A good rifleman could deliver two shots a minute. He used cartridge ammunition; sparing of shells, he would save them and reload them with ball and powder.

The buffalo was a gregarious, herd-bound animal, moving in bands of from twenty-five to three hundred. Poor of eyesight, it relied on scent to detect an approaching hunter. The hunter usually tried to spot a herd at nightfall, then stalked it at daybreak before it was fully roused. Coming in against the wind, sometimes crawling through low brush to keep out of sight and scent, he would approach within two hundred or a hundred yards. If he could find a small eminence from which to shoot, it was an advantage. When possible, he would set up a forked stick or a tripod as a rifle rest, then aim into the middle of a herd. Cows and bulls herded separately except in breeding time; then the bulls rested on the outer edges of the herd, with the cows and calves in the center. Some hunters tried to shoot a cow in the lungs so that she would bleed; the scent of blood would arouse other buffalo, and they would begin to mill, and as they milled aimlessly, they presented good targets.

Since a clever hunter wanted to follow the same herd as long as possible, he tried not to stampede it. If he did so, it would join nearby herds in a thundering black mass, impossible to follow very far across the prairie. When a herd stampeded, the hunter poured into it as many shots as he could, and collected the carcasses later. The trick was to pick the herd leader—it might be either a bull or a cow—whose fall would bewilder the rest of the herd. When a single animal tried to separate from the baffled herd, the hunter would shoot it. The average bag for a professional ranged from a hundred to two hundred a day, although some claimed to have shot three hundred between sunrise and sunset.

When a herd stampeded there was no holding it. It could easily knock a train off the railroad tracks; engineers who thought they could drive their trains through a herd soon learned to stop until it had passed. When buffalo hunting became a mania among nonprofessionals, passengers on Western railways shot buffalo from moving trains, marking a low point in sportsmanship that has been exceeded only by twentieth-century safaris in Africa.

After the day's kill—the average was forty to fifty a day—the hunter's outfit—usually four men, the hunter, a cook, and two skinners—hauled in the carcasses and skinned them at once; a carcass left overnight would bloat and be difficult to flay the next morning. Only the choicest parts of the meat were cut—tongue, liver, hump, or a chunk from the loin—and cooked over the campfire. Some cow meat was cured and sent East, where it was regarded as a delicacy; and a good deal was sold as beef; but this part of the operation was minor; the real profit lay in the hides, which in prime condition were valued as robes and used to make fur coats, and even more could be made from the leather for harness and industrial use. In the evening, the hunter would melt down lead over the campfire, mold it into bullets, which he would put into cartridges with powder.

The hides were stretched and staked on the ground to dry in the sun, a process that took several days. At the height of the buffalo-hunting drive, so many carcasses were left to rot that this, with the drying hides, filled great areas of the open plains with an unbearable stench. The dried hides were treated with poison to keep off wild animals and prevent rot, and stacked in piles to be picked up for shipment from the nearest railway points. In the best years of the great hunt, a quarter of a million hides were shipped from stations on the northern plains, and an equal number from the southern plains. Hardly a bison was left in the Southwest by 1880, and three years later the silent northern prairies were strewn with the whitened bones of the last of the great herds.

The Gore Expedition

Professional hunters killed most of the buffalo in the West, but when the craze was at its peak, buffalo hunting was a fashionable sport for amateurs, and European nobility seemed especially attracted by it. The Grand Duke Alexis of Russia hunted on the North Platte in 1872, and many Englishmen traveled to the West to hunt. Of these the most eccentric and spectacular

[273]

was Sir St. George Gore, whose three-year expedition from 1854 to 1857 is unique in the annals of game hunting. It covered nearly 7,000 miles in largely unexplored territory, it bagged thousands of buffalo, and cost half a million dollars, the equivalent of several million dollars today. Altogether it was a senseless slaughter and adds little glory to the history of sport.

The expedition started out from St. Louis, Missouri, where a train of covered wagons was assembled, with lightweight "express" wagons, a personal carriage which was Gore's version of a stagecoach, and twenty-one two-horse carriages, each painted red.

Each night Gore's servants erected a tent and assembled in it a brass bed, a washstand, and the kind of indoor plumbing known as a commode. Every evening before he retired Gore personally inspected all his firearms, of which he carried about a hundred, including seventy rifles and thirty miscellaneous arms such as shotguns and pistols. Gore brought with him hand guns and shoulder arms made by such outstanding London gunmakers as Manton, Purdey, and Richards; but he soon learned the virtues of the Sharps rifles and reluctantly conceded that for buffalo they were at least the equal of his English guns.

He also brought enough fishing tackle to fill two wagons, and was accompanied by an expert on fishing whose chief task was to tie trout flies and otherwise assist the noble hunter.

Although he was pompous and arrogant, Gore was not entirely stupid about hunting. He had scouts who went ahead of the expedition to sight herds of buffalo. When they found one they erected a tripod on a rise of ground to windward of the herd. Gore took his place at the tripod and his assistants handed him loaded rifles. He placed them one by one on the tripod and fired at buffalo until the rifle was empty, when a servant would hand him a loaded one. Food was brought to him during the day. Thus he could shoot from dawn to sunset as long as the game was within range. On one day alone he killed at least a thousand buffalo.

He brought his own skinners and taxidermists, who selected the best hides. When he shot a buffalo with an especially fine head he would have it prepared for mounting. Hides which his expert rejected were left with the carcasses on the ground.

Most of Gore's shooting was done in the territory that is now Colorado, Wyoming, and New Mexico. After three years Gore had his fill and offered to sell to the American Fur Company at Fort Union everything he had, except enough vehicles and horses to get his party back East. The company's representative, considering this a distress sale, offered only a fraction of what the equipment was worth, so Gore piled up everything he did not need at Fort Union and set fire to it. It was one of the biggest and most expensive bonfires in American history.

The Sharps Rifle

The buffalo rifle was evolved to meet the demands of the professional buffalo hunter, who needed a weapon with long range, accuracy, and extraordinary shock power and penetration for the thick hides and skulls of buffalo; and one which would fire large-caliber ammunition. Before the Civil War, the early American "long hunters" and Indians used any shoulder arms they could get to kill buffalo, including flintlock and percussion muzzle-loaders. But it was not until Christian Sharps evolved the Sharps Buffalo Rifle, caliber .45, after the Civil War that hunters found the ideal weapon.

Sharps (1811–1874) was well-known as the inventor and manufacturer of the Sharps breech-loading pistol, one of the American secondary martial pistols; the Sharps pocket percussion revolver; Sharps cartridge pepperboxes and derringers; and various Sharps percussion and cartridge rifles and carbines. Some of his inventions were marketed under the name of the Sharps Rifle Co., Sharps & Co., and Sharps & Hankins, in all of which companies he was an executive.

His classic buffalo rifle was the caliber .45, single-shot cartridge breechloader, for a cartridge containing a 120-grain powder charge and a bullet weighing 550 grains. It was consequently referred to as the Sharps .45–120–550 (sometimes written .45/120/550). The cartridge case was 2.875 inches long.

Realizing that the hunter would be more successful with a rifle that fired a cartridge with greater shocking power, Sharps later produced a caliber .50 rifle that fired a .50–140–700 cartridge. This meant that he increased the powder load from 120 to 140 grains and the weight of the bullet from 550 to 700 grains, at the same time increasing the cross-sectional area of the bullet. But by the time this rifle appeared, the great herds were already disappearing, and after this, the Sharps rifle, especially designed for buffalo, declined in popularity. Since Sharps never developed a repeating rifle, Winchester outstripped him. The firm closed shop in 1881.

Major H. B. C. Pollard, author of *A History of Firearms*, said, in discussing early breech-loading arms:

"The Sharps rifle is perhaps the most important of all these actions. It was mechanically one of the soundest, and later made a very fine cartridge rifle. Over 18,000 were used during the war and many variations exist for paper, metal or metallic cartridge. Both caps and tape primers were also used. The Sharps principle employed a falling block operated by an under lever which served as a trigger guard. This block fell in a squared box breech exposing the chamber. The cartridge inserted, the closing of the lever pushed up the breech block, which had a sharp cutting edge which cut off the paper base

[275]

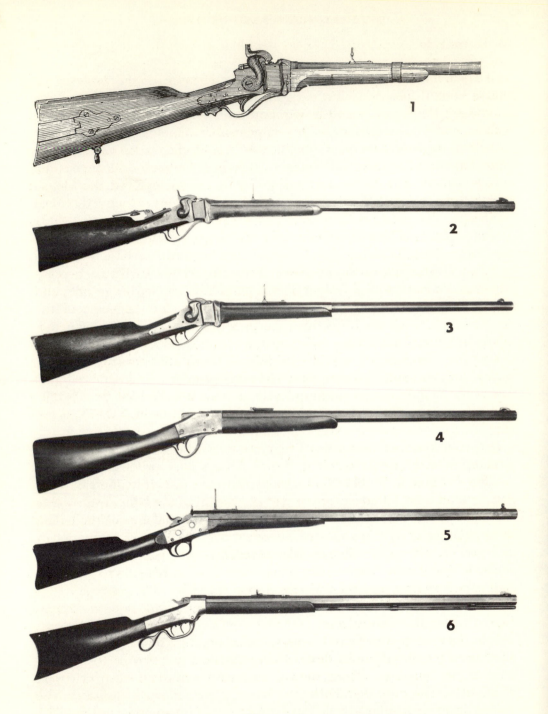

PLATE 1

1. Sharps Breech-Loading Percussion Carbine.	4. The Sharps Model 1878, or Borchardt.
2. Sharps Side-Hammer Rifle.	5. Remington Rolling-Block Rifle.
3. Sharps Bridgeport-made Model 1874.	6. Marlin "Pacific Ballard Model."

of the cartridge, exposing the powder to the cap flash. It was simple, rapid, and effective. The arm was well made and had a high reputation for range and accuracy. The gas escape with paper cartridges was, however, so marked that the arm was never adopted other than as an experimental issue in the British forces and was soon withdrawn as dangerous. The word 'sharpshooter' is a testimony to its reputation."

Pollard neglected to say in his history that in 1877 a British team was defeated in a marksmanship contest by Americans armed with Sharps rifles where shots had to be fired at ranges up to and including one thousand yards. After their defeat, the British team bought Sharps rifles.

Sharps rifles gained wide renown in the Civil War, when Colonel Hiram Berdan armed his Union regiment with them and it became famous for the accuracy of its fire.

It was Sharps rifles which the Rev. Henry Ward Beecher, the crusading abolitionist, sent to John Brown in Kansas in crates labeled "Bibles"—thus the early Sharps rifles were also known as "Beecher's Bibles."

Other rifles were used by buffalo hunters, although not so widely as the Sharps. One was the famous Henry gun, a repeater, which was the forerunner of the Winchester (see Chapter XIV). It was advertised as a buffalo gun as early as 1865. Later on Winchesters were used effectively, but on the whole the buffalo hunter preferred a single-shot rifle because at that time it would usually fire a heavier bullet, was simpler to maintain, repair, and fire; and more accurate than the repeating rifles available.

The following buffalo rifles are from the collection of Richard H. Chamberlain, Whittier, California:

Plate 1, figure 2. Sharps side-hammer rifle made in Hartford, Conn., caliber .50–70, firing either a paper-patched sporting cartridge or the regular U. S. government cartridge. It has a 30-inch barrel and weighs slightly more than 10 pounds.

Figure 3. Sharps Bridgeport-made Model 1874, bearing the stamp or mark of "J. P. Lower," who made many other types, and models of firearms, and was a Denver agent for Sharps at the time this rifle was made. The Sharps and other rifles of the same period made for sporting use often have "set" triggers that can be fired with the front trigger operating either as a conventional trigger or a "hair trigger." The rifle in figure 3 is believed to have been the property of Colonel Frank Meyer, a buffalo hunter, who describes the illustrated rifle in a book written jointly by him and Charles Roth, titled *The Buffalo Harvest*.

The Sharps Bridgeport-made Model 1874 is lighter than most buffalo rifles, although it is powerful enough to kill buffalo. The caliber is .40–70–370, with a bottle-necked cartridge, and the barrel is 28 inches long. The weight is 9.5 pounds. Some buffalo rifles weighed as much as 16 pounds or more, but most of the very heavy cartridges and rifles did not come into use until late in the period of buffalo slaughter, when most of the buffalo were gone and the remainder were easily stampeded and hence had to be shot from longer ranges.

Figure 4, the Sharps Borchardt, or Model 1878 Sharps, which was not widely accepted, probably because it did not have a visible hammer, is what the professional buffalo hunters called a "Business Rifle." It weighs 10 pounds. The cartridge it fires is caliber .40–90–370, using a bottle-necked cartridge. The usual barrel is 28 inches long.

Figure 5 is the Remington rolling-block rifle, caliber .44–77–470, second only to the Sharps side-hammer model among professional buffalo hunters. Remington buffalo rifles were generally lighter in weight than the Sharps rifles and were heavier than this particular specimen, which weighs 10 pounds. The sights of the illustrated rifle folded down when carried and then the open or "field" sight could be used in a hurry if the regular sights were not raised in time for firing.

Figure 6 is the Marlin "Pacific Ballard Model," manufactured especially for Western hunting, known to the manufacturer as Model 5, caliber .40–85–370, but also made in other calibers. The specimen illustrated has a 30-inch barrel and the total weight is 10.5 pounds. There is a cleaning rod under the barrel, which is a rare accessory for the period during which the Marlin was made.

Stagecoach of Overland Mail Co. with Mount Shasta in Background. WELLS FARGO BANK

XVII *The Shotgun Guards the Stage*

THE driver, guards, and passengers on stagecoaches in the Old West had to contend with all the dangers and hardships that beset every other pioneer and traveler—marauding Indians, icy winters and roasting hot summers, starvation or at least poor and insufficient food, every known kind of discomfort; and then one more—the stagecoach robber, or "road agent," as he was politely called. He continued to be a menace long after much of the West had been settled and Indians largely brought under control. For the more prosperous the gold camps and cities grew, the swifter, more frequent and efficient the stage service, the bolder and more persistent the bandit became.

The robbers of the earliest stages had not much to expect in the way of loot except for the U. S. mail and the valuables the passengers carried; these were not negligible because anyone undertaking the long and expensive cross-continent journey had to be well-heeled. But from the 1850's on, when hundreds of thousands of dollars' worth of gold dust, plus the mail, traveled on every coach, the stakes were high. From the early lines that began service in 1849 to the time when the Pacific railroad was completed, the bandits plied a lucrative trade and seized millions of dollars' worth of gold.

Stations on the early lines might be only twelve miles apart, but these were only "swing stations" for changing one pair of the team's six horses. The settled and fortified stations could be many miles apart in wild country, so that stage robbers had plenty of opportunity to waylay a coach. Road agents might operate alone; more often they attacked in bands of four—one to stand guard, one to ransack the treasure box, one to hold up the passenger and one to direct; and in some cases they were part of a huge, well-organized gang, with spies in the employ of the stage company as drivers or station keepers who would send word ahead to their confederates when a rich shipment was expected to pass through.

The stage companies used various devices to thwart them, placing armed guards beside the drivers, building special armored treasure coaches from which the drivers and guards could hold off a large band of attackers, and finally employing scouts to reconnoiter and clear the trail ahead of the coaches. When, as in the Montana gold fields at the height of the boom, the authorities were in league with the bandits, none of these stratagems were foolproof. In fact, for most of the period when the stagecoaches operated through mountains and sparsely settled country, the driver could confidently expect an attack somewhere along the line.

The driver and guard were armed generally with a sawed-off, double-barreled shotgun, the kind employed by hotelkeepers, bartenders, and sheriffs who had to deal with mobs, and the kind still known to prison guards and police as the riot gun. The road agent's technique was to ambush the coach on a steep or curving mountain trail, to appear suddenly at close range. The driver or guard needed a weapon that would disable as many of the gang of robbers as possible with one shot.

Stagecoach drivers, like many other heroes of the Old West, were a special breed of men. They had to be. First, they must be expert drivers to maneuver six horses over mountain trails in all kinds of weather, to ford rivers and cross quicksands, still keeping a fairly exact schedule. They had to have courage, too, and quick wits, to meet the challenge of the road agent who suddenly appeared in front of his team with a six-shooter or a shotgun.

Contrary to popular belief, the road agent was not always a gentleman who could be trusted to leave the driver or passengers alive as long as they handed over their valuables without protest; a good many of them were the most brutal kind of Western desperado, to whom human life meant nothing.

In July 1877 the stage from Virginia City, Montana, carrying seven passengers and a large amount of gold, was held up. The passengers, all tough and well-armed miners, had double-barreled shotguns and sat at the windows with their weapons ready. The "guard" gave the alarm that road agents were attacking and the miners fired a volley. In the returning fire from the robbers' ambush, four of the miners were killed, two seriously wounded, and only one left to escape. In this case, it was found, the so-called guard had been in league with the bandits and had directed the stage into the ambush. The killing of the passengers had been well-planned and took place on cue.

The Wells Fargo company took elaborate precautions to guard passengers and treasure, maintaining a system of scouts and offering large rewards for the capture of bandits that inspired posses and local authorities to hunt down road agents diligently. When a Wells Fargo coach was robbed in May 1866 by three men, and its treasure stolen, near Nevada City, Steve Venard, a former town marshal, set out on his own to capture the robbers, picking up their trail at the scene of the robbery. Armed with a Henry repeating rifle, he stalked them into the hills. Spotting two of the bandits at once, with revolvers leveled at him, Venard delivered two rapid shots with his rifle, killing both of them. He then pursued the third bandit down a ravine, missing him with his next shot. He got him with his fourth bullet, but felt that he must be slipping to have used four bullets to kill three men. He recovered the treasure, and turned it over to the posse. The Wells Fargo company gave him a reward of $3,000, a new 16-shot Henry rifle, and a plaque commemorating his deed.

Not all stagecoach bandits were entirely grim characters. Black Bart, who operated in California in the 1870's, had a pleasant way of leaving a bit of verse of his own composition on the stagecoaches he robbed. One bit, found in 1877 after a robbery, ran:

> Here I lay me down to sleep
> To wait the coming morrow.
> Perhaps success perhaps defeat
> And everlasting sorrow.
> I've labored long and hard for bread,
> For honor and for riches,
> But on my toes too long you've trod,
> You fine-haired sons of bitches.

[281]

Let come what will, I'll try it on.
My condition can't be worse,
And if there's money in that box
Tis money in my purse.

Black Bart
the po8

This seemed to constitute the entire literary remains of the laureate of the stage routes, but the robberies went on and on. Drivers kept reporting that they were held up by a lone bandit wearing a mask and carrying a shotgun, who suddenly appeared and said, "Throw down the box." This always took place in steep mountain country where the horses had to walk. Altogether Black Bart perpetrated twenty-eight robberies before he was caught.

After holding up a coach on the Sonora-Milton road in California he ordered the driver to unhitch his horses and take them over the next hill, so that Black Bart could loot the box at his own leisurely pace. Over the hill the driver met a boy with a rifle, and the two went back and fired on the bandit, who fled. But he had dropped his handkerchief as he ran, and a laundry mark was found on it. The police traced him to San Francisco, where he turned out to be a pleasant gentleman who lived quite near the police station and was known as Charles E. Bolton, which was not his real name any more than was Black Bart. He was not dealt with very severely. Tried only for his last robbery, he was given six years in San Quentin; but he got time off for good behavior. He was rather an endearing figure by this time, and when he was interviewed by reporters on his release from prison, he conversed with them amiably. Then he disappeared and nothing was ever heard of him again.

He carried a double-barreled shotgun in his robberies. It must have looked efficient, but of its mechanical performance we know nothing, because in twenty-eight holdups he never fired a single shot.

Even after repeating rifles had been developed to a fair degree of efficiency the sawed-off shotgun was the stagecoach guard's stand-by. The earliest ones used were old English models; later Winchester shotguns were also used, with their barrels cut down. The official Winchester records do not show that the factory altered any of their shotguns; but the fact that many Winchesters exist that have obviously been factory-altered rather than cut down by local gunsmiths with a hacksaw indicates that the company did alter them by request.

The blunderbuss was the ancestor of the shotgun. Plate 1, figure 1 is an English-made flintlock blunderbuss with a bayonet. It has a 14-inch, round,

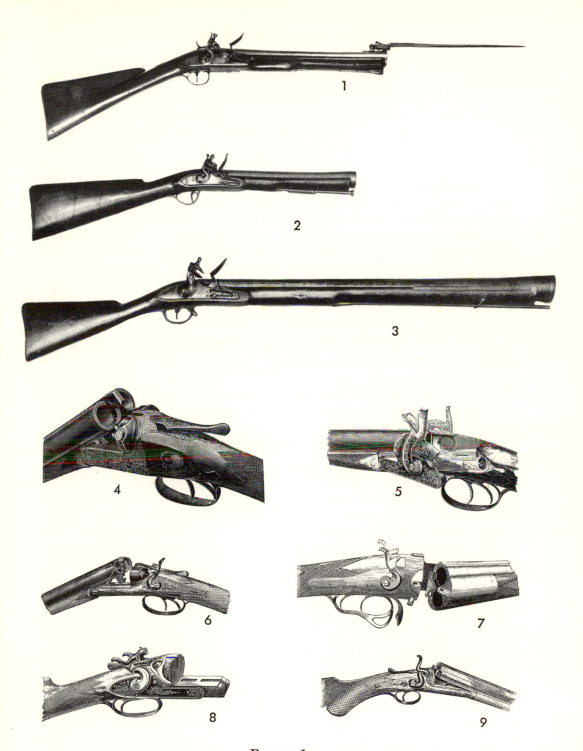

PLATE 1

1. English-made Flintlock Blunderbuss.
2. Flintlock Blunderbuss with British proof marks.
3. British Flintlock Blunderbuss, 1815.
4. Greener's Treble-Wedge-Fast Hammerless Gun.
5. Walsh's Pin-Fire Gun.
6. Top-Lever Gun with back-action locks.
7. Under and Over Wedge-Fast Gun.
8. Greener's Double Gun with single trigger.
9. Top-Lever Rook Rifle.

brass barrel, with a slightly belled muzzle. The muzzle bore is 1.125-inches. The mark is "Rea, London," with British proof marks. A walnut stock goes all the way to the muzzle. All mountings are brass. The flat lock plate is also marked "Rea." There is a gooseneck hammer, an iron pan with a fence, and the spring bayonet has a 11.5-inch blade, hinged on top of barrel at the muzzle, with a catch at the top of the tang.

Figure 2 is a flintlock blunderbuss with British proof marks, bore diameter 1.25 inches at the muzzle, and an average bore diameter of 0.50-inch. The barrel is 12.75 inches long. The total length is 29 inches. There is a full-length walnut stock. The furniture, such as the thimble, trigger guard and butt plate, are brass. There is a double-necked hammer. The lock is marked "Bourn Chambers."

Figure 3 is another British flintlock blunderbuss, bore diameter 2 inches at the muzzle, with a 30-inch barrel and a lock plate dated 1815. There are the usual British proof marks.

All these flintlock British blunderbusses were used in America by stage-coach drivers, stagecoach guards, sea captains, river-boat officers, and others who wanted to repel mobs in a hurry. Contrary to the early pictures of "Pilgrims Going to Church," the muzzle was not belled much; that is, it was not flared out as greatly as the early illustrators indicated.

Among the arms illustrated by Greener in his own book are the Greener's Treble-Wedge-Fast Hammerless Gun, in figure 4; Mr. J. Walsh's Pin-fire Gun, in figure 5; Top-Lever Gun with Back-Action Locks, in figure 6; Under and Over Wedge-Fast Gun, in figure 7; Greener's Double Gun with Single Trigger, in figure 8; and the Top-lever Rook Rifle, in figure 9.

Stalking the Buffalo, from G. F. Berkeley's English Sportsmen on the Western Prairies, *1861.* DENVER PUBLIC LIBRARY

XVIII *The Guns of Teddy Roosevelt*

To sportsmen, historians, and collectors of Western lore, Teddy Roosevelt, in addition to being a great soldier and statesman, personifies the last link between the untamed West and the West of modern times. When Roosevelt went to North Dakota as a young man, the West was still wild. He saw it while the last buffalo still roamed the plains and grizzlies and elks abounded in the hills. By the time he had ended his term as President, that West was almost a thing of the past, and the modern West of fenced range, vast farms, and great national parks and preserves had come into being. As a soldier and a public official he had a special affection and concern for the West; besides loving it he understood its past and future role in the history of the nation.

As a youth, Teddy Roosevelt set out to overcome a constitutional frailty by plunging into "the strenuous life." Outdoor life and hunting coincided with his early interest as a naturalist. At the age of thirteen he was given a pin-fire double-barreled shotgun of French manufacture with which he obtained specimens for his own little natural-history collection. He handled the gun clumsily, the unfired cartridges often got stuck, and he frequently tattooed himself with unburned grains of powder. But by practicing marksmanship he became expert in the use of a rifle.

In 1883, after he had already started an active career in politics, he bought the Elk Horn and Chimney Butte ranches near Medora, North Dakota, on the Little Missouri River, and for the next few years spent much of his time there, hunting fowl, deer, mountain sheep, buffalo, elk, and grizzly bear, using several kinds of rifles which he described in *Hunting Trips of a Ranchman:*

> When I first came to the plains I had a heavy Sharps rifle, 45–120, shooting an ounce and a quarter of lead, and a 50-caliber, double-barreled English express. Both of these, especially the latter, had a vicious recoil; the former was very clumsy; and, above all, they were neither of them repeaters; for a repeater or magazine-gun is as much superior to a single or double-barreled breechloader as the latter is to a muzzle-loader. I threw them both aside, and have instead a 40–90 Sharps for very long-range work; a 50–115 6-shot Ballard express, which has the velocity, shock, and low trajectory of the English gun; and better than either, a 45–75 half-magazine Winchester. The Winchester, which is stocked and sighted to suit myself, is by all odds the best weapon I ever had, and I now use it almost exclusively, having killed every kind of game with it, from a grizzly bear to a bighorn. It is as handy to carry, whether on foot or on horseback, and comes up to the shoulder as readily as a shotgun. It is absolutely sure, and there is no recoil to jar and disturb the aim, while it carries accurately quite as far as a man can aim with any degree of certainty; and the bullet, weighing three-quarters of an ounce, is plenty large enough for anything on this continent . . . it is as deadly, accurate, and handy as any. . . .
>
> Of course every ranchman carries a revolver, a long 45 Colt or Smith & Wesson, by preference the former. . . . I have two double-barreled shotguns: a No. 10 choke-bore for ducks and geese made by Thomas of Chicago; and a No. 16 hammerless built for me by Kennedy of St. Paul, for grouse and plover.

Among hand guns, one of his favorites was the Colt Double-Action Army or Frontier Revolver, Model 1878, caliber .45 c.f., 6-shot; 7.5-inch round barrel, total length 12.5 inches, and weight 2 lbs. 7 oz. (This is not to be confused with the Model 1872, Single-Action Army Revolver, known as the Peacemaker and also as the Frontier Model. The Model 1878 Roosevelt used was a double-action revolver manufactured from 1877 to about 1905 in several variations for military and civilian use. He preferred the military model, with walnut grips, although he used on occasion the civilian type, with hard-rubber grips.)

During his two years of ranch life, Teddy hunted every kind of game to be found in Dakota, including the grizzly bear. On one trip he and a companion, an experienced tracker, between them killed five grizzly bears with seven bullets; in one case Teddy finished off a bear which his companion had wounded; in another case, his companion killed the bear at which Teddy had taken the first shot.

Having seen a wounded grizzly bear, Roosevelt knew what a formidable adversary it was. A blow of its paw could break a man's skull; and he knew of an instance of a grizzly bear's clawing to death two men who had shot at it. In 1892 he himself had a narrow escape. Shooting a grizzly at short range, he managed only to wound it; it charged, and Teddy fired again (he was using a magazine-type Winchester rifle with black-powder cartridges) and killed it barely in time to escape being clawed to death. Later Roosevelt killed lions, elephants, rhinoceroses, and buffalo; but he always thought the Rocky Mountain grizzly bear as dangerous as any game he had ever encountered.

Roosevelt also hunted buffalo—their numbers were dwindling by then— using a heavy rifle such as professional hunters used. But his ranchmen, for whom buffalo hunting was an occasional occupation, often used light Winchester rifles.

After returning to public life Roosevelt made frequent hunting trips to the West, although he was never again a full-time rancher. When the Spanish-American War threatened, in 1898, he was Assistant Secretary of the Navy. In that capacity he began preparations for war. When the Secretary of the Navy was absent for a short rest, Roosevelt ordered supplies and forwarded munitions, and placed various ships in commission with orders to be ready to go to sea at once. At his insistence, detachments of marines were placed aboard vessels recruited to the Navy from the revenue (Coast Guard) service and on converted merchantmen; he knew that the marines were the only really skilled body of riflemen in the services. When war broke out he resigned to join the regiment that was to be known as the Rough Riders.

Congress authorized the raising of three cavalry regiments from among the wild horsemen and riflemen of the Rocky Mountains and Great Plains, designating New Mexico, Arizona, Oklahoma and Indian Territory as the mustering areas. Roosevelt longed to join the men of the West as a soldier, and was offered the command of one of the new regiments. Instead of taking the full rank of colonel, he asked to have Dr. Leonard Wood made colonel while he took the rank of lieutenant colonel, serving under him.

Wood was a seasoned soldier who had served in campaigns against the

Indians in the West, displaying as much strength and endurance as the Indians themselves. He commanded several expeditions against hostile Indians so successfully that he was awarded the Congressional Medal of Honor.

He and Roosevelt chose the rifle with which the Rough Riders were to be armed. In 1892 the Army had adopted magazine rifles and carbines using smokeless powder, to replace the single-shot, black-powder Springfield rifle of the post-Civil War period. However, not all troops went into battle equipped with it.

The new weapon was the one we now describe as the U. S. Magazine Rifle, Model 1892, Krag-Jorgensen, caliber .30, bolt action. It had a 30-inch barrel and a 46-inch stock, and a total length of 49.19 inches. The magazine held five cartridges and was located under the receiver, to the left. A cut-off made it possible to fire it as a single-loader. The top of the barrel was covered with wood to keep the shooter from burning his hand when the barrel was hot. It was the first U. S. rifle to use smokeless-powder cartridges, and also the first of what experts regard as reduced caliber; that is, a smaller caliber than previous martial shoulder arms. The gun was equipped with a knife bayonet.

This gradually was converted into what became known as the U. S. Magazine Rifle Model 1896, slightly shorter and lighter. The magazine cut-off was altered so that when it was in the upright position it indicated that the magazine was functioning; when it was down, the magazine was cut off. Also, the rear sight was improved.

The government also developed the U. S. Magazine Carbine, Model 1896, caliber .30. This was similar to the Model 1896 rifle, but with a 22-inch barrel, a 30.05 stock, and a total length of 40.9 inches. This was the weapon Wood and Roosevelt chose for the Rough Riders.

There were good reasons for choosing it: It was the best available U. S. carbine, and it was the weapon issued to the cavalry of the regular Army, which meant that maintenance and supply in the field would be simple.

A good many volunteer and militia units went into action armed with old-style black-powder rifles. The advantages of the new style rifle were obvious, according to Roosevelt's *The Rough Riders:*

> Our artillery made one or two efforts to come into action on the firing-line of the infantry, but the black powder rendered each attempt fruitless. The Spanish guns used smokeless powder, so that it was difficult to place them. In this respect they were on a par with their own infantry and with our regular infantry and dismounted cavalry; but our only two volunteer infantry regiments, the Second Massachusetts and the Seventy-first New York, and our artillery, all had black powder. This rendered the two volunteer regiments, which were armed with the antiquated Springfield, almost

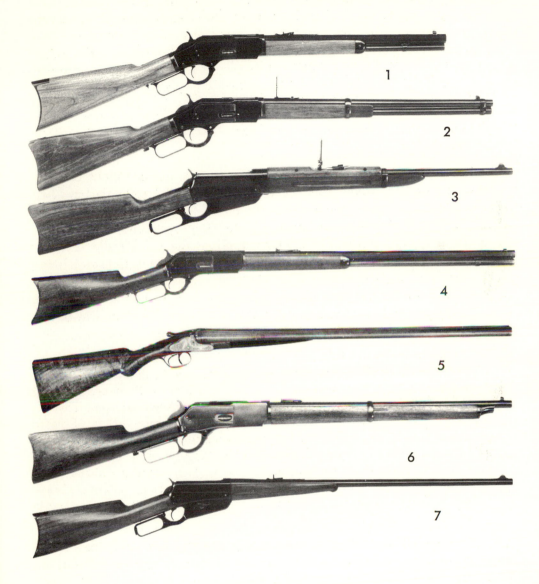

PLATE 1

1. Winchester Lever-Action Repeating Short-Barrel Rifle, Model 1873.
2. Winchester Lever-Action Repeating Carbine, Model 1873.
3. Winchester Lever-Action Repeating Carbine, Model 1895.
4. Winchester Lever-Action Repeating Rifle, Model 1876.
5. Winchester Double-Barrel 12-Gauge Shotgun, English-made.
6. Winchester Lever-Action Model 1876 Carbine.
7. Winchester Lever-Action Repeating Rifle, Sporting Type, Model 1895.

useless in the battle, and did practically the same thing for the artillery wherever it was formed within rifle-range. When one of the guns was discharged a thick cloud of smoke shot out and hung over the place, making an ideal target, and in a half-minute every Spanish gun and rifle within range was directed at the particular spot thus indicated. . . . We got no appreciable help from our guns on July 1st. Our men were quick to realize the defects of our artillery, but they were entirely philosophical about it, not showing the least concern at its failure. On the contrary, whenever they heard our artillery open they would grin as they looked at one another and remark, "There go the guns again; wonder how soon they'll be shut up."

A Model 1898 Carbine was also made. Collectors and historians can distinguish it from the Model 1896 as follows: the Model 1896 Carbine had one band and an elevated section over the barrel that served as a rear-sight protector. The U. S. Magazine Carbine Model 1898 was similar but had an improved rear sight and on the later productions the bolt-handle seat was cut off flush with the receiver, the seat for the bolt handle in the stock being made correspondingly smaller.

The Rough Riders left their horses behind them in Tampa and fought in Cuba as dismounted cavalry. Roosevelt saw action on the ground in trench warfare, in the thick of the fight. He wrote, in *The Rough Riders:*

> Lieutenant Davis's first sergeant, Clarence Gould, killed a Spanish soldier with his revolver, just as the Spaniard was aiming at one of my Rough Riders. At about the same time I also shot one, I was with Henry Bardshar [his orderly] running up at the double, and two Spaniards leaped from the trenches and fired at us, not ten yards away. As they turned to run I closed in and fired twice, missing the first and killing the second. My revolver was from the sunken battleship *Maine,* and had been given me by my brother-in-law, Captain W. S. Cowles, of the Navy. At the time I did not know of Gould's exploit, and supposed my feat to be unique; and although Gould had killed his Spaniard in the trenches, not very far from me, I never learned of it until weeks after.

Regulations allowed officers considerable latitude in the choice of side arms. Roosevelt was carrying a Navy revolver, what we now describe as the Colt New Navy, Double-Action, Self-Cocking Revolver, Model 1892. It was available for caliber .41 short or long Colt cartridges, and also caliber .38 short or long Colt cartridges. It was a six-shot revolver with a six-inch barrel. (See Plate 3, figure 5, Chapter XIII.)

Although officers were not required to carry shoulder arms, Roosevelt took with him a rifle of his own selection, as a protection against enemy snipers. It was not until World War I that the good sense of this practice became apparent, and it did not become common until World War II.

Roosevelt chose a Winchester Model 95, caliber .30 U. S. Army carbine (see Plate 1, figure 3) which used the government cartridge. But he parted with it when one of his troopers needed a gun. "He [Bob Wrenn] had joined us very late and we could not get him a Krag carbine; so I had given him my Winchester, which carried the government cartridge; and when he was mustered out he carried it home in triumph, to the envy of his fellows, who themselves had to surrender their beloved rifles."

Throughout the campaign in Cuba Roosevelt observed that both sides were distinguished by generally poor marksmanship. This may not have been the case with the Westerners in his own outfit. Years before, he had written, "Beyond question our Western hunters are, as a body, to the full as good marksmen as, and probably much better than, any other body of men in the world, not even excepting the Dutch Boers or Tyrolese Jägers, and a certain number of them who shoot a great deal at game, and are able to squander cartridges very freely, undoubtedly become crack shots, and perform really wonderful feats."

But in general there was a lack of well-aimed fire, and Roosevelt the rest of his life strenuously advocated marksmanship training for civilians as part of a general preparedness program. In 1901 by an act of Congress the Secretary of War was directed to establish the National Board for the Promotion of Rifle Practice, including in its membership representation from the regular services, the National Guard, and the National Rifle Association of America. Small-arms competitions were to be held, the expenses of regular and National Guard teams were to be paid, and trophies paid for with funds provided by Congress were to be awarded. This recognition greatly strengthened the National Rifle Association of America by making it part of an official program.

After his second term as President, Roosevelt made several game-hunting and exploratory expeditions to Africa and South America, during which he used a variety of rifles, most of them provided by Winchester. These weapons he chose with great care, having the Winchester company fit them with special sights and stocks. He liked especially his .45-70 Winchester, Model 86, which he had shot moose with, and thought of taking it to Africa for shooting heavier game. The Winchester company doubted that it would be powerful enough, and suggested their .405 instead. Roosevelt finally took three of these, sending in his .30-30 to be used as a model for the stocks and sights. After some difficulty, since Roosevelt was extremely particular about the details of his rifles, Winchester produced the guns. In addition he carried a Springfield, a double-barreled Holland rifle, and a Mannlicher. Winchester supplied ammunition to specifications, sending a huge supply ahead to Mombasa, the port of entry for the expedition into the interior of Africa.

The African expedition lasted eleven months, during which Roosevelt and his companions bagged 4,897 specimens of mammals, more than 4,000 birds, and about 2,000 reptiles. In *African Game Trails*, Roosevelt wrote: "The Winchester and the Springfield were the weapons one of which I always carried in my own hand, and for any ordinary game I much prefer them to any other rifles. The Winchester did admirably with lions, giraffes, elands, and smaller game, and, as will be seen, with hippos. For heavy game like rhinoceros and buffalo, I found that for me personally the heavy Holland was unquestionably the proper weapon."

Roosevelt died in 1919. In addition to being honored as a statesman, soldier, sportsman, naturalist, and writer, he holds a special place in the affections of Westerners as one of the last of the great figures of the vanishing frontier. Some of his guns are now in museums, a few are owned by his descendants, but most of them are where he would have wished them to be, hanging on the walls of houses in the West.

James J. Clarke, of the Winchester-Western Division, Olin Mathieson Chemical Corporation, New Haven, Connecticut, has selected the seven firearms illustrated in Plate 1; they typify the shoulder arms that Teddy Roosevelt bought from Winchester. Other firearms owned or used by Roosevelt are discussed and illustrated in other chapters of this text.

Bibliography

Albaugh, William A., III, and Edward N. Simmons. *Confederate Arms*. Harrisburg, Pa.: The Stackpole Co., 1957.

Asbury, Herbert. *The Barbary Coast*. New York: Alfred A. Knopf, Inc., 1936.

————. *The French Quarter*. New York: Alfred A. Knopf, Inc., 1936.

Ashton, Wendell J. *Voice in the West, Biography of a Pioneer Newspaper*. New York: Duell, Sloan & Pearce, 1950.

Baker, Ezekiel. *Remarks on Rifle Guns*, also titled *Baker's Remarks on the Rifle*. London: Joseph Mallett, 1835.

Bancroft, Hubert Howe. *History of California*, Vols. I to VII. San Francisco: A. L. Bancroft & Co., 1884–1890.

Bannerman, David B. *Military Goods Catalogue*. New York: Francis Bannerman Sons, 1955, et seq.

Banning, George William, and George Hugh Banning. *Six Horses*. New York: The Century Co., 1930.

Bartholomew, Ed. *The Biographical Album of Western Gunfighters*. Houston: The Frontier Press, 1958.

Beebe, Lucius. *Comstock Commotion, the Story of the Territorial Enterprise and the Virginia City News*. Stanford, Calif.: Stanford University Press, 1954.

Beebe, Lucius, and Charles M. Clegg. *The American West*. New York: E. P. Dutton & Co., Inc., 1955.

————. *Dreadful California*. New York and Indianapolis: The Bobbs-Merrill Co., 1948.

————. *Hear the Train Blow*. New York: Grosset & Dunlap, 1952.

————. *The Saga of Wells Fargo*. New York: E. P. Dutton & Co., Inc., 1949.

Bosworth, N. *A Treatise on the Rifle, Musket, Pistol and Fowling Piece*. New York: J. S. Redfield, 1846.

Botkin, B. A. *A Treasury of American Folklore*. New York: Crown Publishers, 1944.

Breihan, Carl W. *The Complete and Authentic Life of Jesse James*. New York: Frederick Fell, Inc., 1953.

Brooks, Juanita. *The Mountain Meadows Massacre*. Stanford, Calif.: Stanford University Press, 1950.

Brown, Dee. *Trail Driving Days*. New York: Charles Scribner's Sons, 1952.

Bruce, John. *Gaudy Century*. New York: Random House, 1948.

Brown, Mark H., and W. R. Felton. *Before Barbed Wire*. New York: Henry Holt & Co., 1956.

Brown, F. R. ("Bob"). *Encyclopedia of Modern Firearms—Parts & Assembly*, Vol. I. Montezuma, Iowa: F. R. ("Bob") Brownell, 1959.

Burns, Walter Noble. *Tombstone—An Iliad of the Southwest*. New York: Doubleday Doran & Co., 1929.

Burrard, Gerald. *The Modern Shotgun* (in two volumes). New York: Charles Scribner's Sons, 1931.

Casey, Robert J. *The Black Hills and Their Incredible Characters*. Indianapolis: The Bobbs-Merrill Co., 1949.

————. *The Texas Border and Some Borderliners*. Indianapolis: The Bobbs-Merrill Co., 1950.

Casey, Brigadier General Silas. *Infantry Tactics* (in three volumes). D. Van Nostrand, 1865.

Chalfant, W. A. *Gold, Guns & Ghost Towns*. Stanford, Calif.: Stanford University Press, 1947.

Chapel, Charles Edward. *The Art of Shooting*. New York: A. S. Barnes & Co., Inc., 1960.

————. *The Boy's Book of Rifles*. New York: Coward-McCann, Inc., 1948.

————. *The Complete Book of Gun Collecting*. New York: Coward-McCann, Inc., 1961.

————. *Field, Skeet, and Trap Shooting*. New York: Coward-McCann, Inc., 1949.

————. *Forensic Ballistics*. Chicago: Institute of Applied Science, 1933.

————. *Gun Collecting*. New York: Coward-McCann, Inc., Revised Edition, 1947.

————. *Gun Care and Repair—A Manual of Gunsmithing*. New York: Coward-McCann, Inc., 1943.

————. *The Gun Collector's Handbook of Values*. New York: Coward-McCann, Inc., Revised Edition, 1960.

————. *Guns of the Old West*. New York: Coward-McCann, Inc., 1961.

————. *Simplified Pistol and Revolver Shooting*. New York: Coward-McCann, Inc., 1950.

————. *Simplified Rifle Shooting*. New York: Coward-McCann, Inc., 1950.

Chapman, Arthur. *Pony Express*. New York: G. P. Putnam's Sons, 1932.

Clemens, Samuel Langhorne (Mark Twain). *Roughing It*. New York: Harper & Brothers, 1903.

Clephan, Robert Coltman. *An Outline of the History and Development of Hand Fire-arms, Etc.* London: The Walter Scott Publishing Co., 1906.

Cline, Walter M. *The Muzzle-Loading Rifle, Then and Now*. Huntington, W. Va.: Standard Printing and Publishing Co., 1942.

Connecticut Historical Society. *Samuel Colt's Own Record of Transactions with Captain Walker and Eli Whitney, Jr., in 1847*. Hartford, Conn.: The Connecticut Historical Society, 1949.

Cook, D. J. *Hands Up: Or, Thirty-five Years of Detective Life in the Mountains and on the Plains*. Denver: W. F. Robinson Printing Co., 1897.

————. *Hands Up: Or, Twenty Years of Detective Life in the Mountains and on the Plains*. Norman, Okla.: University of Oklahoma Press, 1958.

Corle, Edwin. *Billy the Kid*. New York: Duell, Sloan and Pearce, 1935.

Custer, George Armstrong. *My Life on the Plains or Personal Experiences with Indians*. New York: Sheldon & Co., 1874.

Damon, G. E. *Gun Fun with Safety*. Huntington, W. Va.: Standard Publications, Inc., 1947.

Daniels, Zeke. *The Life and Death of Julia C. Bulette, "Queen of the Red Lights."* Virginia City, Nev.: Lamp Post, 1958.

Davis, Samuel P. *The History of Nevada*. Reno: Elms Publishing Co., 1913.

Deane. *Deane's Manual of the History and Science of Fire-Arms*. London: Longman, Brown, Green, Longman's & Roberts, 1858.

De Quille, Dan (William Wright). *The Big Bonanza*. New York: Alfred A. Knopf, 1947.

De Voto, Bernard. *Across the Wide Missouri*. Boston: Houghton Mifflin Co., 1947.

————. *The Year of Decision, 1846*. Boston: Little, Brown & Co., 1943.

Dick, Everett. *Vanguards of the Frontier*. New York: Appleton-Century-Crofts, 1941.

Dillin, John G. W. *The Kentucky Rifle*. Wilmington, Del.: George N. Hyatt, 1959.

Dimsdale, Thomas J. *Vigilantes of Montana*. Norman, Okla.: University of Oklahoma Press, 1953.

Dobie, Charles Caldwell. *San Francisco: A Pageant*. New York: D. Appleton-Century Co., Inc., 1937.

Dodge, Richard Irving. *The Plains of the Great West and Their Inhabitants*. New York: G. P. Putnam's Sons, 1877.

Dougall, James Dalziel. *Shooting: Its Appliances, Practice, and Purpose*. London: Sampson Low, Marston, Searle & Rivington, 1881.

Dunn, J. P., Jr. *Massacres of the Mountains*. New York: Harper & Brothers, 1886.

Drury, Wells. *An Editor on the Comstock Lode*. Palo Alto, Calif.: Pacific Books, 1936.

Edwards, William B. *The Story of Colt's Revolver*. Harrisburg, Pa.: The Stackpole Co., 1957.

Foertsch, Hermann. *The Art of Modern Warfare*. New York: Oscar Piest, 1940.

Fowler, Gene. *Timber Line, A Story of Bonfils and Tammen*. New York: Covici-Friede, 1933.

Freidel, Frank. *The Splendid Little War*. Boston: Little, Brown & Co., 1958.

Frémont, John C. *The Exploring Expedition to the Rocky Mountains, Oregon and California*. Buffalo: Derby, Orton & Mulligan, 1854.

Fuller, Claud E. *The Breech-Loader in the Service*. Topeka, Kan.: F. Theodore Dexter, 1933.

————. *The Rifled Musket*. Harrisburg, Pa.: The Stackpole Co., 1958.

————. *Springfield Muzzle-Loading Shoulder Arms*. New York: Francis Bannerman Sons, 1930.

————. *The Whitney Firearms*. Huntington, W. Va.: Standard Publications, Inc., 1946.

Fuller, Claud E., and Richard D. Steuart. *Firearms of the Confederacy*. Huntington, W. Va.: Standard Publications, Inc., 1944.

Furlong, Thomas. *Fifty Years a Detective*. St. Louis: C. E. Barnett, 1912.

Gard, Wayne. *Frontier Justice*. Norman, Okla.: University of Oklahoma Press, 1949.

Gardner, Robert E. *American Arms and Arms Makers*. Columbus, Ohio: The F. J. Heer Printing Co., 1938.

George, J. N. *English Guns and Rifles*. Plantersville, S. C.: Small-Arms Technical Publishing Co., 1947.

————. *English Pistols and Revolvers*. Onslow County, N. C.: Small-Arms Technical Publishing Co., 1938.

Glasscock, C. B. *The War of the Copper Kings*. Indianapolis: The Bobbs-Merrill Co., 1935.

Gluckman, Arcadi. *Catalogue of United States Martial Pistols*. Buffalo: Otto Ulbrich Co., 1939.

————. *United States Martial Pistols and*

Revolvers. Buffalo: Otto Ulbrich Co., 1939.

―――――. *United States Muskets, Rifles and Carbines.* Buffalo: Otto Ulbrich Co., Inc., 1948.

Gluckman, Arcadi, and L. D. Satterlee. *American Gun Makers.* Harrisburg, Pa.: The Stackpole Co., 1953.

Grant, James. *More Single-Shot Rifles.* New York: William Morrow & Co., 1959.

―――――. *Single-Shot Rifles.* New York: William Morrow & Co., 1947.

Gunther, Jack Disbrow, and Charles O. Gunther. *The Identification of Firearms.* New York: John Wiley & Sons, Inc., 1935.

Hagan, William T. *The Sac and Fox Indians.* Norman, Okla.: University of Oklahoma Press, 1958.

Hale, William Harlan. *Horace Greeley, Voice of the People.* New York: Harper & Brothers, 1950.

Hardee, W. J. *Rifle and Light Infantry Tactics* (two or more volumes). Philadelphia: Lippincott, Grambo & Co., 1855.

Harlow, Alvin F. *Old Waybills, the Romance of the Express Companies.* New York: D. Appleton-Century Co., 1934.

Hatch, Alden. *Remington Arms in American History.* New York: Rinehart & Co., Inc., 1956.

Hartley, Rachel M. *The History of Hamden, Connecticut.* Hamden, Conn.: Published by the Town, 1943.

Hatcher, Julian S. *Hatcher's Notebook.* Harrisburg, Pa.: Military Service Publishing Co., 1947.

―――――. *Textbook of Firearms Investigation, Identification and Evidence.* Marines, Onslow County, N. C.: Small-Arms Technical Publishing Co., 1935.

Haven, Charles T., and Frank A. Belden. *A History of the Colt Revolver.* New York: William Morrow & Co., 1940.

Held, Robert. *The Age of Firearms.* New York: Harper & Brothers, 1957.

Helper, Hinton R. *The Land of Gold, Reality Versus Fiction.* Baltimore: Henry Taylor, 1855.

Hicks, James E. Author's Notice: The books by James E. Hicks were published by him at Mt. Vernon, N. Y., thus:

Notes on United States Ordnance, Vol. I, *Small Arms,* 1940.

Notes on United States Ordnance, Vol. II, *Ordnance Correspondence,* 1940.

Notes on German Ordnance, 1937.

Notes on French Ordnance, 1937.

Notes on French Ordnance (Translation of *Memoires d'Artillerie*), 1939.

U. S. Firearms (Revision of Vol. I, above), 1946.

Hicks, John Edward. *Adventures of a Tramp Printer, 1880–1890.* Kansas City: Mid Americana Press, 1950.

Holbrook, Stewart H. *Far Corner, A Personal View of the Pacific Northwest.* New York: The Macmillan Company, 1952.

―――――. *Holy Old Mackinaw.* New York: The Macmillan Company, 1938.

Holcomb, Robert N. *Story of Connecticut* (in three volumes). Hartford, Conn.: 1936.

Holloway, Carroll C. *Texas Gun Lore.* San Antonio, Texas: The Naylor Co., 1951.

Horan, James D. *Desperate Men.* New York: G. P. Putnam's Sons, 1949.

―――――. *Desperate Women.* New York: G. P. Putnam's Sons, 1952.

―――――. *The Great American West.* New York: Crown Publishers, 1959.

Horan, James D., and Paul Sann. *Pictorial History of the Wild West.* New York: Crown Publishers, Inc., 1954.

Howard, Joseph Kinsey. *Montana, High, Wide, and Handsome.* New Haven, Conn.: Yale University Press, 1943.

Howard, Robert West (Ed.). *This Is the West.* Chicago: Rand McNally & Co., 1957.

Hunter, J. Marvin, and Noah H. Rose. *The Album of Gun-Fighters.* Bandera, Tex.: Published by the Authors, 1951.

Inman, Henry. *The Old Santa Fe Trail, the Story of a Great Highway.* New York: The Macmillan Company, 1899.

Jackson, Joseph Henry. *Anybody's Gold.* New York: D. Appleton-Century, 1941.

Johnson, Melvin M., Jr., and Charles T. Haven. *Automatic Weapons of the World.* New York: William Morrow & Co., 1945.

Kahn, Edgar M. *Cable Car Days in San Francisco.* Stanford, Calif.: Stanford University Press, 1940.

Kalman, James M., and C. Meade Patterson. *Pictorial History of U. S. Single-Shot Martial Pistols.* New York: Charles Scribner's Sons, 1957.

Kaltenborn, H. V. *It Seems Like Yesterday.* New York: G. P. Putnam's Sons, 1956.

Karr, Charles Lee, Jr., and Caroll Robbins. *Remington Handguns.* Harrisburg, Pa.: The Stackpole Co., 1951.

Karsner, David. *Silver Dollar, the Story of the Tabors.* New York: Covici-Friede, 1932.

Knox, Dudley W. *A History of the United States Navy.* New York: G. P. Putnam's Sons, 1936.

Lake, Stuart N. *Wyatt Earp, Frontier Marshal.* New York: Houghton Mifflin Co., 1931.

Langford, Nathaniel Pitt. *Vigilante Days and Ways.* Chicago: A. C. McClurg & Co., 1931.

Lavender, David. *The Big Divide.* New York: Doubleday & Co., Inc., 1948.

Leffingwell, William Bruce. *The Art of*

Wing Shooting. Chicago: Rand, McNally & Co., 1894.

Lenz, Ellis Christian. *Muzzle Flashes.* Huntington, W. Va.: Standard Publications, Inc., 1944.

————. *Rifleman's Progress.* Huntington, W. Va.: Standard Publications, Inc., 1946.

Lewis, Oscar. *The Big Four.* New York: Alfred A. Knopf, 1938.

————. *Silver Kings.* New York: Alfred A. Knopf, 1947.

Lindsay, Charles. *The Big Horn Basin.* Lincoln: University of Nebraska Press, 1932.

Logan, Herschel C. *Cartridges—A Pictorial Digest of Small Arms Ammunition.* Huntington, W. Va.: Standard Publications, Inc., 1948.

————. *Hand Cannon to Automatic.* Huntington, W. Va.: Standard Publications, Inc., 1944.

Lord, Eliot. *Comstock Mining and Miners* (Reprint of 1883 Edition). Berkeley, Calif.: Howell-North, 1959.

Lyman, George D. *The Saga of the Comstock Lode—Boom Days in Virginia City.* New York: Charles Scribner's Sons, 1937.

McClellan, George B. *Manual of Bayonet Exercises, Prepared for the Use of the United States Army.* Philadelphia: J. B. Lippincott & Co., 1852.

McGivern, Ed. *Ed McGivern's Book on Fast and Fancy Revolver Shooting and Police Training.* Springfield, Mass.: King Richardson Co., 1938.

McHenry, Roy C., and Walter F. Roper. *Smith & Wesson Hand Guns.* Harrisburg, Pa.: The Stackpole Co., 1958.

Mack, Effie Mona. *Mark Twain in Nevada.* New York: Charles Scribner's Sons, 1947.

Majors, Alexander. *Seventy Years on the Frontier.* Chicago: Rand, McNally & Co., 1893.

Marshall, James. *Santa Fe, the Railroad that Built an Empire.* New York: Random House, 1945.

Marryat, Frank (Francis Samuel Marryat). *Mountains and Molehills.* New York: Harper & Brothers, 1855.

Martin, Douglas D. *Tombstone's Epitaph.* Albuquerque, N. M.: University of New Mexico Press, 1951.

Mayer, Dr. Joseph R. *Five Centuries of Gunsmiths, Swordsmiths and Armourers, 1400-1900.* Columbus, Ohio: Walter F. Heer, 1948.

Metcalf, Clyde H. *A History of the United States Marine Corps.* New York: G. P. Putnam's Sons, 1939.

Metschl, John. *The Rudolph J. Nunnemacher Collection of Projectile Arms.* Milwaukee: The Milwaukee Public Museum, 1928.

Miller, Joseph. *The Arizona Story.* New York: Hastings House, 1952.

Murphy, Bill. *A Pictorial History of California.* San Francisco: Fearon Publishers, 1958.

Myers, John. *The Last Chance, Tombstone's Early Years.* New York: E. P. Dutton & Co., Inc., 1950.

Neider, Charles. *The Great West.* New York: Coward-McCann, Inc., 1958.

Nevada State Historical Society. *Nevada State Historical Society Papers, 1925–1926.* Reno: Nevada State Historical Society, 1926.

Nichols, Alice. *Bleeding Kansas.* New York: Oxford University Press, 1954.

Nutter, Waldo E. *Manhattan Firearms.* Harrisburg, Pa.: The Stackpole Co., 1958.

Palmer, John McAuley. *General Von Steuben.* New Haven: Yale University Press, 1937.

Parkhill, Forbes. *The Wildest of the West.* New York: Henry Holt & Co., 1951.

Parkman, Francis. *The Oregon Trail.* Boston: Little, Brown & Co., 1872.

Parsons, John E. *Henry Deringer's Pocket Pistol.* New York: William Morrow & Co., 1952.

————. *The Peacemaker and Its Rivals.* New York: William Morrow & Co., 1950.

————. *Smith & Wesson Revolvers: The Pioneer Single-Action Models.* New York: William Morrow & Co., 1957.

Parsons, John E., and John S. du Mont. *Firearms in the Custer Battle.* Harrisburg, Pa.: The Stackpole Co., 1954.

Pearl, Cyril. *The Girl with the Swansdown Seat.* Indianapolis: The Bobbs-Merrill Co., Inc., 1955.

Peattie, Roderick. *The Black Hills.* New York: The Vanguard Press, 1952.

Penfield, Thomas. *Western Sheriffs and Marshals.* New York: Grosset & Dunlap, 1955.

Pollard, H. B. C. *A History of Firearms.* London: Geoffrey Bles, 1931. Boston: Houghton Mifflin Co., 1931.

Rathbone, Perry T. (Ed.). *Mississippi Panorama.* St. Louis: City Art Museum, 1950.

Richardson, Albert D. *Beyond the Mississippi.* Hartford, Conn.: American Publishing Co., 1867.

Rohan, Jack. *Yankee Arms Maker.* New York: Harper & Brothers, 1948.

Roosevelt, Theodore. *African Game Trails.* New York: Charles Scribner's Sons, 1910.

————. *Hunting Trips of a Ranchman.* New York: G. P. Putnam's Sons, 1900.

————. *The Rough Riders.* New York: G. P. Putman's Sons, 1899.

Rosebush, Waldo E. *Frontier Steel, Their Men and Their Weapons.* Appleton, Wis.:

C. C. Nelson Publishing Co., 1958.

Russell, Carl P. *Guns of the Early Frontiers.* Berkeley, Calif.: University of California Press, 1957.

Rywell, Martin. *Samuel Colt, a Man and an Epoch.* Harriman, Tenn.: Pioneer Press, 1952.

Sandburg, Carl. *Abraham Lincoln, the Prairie Years and the War Years.* New York: Harcourt, Brace & Co., 1954.

Sandoz, Mari. *The Buffalo Hunters.* New York: Hasting House Publishers, 1954.

Satterlee, L. D. *A Catalog of Firearms for the Collector.* Detroit: Published by the author, 1939.

Sawyer, Charles Winthrop. (Author's Notice: All of the following four titles were originally published by Charles Winthrop Sawyer.)

Firearms in American History, 1600–1800.

Firearms in American History, Vol. II, *The Revolver, 1800–1911.* (An authorized reprint edition of 1,000 copies was published in 1939 by Charles Edward Chapel.)

Firearms in American History, Vol. III, *Our Rifles.*

United States Single-Shot Martial Pistols.

Schmitt, Martin F. and Dee Brown. *Fighting Indians of the West.* New York: Charles Scribner's Sons, 1948.

Schultz, James Willard. *Signposts of Adventure.* Boston: Houghton Mifflin Co., 1926.

Scott, Winfield. *Abstract of Infantry Tactics.* Boston: Hilliard, Gray, Little & Wilkins, 1830.

——. *Infantry Tactics in Three Volumes.* New York: Harper & Brothers, 1858.

Serven, James E. *Colt Firearms.* Santa Ana, Calif.: James E. Serven, 1954.

Settle, Raymond W., and Mary Lund. *Empire on Wheels.* Palo Alto, Calif.: Stanford University Press, 1953.

Sharpe, Philip B. *The Rifle in America.* New York: Funk & Wagnalls Co., 1938.

Sherlock, Herbert Arment. *Black Powder Snapshots.* Huntington, W. Va.: Standard Publications, Inc., 1946.

Shields, Joseph W. *From Flintlock to M-1.* New York: Coward-McCann, Inc., 1954.

Shirley, Glen. *Toughest of Them All.* Albuquerque: University of New Mexico Press, 1953.

Smith, Lawrence B. *Shotgun Psychology.* New York: Charles Scribner's Sons, 1938.

Smith & Wesson, Inc. *Burning Powder.* Springfield, Mass.: Smith & Wesson, Inc., 1921, et seq.

Spaulding, Oliver L. *The Story of the United States Army in War and Peace.* New York: G. P. Putnam's Sons, 1937.

Sprague, Marshall. *Money Mountain—The Story of Cripple Creek Gold.* Boston: Little, Brown & Co., 1953.

Spaulding, Oliver Lyman. *The United States Army in War and Peace.* New York: G. P. Putnam's Sons, 1937.

Stevens, Captain C. A. *Berdan's United States Sharpshooters in the Army of the Potomac, 1861–65.* St. Paul, Minn.: Price-McGill Co., 1892.

Stormy, Barry. *Thunder Gods Gold.* Tortilla Flat, Ariz.: Southwest Publishing Co., 1945.

Strickland, W. P. *The Pioneers of the West or Life in the Woods.* New York: Carlton & Phillips, 1856.

Sunset Books and Sunset Editors. *Gold Rush Country—A Guide to California's Mother Lode and Northern Mines.* Menlo Park, Calif.: Lane Publishing Co., 1957.

Taft, Robert. *Artists and Illustrators of the Old West, 1850–1900.* New York: Charles Scribner's Sons, 1953.

——. *Photography and the American Scene.* New York: The Macmillan Co., 1942.

Tallant, Robert. *The Romantic New Orleanians.* New York: E. P. Dutton & Co., Inc., 1950.

Thompson, Thomas H., and Albert Augustus West. *History of Los Angeles County, California.* Oakland, Calif.: Thomson & West, 1880.

Turnbull, Agnes Sligh. *The Day Must Dawn.* New York: The Macmillan Co., 1942.

Ulrich, Arthur L. *A Century of Achievement, 1836–1936, Colt's 100th Anniversary Fire Arms Manual.* Hartford, Conn.: Colt's Patent Fire Arms Manufacturing Co., 1936.

Van Every, Edward. *Sins of America as "Exposed" by the Police Gazette.* New York: Frederick A. Stokes Co., 1931.

——. *Sins of New York as "Exposed" by the Police Gazette.* New York: Frederick A. Stokes Co., 1930.

Van Rensselaer, Stephen. *An Histology of American Gunsmiths, Arms Manufacturers, and Patentees With Detailed Description of Their Arms.* Morristown, N. J.: Mrs. Stephen Van Rensselaer, 1947.

Vestal, Stanley (Pen name of Walter Stanley Campbell). *Joe Meek, The Merry Mountain Man.* Caldwell, Idaho: Caxton Printers, Ltd., 1952.

——. *Queen of Cowtowns, Dodge City.* New York: Harper & Brothers, 1952.

Ward, Fay E. *The Cowboy at Work.* New York: Hastings House Publishers, 1958.

Webb, Robert N. *The Illustrated True Book on American Railroads.* New York: Grosset & Dunlap, 1957.

Wellman, Paul I. *The Trampling Herd.* New York: Garrick & Evans, Inc., 1939.

Wells, Evelyn, and Harry C. Peterson. *The '49ers.* New York: Doubleday & Co., 1949.

Western Historical Co. *The History of*

Delaware County, Iowa. Chicago: Western Historical Co., 1878.

Williamson, Harold F. *Winchester, The Gun That Won the West.* Washington, D. C.: Combat Force Press, 1952.

Willison, George F. *Here They Dug the Gold.* New York: Harcourt, Brace & Co., 1946.

Wilson, Neill C. *Silver Stampede.* New York: The Macmillan Co., 1937.

————. *Treasure Express—Epic Days of Wells Fargo.* New York: The Macmillan Company, 1936.

Wilstach, Frank J. *Wild Bill Hickok, the Prince of Pistoleers.* New York: Doubleday, Page & Co., 1926.

Winant, Lewis. *Early Percussion Firearms.* New York: William Morrow & Co., 1959.

————. *Firearms Curiosa.* New York: Greenberg, Publisher, 1955.

————. *Pepperbox Firearms.* New York: Greenberg, Publisher, 1952.

Winther, Oscar Osburn. *Via Western Express and Stagecoach.* Stanford, Calif.: Stanford University Press, 1945.

Wood, Richard Coke. *Murphys, Queen of the Sierra.* Angels Camp, Calif.: Calaveras Californian, 1948.

Young, G. O. *Alaskan-Yukon Trophies Won and Lost.* Huntington, W. Va.: Standard Publications, Inc., 1947.

INDEX